How YOU™ are like Shampoo

For COLLEGE GRADUATES

Here's to YOU™!

A Personal Note from the Author

I am proud to support Dress for Success®, an international organization whose mission is "to promote the economic independence of disadvantaged women by providing professional attire, a network of support, and the career development tools to help women thrive in work and in life." To demonstrate our commitment for this strong cause, my husband, Daniel, and I will donate $1.00 to Dress for Success for every copy sold of the *How YOU™ are like Shampoo* book series.

I believe strongly in the mission of Dress for Success and, through this partnership, we know we are empowering disadvantaged women to take charge of their lives and careers. Many thanks to you for your purchase of *How YOU™ are like Shampoo for College Graduates*. By doing so, you have made a difference in the lives of thousands of women, and we are grateful to you for helping us to support such a purposeful organization.

To find out more about Dress for Success, turn to page 274 or visit www.dressforsuccess.org.

How YOU™ are like Shampoo

For COLLEGE GRADUATES

The Complete **Personal Branding System**
to Define, Position, and Market Yourself
and Land a Job You Love

Brenda Bence

BRANDING EXPERT AND CAREER COACH

Copyright © 2010 by Brenda S. Bence. All rights reserved.

Published by Global Insight Communications LLC, Las Vegas, Nevada, U.S.A.

ISBN: 978-0-9799010-9-6
Library of Congress Control Number: 2009936995

Cover design by George Foster, Foster Covers (www.fostercovers.com)
Front cover photography by Kurt Heck (www.kurtheck.com)
Graphic design by Jay Cotton, Hot Ant Design (www.hotant.com.au)
Cartoons by Brenda Brown (http://webtoon.com)
Interior design and typesetting by Eric Myhr

The stories in this book are based on real events and real people. Where requested, and in order to protect the privacy of certain individuals, names and identifying details have been changed.

No part of this publication may be reproduced, stored in a retrieval system, or transmitted in any form or by any means, electronic, mechanical, photocopying, recording, scanning, or otherwise, without the prior written permission of the publisher. Requests to the publisher for permission should be addressed to the Permission Department, Global Insight Communications, P.O. Box 28909, Las Vegas, NV 89126, U.S.A. Phone: +1-702-851-7697; Fax +1-702-220-6444 or by e-mail at info@globalinsightcommunications.com.

Limit of Liability/Disclaimer of Warrant: While the publisher and author have used their best efforts in preparing this book, they make no representations or warranties with respect to the accuracy or completeness of the contents of this book and specifically disclaim any implied warranties of merchantability or fitness for a particular purpose. No warranty may be created or extended by sales representatives or written sales materials. The advice and strategies contained herein may not be suitable for your situation. You should consult with a professional where appropriate. Neither the publisher nor author shall be liable for any loss of profit or any other commercial damages, including but not limited to special, incidental, consequential, or other damages.

Publisher's Cataloging-in-Publication Data:

Bence, Brenda S.
   How you(tm) are like shampoo for college graduates : the complete personal branding system to define, position, and market yourself and land a job you love / Brenda Bence.
   p. cm.
   ISBN 978-0-9799010-9-6
   1. Job hunting. 2. College graduates--Employment. 3. Résumés (Employment) 4. Employment interviewing. 5. Career development. 6. Vocational guidance. I. Title.
HF5381 .B 3563 2010
650.1--dc22   2009936995

*To Kathie and Arlyn Uhrmacher
who have dedicated their lives not just to educating students,
but to inspiring them to follow their passions
and to do what they love.*

Contents

Preface	9
Introduction: Your Job Search — How *Are* YOU™ Like Shampoo?	15
The Power of Brands	21

Step 1: Define It

Defining Your Personal Brand	29
Element #1: *Audience*	37
Element #2: *Need*	59
Element #3: *Comparison*	71
Element #4: *Unique Strengths*	83
Element #5: *Reasons Why*	97
Element #6: *Brand Character*	107
Pulling It All Together	119

Step 2: Communicate It

Taking YOU™ on Interviews	135
Launching Your College Graduate Personal Brand	139
Activity #1: *Actions*	147
Activity #2: *Reactions*	167
Activity #3: *Look*	179

Activity #4: *Sound*   195

Activity #5: *Thoughts*   215

Your Complete College Graduate Personal Brand Marketing Plan   235

Step 3: Avoid Damaging It

College Graduate Personal Brand Busters®   243

Quiz: The Top 20 College Graduate Personal Brand Busters®   247

Assuring Long-Term Success   263

Appendix A: *Great Interview Questions for YOU™*   267

Appendix B: *Personality Profiles and Tests*   270

Suggested Books   272

About the Author   273

Acknowledgments   275

Contact Information   277

Preface

Each one of us has a fire in our heart for something. It's our goal in life to find it and to keep it lit.

— Mary Lou Retton, Olympic Gold Medal Gymnast

I just might be the kind of person you love to hate. Why? Well, I wake up every single morning happy, with a smile on my face. I can't wait to get out of bed and head off to work. I thoroughly enjoy what I do for a living. And because I'm so satisfied in my professional life, this rolls over into the rest of my life. I have a terrific marriage, fantastic relationships with family, wonderful friends, and an active social life ... and the list goes on and on.

But before you decide that you hate me *too* much, I should tell you: It wasn't always this way.

When I graduated from college, I had absolutely no idea what I wanted to do. I had spent four years in school, had worked hard to get good grades, my father had spent all that money on tuition, and there I stood — diploma in hand — with a blank expression on my face. I didn't have a *clue* what I should do with it. The only thing I knew for sure is what I *didn't* want to do — and that was business! (Funny when I think about that now...)

So, what happened? Well, suffice it to say that the universe kicked me in the pants a few times but, ultimately, led me in the right direction during the five years that followed college. As a result, I eventually learned that I would not only do well in business but that I would absolutely love it. Still, getting there was a rocky road, akin to being in a haunted house ... crawling along the walls, feeling my way, not sure where I was heading or what was around the next corner. And just like a haunted house visit, all turned out well in the end, but it was pretty scary going through the process.

Why am I telling you this? For the same reasons I wrote this book: to spare you, as you prepare to graduate, the same kind of floundering that I went through. Defining and communicating a powerful personal brand for your job search can do just that. It can save you time, energy, money, and frustration so that you don't have to spend your next five years like I did, wondering what you *really* want to do with your life.

Personal branding helps you cut to the chase, allowing you to carefully define and hone in on your passions. Then, it shows you how to communicate who you are and what you have to offer. And, most importantly, it helps you to get where you want to be — in a job that you love — *now,* not five years from now.

Branding yourself as a college graduate can prevent you from becoming one of 75% of all people who are unhappy in their jobs. Yes, that's right — statistics show that as many as 75% of people working today are dissatisfied in their professions. Think about that: If you're not happy with how you make your living — where you'll be spending about half of your waking hours — how can you lead a full, productive, and complete life? If you're not happy in such an important part of your life as your work, how can you be completely fulfilled in the hours that are left over?

There's just no reason why you shouldn't feel as passionate about your work as I feel about mine. If it can happen for me, it can happen for you. And wouldn't the world be a different place if everyone loved their work as much as that? We would be more fulfilled as a whole, our relationships would be better, and our family lives would be happier. What a difference it would make.

And that's exactly what *How YOU™ are like Shampoo for College Graduates* is all about. I created the *How YOU™ are like Shampoo* series of personal branding books with this dream in mind.

So, how did I get from floundering five years out of college to becoming the author of a series of personal branding books?

Well, to start with, I've spent quite a few years coaching clients to develop their personal brands. Besides coaching individuals, I work as an international branding and marketing trainer and a professional speaker. Not only has this work allowed me to visit almost 70 countries, but I've also gotten to live and work in quite a few countries outside the U.S., too. It's been an incredible experience!

You've heard of serial killers? Well, think of me as a "serial brander"—I just can't stop branding! For many years, I marketed big-name brands like Pantene and Vidal Sassoon when I worked for corporations like Procter & Gamble and Bristol-Myers Squibb. Throughout all of that, I used an established process and framework that name-brand marketers have used for a long time to craft and communicate brands. You may not have known such a process exists, but trust me: Great brands don't become great brands by accident! It's only because of a powerful process put into place by good, strategic marketers that these brands make millions. And it's only because of this process that successful brands continue to survive and thrive through economic ups and downs.

Several years ago, when I began coaching people to reach their goals and develop their individual personal brands, I started to experiment and apply these same principles of corporate branding to personal branding. I took the elements and framework used by name-brand marketers and adjusted them to fit personal brands, so that all of us—as individuals—could thrive in our careers the same way those great name brands we love have thrived in the marketplace. That's how the personal branding system in this book was born.

Now, you may be thinking, "But Brenda, you weren't coaching college grads, were you?" Well, yes, eventually I was! At first, as you'd expect, I mostly coached executives, but those executives had sons and daughters just like you who were getting ready to graduate from college. That's why I took my system one step further and adapted it especially for college grads. So, I've witnessed firsthand just how powerful this personal branding process can be when applied to college graduates, and that's how this book came about.

In the pages that follow, we'll walk together through the process of building your college graduate personal brand step by step by step, helping you to craft and effectively communicate YOU™. That's right—the trademarked *you*.

Today, you—or YOU™—can apply the same system in your job search that big-company marketers have used for years to build enormously successful corporate brands. Can you see now "how YOU™ are like shampoo?" Just as a corporate marketer uses this proven process to build the mega-brand of a shampoo like Pantene or Vidal Sassoon or Head & Shoulders, you, too, will build the brand of YOU™. It doesn't matter if you are looking for your first full-time job. It doesn't matter if you don't have any work experience or if you've "only" ever worked at a fast food chain. You'll learn how to use your education and *all* of your experiences (even outside of work and school) to your advantage during your job search.

Since the advent of personal branding over a decade ago, several books have been written on the subject. What makes *How YOU™ are like Shampoo for College Graduates* different is that it offers a complete system specifically for job-seeking college grads, covering every possible aspect of how to use personal branding to sail through your job search with a successful result. This book goes beyond the theories about personal branding to bring you practical tools that you can apply immediately to your job search!

My hope is that this book will:

- Open you up to the power that comes from successfully branding yourself.
- Show you how your job search can actually be energizing and fun.
- Expand your vision of the kind of job and career you're capable of achieving.
- Offer you empowering tips and tools you can use before, during, and after your interviews so that you'll feel confident and fully ready to wow your interviewers.
- Give you the satisfaction of knowing you're reaching your full potential and starting the gratifying life that will put a smile on *your* face every morning.

This is probably both an exciting and scary time in your life. Up until now, your primary role has been to study, learn, and grow. Your parents have probably taken care of putting a roof over your head and food on the table. Now, for the first time, it's going to be up to you to step up to the plate and fend for yourself. Personal branding can help you do just that, and that's what this book is all about. Your personal brand can serve as a compass to guide you in a future direction toward a job that doesn't just look good on paper but that feels absolutely "right" down in your bones. I want you to wake up every day, revved up about going to work.

It's exciting for me to share with you my personal branding system tailored specifically for college grad job seekers! I hope you'll have fun with it, too, as we move through this process together.

> *Today, you — or YOU™ — can apply the same system in your job search that big-company marketers have used for years to build enormously successful corporate brands.*
>
> *Can you see now 'how YOU™ are like shampoo?'*

The Proven Pathway to Getting YOU™ a Great Job

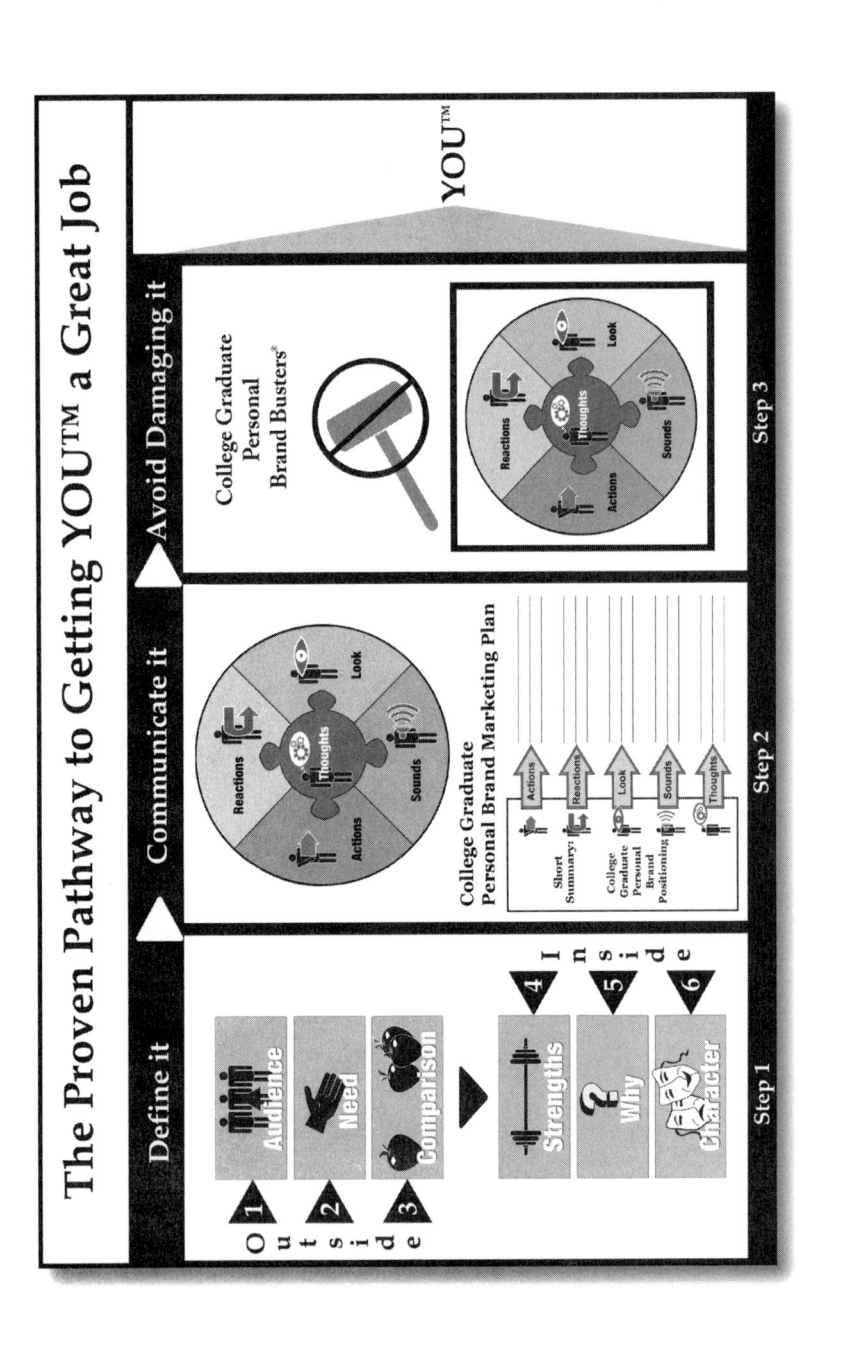

Define it	Communicate it	Avoid Damaging it

Step 1

O u t s i d e

1. Audience
2. Need
3. Comparison

I n s i d e

4. Strengths
5. Why
6. Character

Step 2

College Graduate Personal Brand Marketing Plan

- Short Summary:
- College Graduate Personal Brand Positioning:
  - Actions
  - Reactions
  - Look
  - Sounds
  - Thoughts

Step 3

College Graduate Personal Brand Busters®

YOU™

Introduction

Your Job Search— How *Are* You™ Like Shampoo?

It's better to look ahead and prepare than to look back and regret.
— Jackie Joyner-Kersee, Olympic Gold Medalist

Alfred Nobel was a successful and wealthy Swedish man who lived in the late 1800s. He was famous for having invented two things: dynamite and the detonator, the device that makes dynamite go off from far away. Thanks to these two inventions, Alfred Nobel had made millions, and he was living a wonderful millionaire's life.

Alfred's brother, Ludwig Nobel, who was also famous and wealthy, died in 1888. But the obituary that showed up the next day in the newspaper was switched, and it was *Alfred's* obituary that got printed, not Ludwig's. So, Alfred Nobel had the mind-boggling experience of opening up the morning paper … and reading his own life story.

Can you imagine how powerful that would be?

But Alfred must have cringed when he read the title of his obituary. It called him "The Merchant of Death" because of all the work he had done with dynamite and detonators. In that single moment, Alfred Nobel realized that his personal brand would always be associated with death and destruction — unless he took control and did something about it.

So, he decided to change what his brand stood for. He made a plan to develop the Nobel Prizes to make a difference in important subjects that he really cared about. And when he died in 1895, Alfred Nobel left most of his millions to establish those prizes. He didn't want his name, "Nobel," to stand for destruction and death. Did he succeed? Well, just look at what the name Nobel stands for today — the world's most prestigious prizes awarded for outstanding achievements in Physics, Chemistry, Medicine, Literature, and Peace.

You've heard of the Nobel Prizes, right? But you probably didn't know the other work that Nobel had done in his life. That's because Alfred Nobel was successful in changing his personal brand so that his name could stand for what he *wanted* it to stand for.

You can change what you stand for, too, by creating your own personal brand and using it to energize your job search. As author Carl Bard said, "Though no one can go back and make a brand new start, anyone can start from now and make a brand new ending."

Did You Know You Already Have a Personal Brand?

So, maybe you're thinking, "Good story, Brenda, but what does that have to do with me? I'm just getting started in my career. How could I already have a personal brand?"

That's a fair question — and here's my answer: Even if you've never had a full-time job in a company, you already have a personal brand. (And you didn't have to do anything as earth-shattering as invent dynamite to get it!)

It's true. To have a personal brand, you don't have to be an inventor or even sit down and give your personal brand any thought. Just by virtue of being *you* in a job interview or at school or wherever you are, you have a personal brand. The question is whether you have the personal brand you *want*. If not, you're leaving too much of your job search and your future to chance.

Just like Alfred Nobel, you have the power to change your personal brand and create the one that you desire. In other words, you have to make a decision about how you want to come across before, during, and after interviews in order to get the kind of work you really want. And there's no better time to work on your personal brand than now as you think about your first job after college and as you get ready to launch yourself into the professional marketplace.

Personal Branding and Your Job Search

But what if you're starting at the bottom of the totem pole with little or no experience, and you're convinced it's going to be hard as nails to find a job that keeps you happy and excited? Well, I'm here to tell you: With personal branding, you can do it. If you want the kind of job where you can't wait to get up in the morning and get to work, personal branding is the answer.

Defining your college graduate personal brand can be the missing link to helping you find the type of job you've been daydreaming about. Knowing who "YOU™" are — the trademarked you — will give you a clear edge in your job search. In fact, once you carefully define the college graduate personal brand you want to communicate in interviews, you'll be able to look at your job search with new meaning and confidence. That's how you make every moment of your job hunt count. And yes — even though it's hard to believe — you may actually begin to find interviews *fun*.

Yep, personal branding can do all of that, but here's the scoop: It really is up to you. If you want a great first job out of college that sets you up for success both short-term and long-term, you have to do something about it. If you don't, I can guarantee you one thing: Nothing will happen.

Now, I can almost hear you saying, "But Brenda, I don't have control over whether an interviewer likes me or not. If they decide not to hire me, what can I do?" Even though it may feel like your job search is at the mercy of potential employer "decision-makers" out there, a big part of your job search success *is* in your control. The key to that control is learning how to master your college graduate personal brand. In *How YOU™ are like Shampoo for College Graduates*, we will focus on those fundamental parts of your job search that *are* in your control.

My Personal Branding System

So, let's recap. Here's the reality: You already have a personal brand. Every time you've gone on an interview or shown up at school or at a meeting, your personal brand was front and center, even though you didn't know it. Now, it's time to take control and learn how to manage it. That's how you will have better success before, during, and after job interviews, and — ultimately — that's how you'll land a great position in a company where you want to work.

How YOU™ are like Shampoo for College Graduates is a do-it-yourself, no-nonsense guide to getting the job you want through successfully branding yourself. It's simple, easy to read, and it works. I custom-designed the personal branding system in this book to help graduating students like you take the guesswork out of personal branding. This system will show you exactly how to figure out (1) what your personal brand is and (2) how to use it to get the job you want *faster*. In this book, I'm going to walk you through my proven step-by-step personal branding process — using exercises and worksheets — to help you define the most powerful college grad personal brand you can possibly have. This system is all about applying it in the real world.

Most importantly, your brand won't just stay a nice idea in your head. I mean, think about it: It makes no sense to spend the time defining your brand just to leave it in a drawer while you continue on the same as always, right?

No, you need a plan to make sure you're communicating the brand you want to potential employers. That's how you find your dream job. That's how you take the steering wheel at the beginning of your career and drive it where you want it to go.

As you read on, here's what you'll learn:

- How to define your personal brand using the College Graduate Personal Brand Positioning Statement format modeled off of the six core elements used by the most successful name brands in the world. It's worked for Nike, Starbucks, and McDonald's, and it will work for YOU™, too.

- How to communicate your personal brand through your College Graduate Personal Brand Marketing Plan so that potential employers will see you as you *want* to be seen. This will help you master the five most important activities you do throughout your job search that will impact your personal brand — and your ability to get the job you want.

- How to avoid damaging your college grad personal brand by learning from the mistakes that other grads like you have made during their job search. This is one of the most unique and fun parts of the system — our top 20 most damaging College Graduate Personal Brand Busters®. Knowing these will help you bypass the most common traps that have prevented other grads from getting the job they wanted. You'll know what to watch out for before you even get there.

- Lots of amazing interview success tips and secrets from dozens of college recruiters and human resources experts all across the U.S. that I interviewed for this book. They've been in the trenches and have seen it all!
- How to use the graphic called "The Proven Pathway to Getting YOU™ a Great Job" that is on page 14. It will guide you kind of like a map as we work through each step of the personal branding system together. Don't worry if it doesn't make sense to you yet. It will — I promise.

As you read these pages, I hope that you will experience that "ah-ha!" moment that comes from the power of thinking of yourself as a unique personal brand. I hope you'll see how you can use personal branding to make real changes in your life that can lead to a terrific job with a sweet paycheck, great job satisfaction, and exciting career opportunities.

Input Equals Output

How YOU™ are like Shampoo for College Graduates is an interactive, action-oriented experience, but your personal brand won't be handed to you on a silver platter. I can guarantee you one thing for sure: What you put *in* to defining and communicating your college grad personal brand is exactly what you'll get *out* of it. As I said, it's up to you! The more time and energy you give to this process, the faster you will get the job you want.

I know, I know … you've had it with homework. You're near the end of your time at college, and you want to just put it all on autopilot. But trust me: You'll be glad that you took your personal brand seriously and followed this process step-by-step. When you're driving down the street in the new car you bought thanks to your great new job, you'll be thanking me and patting yourself on the back for making it happen.

Of course, it isn't just about a new car that you can buy with your earnings. It's about finding a job that you love that doesn't even seem like work. Get ready to feel pumped as you take charge of your college graduate personal brand and become the Brand Manager of YOU™.

"This is our best-selling brand!"

1

The Power of Brands

Is Google a 'better' search engine? Is Red Bull a 'better' energy drink? Is Microsoft a 'better' operating system? Or did these companies just build better brands?
— Laura Ries, Media commentator

A book on personal branding wouldn't be complete without taking some time to understand the powerful role that brands play in our lives every single day. Not that long ago, a *Time* magazine article reported that the average American citizen runs across about 3,000 brands per day. When I first heard that, I found it hard to believe! But, then, I stood at a busy intersection in downtown Los Angeles and looked at all of the signs … I drove to the Dallas-Fort Worth airport with hundreds of billboards lining the way … I walked down a grocery store aisle in Philadelphia and saw brand after brand peering down at me. Maybe 3,000 brands per day isn't all that hard to believe after all!

Think about it for a second. How many brands have *you* seen today on can labels, the side of a bus, the top of a taxi, or on the web? No matter where you look, brand names are screaming for your attention. Let's face it: Brands are everywhere and are such a part of our day-to-day lives that we often don't even think about them.

But, if you're like most of us, you will probably be loyal to at least one or two name brands for the rest of your life. Are *you* loyal to a favorite brand? Would you consider it out of the question, for example, to wear anything but Adidas tennis shoes or to switch from your favorite brand of MP3 player? Why? What is it about that favorite brand of yours that gets you to buy it time and time again? Great brands make us intensely loyal.

Great brands can be incredibly big and influential, too. Take Coca-Cola, for example. People all around the world buy an estimated $15 billion of Coke every single year — that's more than $1 billion worth of Coke *per month*. To fully get the picture, that's more than the GDP of about 85 countries in the world. How's *that* for powerful?

The Untouchables

So, what do we know so far? We know that brands are everywhere, that they can create intense loyalty, and that they can have a powerful influence on us. Is there any question why I find brands so fascinating?

But what's even more amazing about brands is that, even though they have all of this power and influence, you can't touch a brand. It's true. You can smell the aroma of a cup of Starbucks coffee, you can taste the kick of an Altoid when you pop one in your mouth, you can hear the sound of Windows starting up on your computer, you can feel an ice cold can of Red Bull in your hand, and you can see the golden arches of the McDonald's logo, but you cannot *touch* a brand. The smell, touch, or sight of a product is really just a representation of that brand. The brand itself is invisible. Its power only exists in your mind.

So, can these untouchable things called "brands" actually change the way we act and think? Let's see…

Powerful Brand Images

Great brands are like people. They have a personality and a character all their own. Stop for a second, look around you, and find two doorways that you can see from where you are. In the first doorway, imagine that Mercedes Benz — the brand — is standing there as a *person* (not the car, but the brand of Mercedes Benz itself). What kind of person would the Mercedes Benz brand be? Is it a man or a woman? What does this person do for a living? How is this person dressed? What is this person's income — low, medium, or high? What does this person do for fun?

Now, look at that second doorway, and imagine that Ferrari — the brand — is standing there as a person. What kind of person would the Ferrari brand be? Is it a man or a woman? What does this person do for a living? How is this person dressed — more formally or more casually than Mercedes Benz? Is the income of this person higher or lower than Mercedes Benz? What does this person like to do for fun?

Now, compare the answers to both sets of questions. They're very different, right? Even though Mercedes Benz and Ferrari are both high-end luxury cars that get you from one place to another, the brand images of Mercedes Benz and Ferrari aren't the same. Why is that? It's because you *perceive, think,* and *feel* differently about these two brands. Your perceptions, thoughts, and feelings have been carefully created in your mind by smart marketers who understand the art and science — and the power — of branding.

That's right. Branding, whether we're talking about a product or a person, is both an art *and* a science. On the one hand, brands appeal to our logic — they're "rational" in terms of how we think about them, and that's where the science comes in. But branding is also an art form because brands make us feel a certain way about them.

Take a minute and think about the brands you're loyal to. Maybe you've even traveled out of your way to find and buy that one special brand that you just *had* to have. What if you could grab hold of that same kind of power in your own job search as you get ready to graduate? How would *you* like to have that kind of influence over a recruiter or a potential boss?

Branding People?

I really believe that people — just like shampoo and other products — are brands, too. Consider some examples of people we all know — starting with celebrities. What do you perceive, think, and feel when you hear the name "Brad Pitt?" What do you perceive, think, and feel when you hear the name "Will Smith?" Both of these actors are good-looking leading men, but you don't have the same perceptions, thoughts, and feelings about them, do you? Now, let's throw "Johnny Depp" into the picture ... you have different perceptions, thoughts, and feelings about him, too, right?

Think of any category of well-known people — let's try singers this time. Think Taylor Swift ... Madonna ... Beyoncé. Again, they're all very different. That's because each of these singers has a very specific personal brand that is absolutely unique and ownable as compared to the others. And it's not just because they all *look* different!

"But hold on a second," you may be saying. "Those people are all celebrities and have a lot of money, so they can all hire full-time image specialists to manage their personal brands!"

Fair point. But you don't need high-priced help to define and communicate your personal brand as you get ready to join the professional world. The personal branding system shared in *How YOU™ are like Shampoo for College Graduates* will help you build your brand without handing bundles of cash to a publicist. It's designed for the millions of grads all around the world who aren't famous and who don't plan on turning their personal brand into a global household name. What you want to do is define yourself in *your world* to reach your ultimate personal career goal: to land that first great job that you can really love so that you can get your career off to a fantastic start.

So, if Johnny Depp and Beyoncé have one, and you have one, too, just what is a personal brand anyway?

Taking Your Brand on a Job Search

When it comes to looking for a job, your personal brand is defined as:

> *The way you want potential employers to*
> *perceive, think, and feel about you*
> *compared to other candidates.*

Just as name brands exist in our minds, your personal brand as a college grad exists in the minds of recruiters and potential bosses in the way they perceive, think, and feel about you when they compare you to other candidates. Let's dive deeper into this definition, and focus on three key words: perceive, think, and feel. They've been carefully chosen for a reason.

> **Perceive:** In marketing, the way you perceive something is reality. When it comes to your college grad personal brand, it doesn't matter who *you* think you are. What matters instead is how the *interviewer* perceives you. If a potential boss sees you as very different from who you actually believe you are inside, you're probably not communicating the personal brand you want. You'll need to do some work to make sure you're presenting your best possible brand in interviews.
>
> **Think:** On the one hand, our brains have a lot to do with how we *think* about brands, so branding is a fairly rational exercise. There are some good solid reasons we choose one brand over another. The same holds true when it comes to personal branding for a job search—you need to consider what your potential employers will *think* about you. What are the reasons a potential boss might believe you are better for the job than another candidate?
>
> **Feel:** On the other hand, branding is also a very emotional process. Stop and consider that one brand from earlier in this chapter that

you said you are intensely loyal to. What do you feel when you think about that brand? Trust? Reliability? We establish relationships with name brands, and these relationships are based on much more than just what the products do for us. We're loyal to these brands because of the emotional connection we have with them. It's the same in personal branding. The way recruiters and potential bosses *feel* about you can make or break your success.

Here's the stark reality: Interviewers hire people they like. In fact, some recruiters estimate that as much as 40% of the hiring decision is based on whether or not you were liked in your interview. If you think about it, this is also the case with name brands. After all, you buy name brands you like, right? The same holds true on the job. Don't you prefer being around people you like, and, if the hiring decision were up to you, wouldn't you hire someone you'd like to spend time with?

It's no different with employers. They hire people they believe they'll like working with, and YOU™ are no exception. The truth is: Interviewers will hire you because they like you and because you've made a connection with them. This doesn't mean, of course, that you'll be hired if you're completely unable to do the job, but even if your skills aren't as good as someone else's, you *could* get hired if you hit it off with the recruiter.

The stronger the connections you create before, during, and after your job interviews, the more powerful your personal brand will be throughout your entire job search process.

✓ Your Brand Doesn't Just Exist on Web 2.0

If potential employers are having perceptions, thoughts, and feelings about you, trust me: It isn't happening just on the Internet through social media networks. While you definitely want to make sure your personal brand stays intact on Web 2.0 applications like Facebook and Twitter, remember that your brand is out there everywhere you are — in person, in e-mails, *and* on the Internet. Later on in the book, we'll talk more about how to protect your brand online, but don't make the mistake of thinking that your personal brand is *only* your brand on the computer. Personal branding is much more than that!

Your Professors' Brands

Still don't believe the average person has a brand? Think of your favorite professor — the one teacher you actually looked forward to listening to. Stop for a second and consider: How do you perceive that professor? How does he or she make you feel? What are your thoughts about him or her?

Now, consider a different prof you've had ... and let's be honest ... who you really didn't enjoy listening to all that much! It was that one instructor who was so boring that you almost needed intravenous caffeine just to stay awake. Or maybe it was a teacher who was an incredibly hard grader. Just the thought of turning in a paper to this professor tied your stomach into knots. How does *this* person make you feel? What do you think about this teacher, and how do you perceive him or her?

Can you see how these teachers have very different personal brands? And their brands have nothing to do with who *they* think they are. Their brands exist in *your* mind, based on how you perceive, think, and feel about them.

Taking Control of YOU™

Now, apply this thinking to you and your job search. As I said earlier, you already have a personal brand even if you didn't think you needed or wanted one. Your college grad personal brand may be out there doing its thing, creating perceptions about YOU™ without you even being aware of it. Recruiters may think and feel about you in ways that aren't at all how you want to be perceived, just like Alfred Nobel before he created his prizes.

Most people I've met find this idea pretty exciting ... and a little bit scary. They don't like the idea that their personal brand may be running wild — maybe even preventing them from getting the job they want — without knowing what to do about it.

So, how do you take control of YOU™ during your job hunt if your college grad personal brand exists in the minds of your potential bosses? What can you do to make sure your personal brand is what you want it to be in interviews and beyond? And how do you want potential bosses to perceive, think, and feel about you? What steps can you take to make your personal brand something that is definable and that you can own? Then, how can you communicate that brand effectively — before, during, *and* after a job interview?

That's a lot of questions, but these are exactly the ones we'll answer as you move through the steps of our college graduate personal branding system. Once you carefully define your personal brand and put it to work, you'll truly be able to stick out from the pack of other job applicants. And, just like you pay more for a Starbucks coffee than you pay for a standard cup of coffee at a local café, you can also create a premium-image personal brand for yourself that brings you a better job, higher starting salary, nicer perks, and — in the end — a great start to a more satisfying career.

Think of it this way: Your personal brand in the job search process is what you want to stand for in the minds of potential future bosses. Who is _____™? Write your name in the blank, and let's get started!

"Personal Branding? You'll find that under 'Arts and Science'."

Step 1
Define it

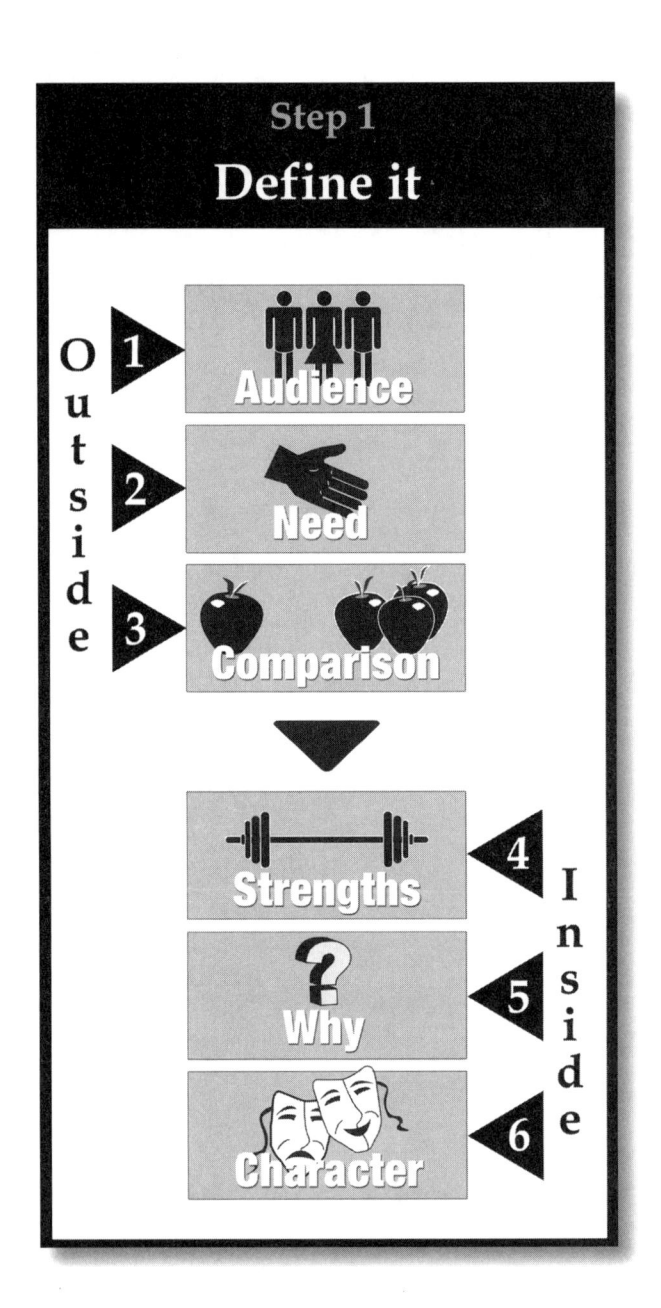

Outside
1. Audience
2. Need
3. Comparison

Inside
4. Strengths
5. Why
6. Character

2

Defining Your Personal Brand

*I always wanted to be somebody,
but I should have been more specific.*
— Lily Tomlin, Actress and comedian

Now, you know you can't touch your personal brand because it exists in the minds of others. So, if you can't touch your brand, how can you take charge of it in a way that actually helps you get the job you want as you get ready to leave college? It may seem like an incredibly tough challenge, but name brands have been successfully created in the minds of millions of consumers for years and years. You can absolutely take control of your college graduate personal brand, too. Just like smart marketers have helped buyers choose one brand over another, you can use the same strategies to help company recruiters choose you over the next candidate. The key is to do what all great brands out there do as a first step: *Define it.*

Fact: Every name brand you know and love uses six "positioning elements" to carefully define that brand. It doesn't even matter if the people in charge of managing those brands know about these elements. Trust me: All six are a big part of what makes the brand tick, and it's a tried-and-true formula.

You've already asked yourself the question, "Who is _____™ — the trademarked YOU™? And maybe you're saying, "But Brenda, give me a break! I have no idea how to answer that question!" If this is the case, don't worry. We're going to work with a step-by-step formula that borrows from those same six positioning elements used by the most successful marketing experts around the world. That formula will help you pinpoint the best possible personal brand for you as a college grad—a personal brand that will present your best talents, strengths, and attributes and that distinguishes you from other people applying for the kinds of jobs you want most.

The Power of a Framework

Let's take a look at the six parts of this formula and see first how they work for the name brands we all love and use every day. Then, you will see how to apply those same elements to YOU™.

THE SIX-ELEMENT BRANDING FORMULA

Name Brands	Personal Brands for Job Seekers
Target: When it comes to name brand products, this is the Target Market. Who will buy the product—men, women, college graduates, people with high incomes or low incomes? What are their hopes, dreams, and fears? What attitudes do they have toward the brand or the type of product in question? What can you tell about them by the way they act toward a particular brand?	*Audience:* Like a Target Market, your Audience consists of the people you want to influence with your personal brand as you look for a job. Maybe your Audience is a single person—like a potential boss—or a group of people, like a department of a company. Who do you want to influence with your college graduate personal brand?

Need: What does the Target Market need? When a company creates a brand, they try to respond to a Need of ours that hasn't been met yet. Or maybe they aim at filling a Need we already have in a way that's better than the competition.	*Need:* If your Audience is a potential boss, what does he or she need? Is there a gap that hasn't been filled in the company? For example, it's possible your future supervisor needs someone to take some responsibility off his or her shoulders.
Competitive Framework: When it comes to name brands, competitive framework is all about the brands that compete for your attention. You have lots of brands all trying to get you to buy them — why do you choose one brand over another?	*Comparison:* In personal branding, this is more about *comparing* than competing. Who will your Audience compare you with when it comes to meeting a Need you've identified? Even if you have less direct work experience, what do you have to offer that will set you apart from other candidates?
Benefits: What does a brand offer its customers? Your toothpaste brand, for example, can whiten your teeth and, therefore, help you feel more confident.	*Unique Strengths:* In personal branding, your Unique Strengths are the promises that you bring to the table. Just like with name brands, your Strengths are the *benefits* you can offer to a potential boss.

Reasons Why: Why should the Target Market believe a name brand will do what it says it can? These are a brand's Reasons Why. They can be based on a variety of things like what it's made of, what experience it has in the market already, how the product is created, or maybe a strong endorsement.	***Reasons Why:*** Why should a future boss believe you can deliver the Unique Strengths you promise? This is where you prove you can do what you say you can.
Brand Character: Think of this as the personality of a brand. What words would you use to describe a name brand if that brand were a person?	***Brand Character:*** What is the Character of your personal brand? Think of it as your personality, your overriding attitude, and your temperament. Like the foundation of a house, it's the base of who YOU™ are.

Your College Graduate Personal Brand Positioning Statement

Hopefully, by now, you've asked yourself: "Who really is [insert your name here]™?" If you're not sure how to answer that question yet, stick around. We're going to walk through each part together in detail as you go through the book.

As we work our way through Step 1 — the "Define it" step — I'll share with you what you need to complete your "College Graduate Personal Brand Positioning Statement." Your Positioning Statement will show you exactly how to define who YOU™ really are — which will help you to get the absolute best job for you upon graduation.

Bottom line: This is where "you" become "YOU™."

As we work our way through each of the next six chapters, you'll be able to fill in each portion of your College Graduate Personal Brand Positioning Statement, just like the one below. Then, we'll get into how to communicate that well-defined personal brand before, during, and after job interviews. After that, we'll focus on how to avoid damaging the personal brand you've worked so hard to create.

YOUR College Graduate Personal Brand Positioning Statement

Audience

My Audience is:

Company Facts:

Company Culture:

Division/Department Culture:

Interviewer/College Recruiter:

Potential Boss/Supervisor:

Needs

Functional:

Emotional:

Comparison

Job Title:

Desired Label: I want to be the brand of (*the way I would like to be perceived*):

Unique Strengths

My Existing Unique Strengths are:

The Future Unique Strengths That I Want to Work on Are:

Reasons Why

My Existing Reasons Why (*why my Audience should believe I can deliver my Unique Strengths*) *are:*

The Future Reasons Why That I Want to Work on Are:

> ### Brand Character
>
> *My Personal Brand Character (how I want my personal Brand Character to be perceived, including my overriding attitude, temperament, and personality)* ***is:***

By the time you've finished working with the six parts of your College Graduate Personal Brand Positioning Statement, you'll be ready to put YOU™ into action. Armed and ready with that, you will be able to make clear to your ideal employers exactly what you can offer them. So, roll up your sleeves! Your personal brand — and that amazing job you want — is waiting....

Define it

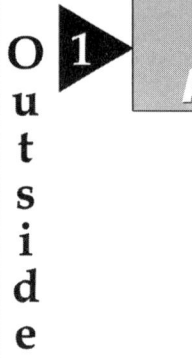

Outside

1 ▶ Audience

Step 1

3

Audience

College Graduate Personal Brand Positioning Element #1

It's up to the Audience. It always has been.
— Kate Smith, Singer

When you're just graduating from college and looking for your first full-time job, let's face it: It's hard not to focus on yourself. All you want is to find a job that you love with great people to work with and a steady paycheck. But the surprising truth about using personal branding in your job search is this:

The best way to land the job you want the most is to focus on your Audience.

After all, potential bosses (your personal brand "Audience") are interested in what you can do for *them*. How are you going to make their jobs easier? What have you learned in school that the company can benefit from? While it's human nature to wonder what the company can do for you, showing them what YOU™ can offer a company is how you land a great job.

One of the most common myths about personal branding is that it's "all about you." But think about it: If your brand exists in the minds of your Audience, how can personal branding be all about you? It can't, and it isn't. The focus has to be on your Audience. So, the more you learn about your Audience, the more in sync you will be with the interviewer. And the more you learn about what the company needs, the faster you'll get the great job you really want.

Now, you may be thinking, "Sounds good, Brenda, but I don't even know where to begin." Well, the key is to get as much information about the company as possible. In fact, one of the recruiters I interviewed said: "You want to stick out in an interview? Be knowledgeable about the company. You wouldn't believe how many students know virtually nothing about the company they're interviewing with. It's a big mistake." Some company recruiters told me that college grads have actually walked into an interview and asked, "What does your company do?" How will a recruiter react to that? Your resume will get thrown in the trash!

One of the HR pros I spoke with said: "It isn't enough in an interview to simply say, 'You have a job I'm interested in, and I know this is a good company.' But you'd be surprised how many candidates do exactly that." Interviewers will see this kind of thinking as lazy, so not knowing about the company just won't cut it. You need to have a very specific reason for wanting a particular job at a particular company. And the only way you can figure out if a company is right for you is to learn about it. Then, you'll be prepared to tell your interviewer that reason.

The more you learn about your Audience, the more you'll have a head start on the interview process because you'll already know more about the company than most of the other applicants. Bottom line: Your interviewers will remember you if you can give them a detailed reason why you want to work there, if you've taken the time to read about the company's background, and if you've learned about the company's recent news.

Who is Your Audience?

So, how do you go about getting that information in order to connect with your interviewer? Let's pretend you're a top-notch marketer — the newly-promoted Brand Manager of YOU™. You're in charge, and it's your job to see that your brand reaches the top.

If YOU™ were a product, your Audience would be called the "Target Market," and you would find out all you could about your Target Market through surveys and questionnaires that ask questions about who they really are. You would want to know provable facts about the people in your Target Market, like their age, sex, income, education, etc. How much do they earn? Do most of them live in the city or in the suburbs? In marketing-speak, these provable facts are called "demographics."

Now, an average marketer might stop there, but provable facts are only the tip of the iceberg when it comes to learning about the Target Market. Think about it for a second: If you really want to get to know someone, it wouldn't be enough only to find out this person's age, how much they earn, and where they were born and lived, right? Those kinds of "facts" wouldn't really tell you much about a person. You would only have scratched the surface, and you would need to base all of your beliefs about that person on less than what they'd write on a doctor's office form.

That's why top-notch marketers take the time to go deeper. They want to know much more about their Target Market. They want to get into the heads of the people who are buying their brands and understand their behavior. In marketing, this information is called "psychographics," which sounds pretty heavy, but basically means personal information that tells you what makes a particular person or group of people tick.

How does this apply to personal branding? Well, in general, your Audience is anyone or any company you want to impact with your personal brand. In your job search process, this includes the people who could hire you for the kind of job you want after graduation. Your Audience might simply be the person who interviews you, but you may not know at first who your interviewer or even your potential immediate supervisor will be. So, in the beginning of your job search, your job-seeking personal brand Audience might be the entire company or a group of people within the company, such as the division or department where you'd like to work.

Now, you're probably thinking: "But how can I know so much about an Audience that I haven't even met yet? I don't know anyone at most of the companies where I want to apply for a job. In fact, I don't even know which *companies* I'm interested in yet!"

That's fair. It's true that when you're looking for a new job, learning about your Audience may seem challenging at first. Even choosing companies to target can be confusing, especially when you're looking seriously at the professional job market for the first time. But don't worry. We're going to walk through this process together. Learning about your Audience before you land a job is definitely doable, and all it takes is some smart investigating, which can actually be fun if you let it. With a little bit of research, you can find out which companies are the best fit for YOU™. In fact, you may be surprised how much you can learn about a company and its people with just a little bit of effort.

Getting Ready to Get Ready

When you're at the very beginning of your job search after (or just before) graduation, you're in more of a *company* search than anything else. There are literally thousands of companies out there, so choosing the right ones to target may feel like looking for a needle in a haystack. But as the determined Brand Manager of YOU™, it's your task to decide which companies should receive your resume — the ones that will truly turn into an Audience for your job-seeker personal brand.

How do you do that? Start by asking yourself some questions about the "type" of companies you would be interested in. What is most important to you?

- Location?
- Size of the company?
- Culture of the company?
- Learning and training focus?
- Opportunities for advancement?
- Whether the company gives back to the community?

You might even rate these elements from 1 to 6 — with 1 as your highest priority and 6 as your lowest priority. Once you've decided what aspects of a company matter most to you, it will be easier to dig deeper and find out more about the companies that feel right to you.

If you don't know which companies in your field are out there, do an Internet search, and begin to gather names. Then, you can look through their websites and see how they measure up on your rating scale. As you start to see which companies have the qualities and the types of opportunities you're looking for, you can narrow down your choices.

Become a Creative Detective

Once you've selected your top companies, it's time to do some digging. At this point, the Audience for your job-seeker personal brand is the entire company you're targeting. Of course, that doesn't mean you're expected to learn about every single person in a big company! Not only is that impossible, but it's not necessary either.

Instead, you can think of the entire company as an "individual" with its own set of facts and attitudes. As a great marketing detective, you can take what you learn about a company and begin to piece together a profile of how it operates, just as you would if you were learning about one specific person. You'll discover if the company has a relaxed, more casual atmosphere or a more structured, buttoned-down setting. You'll find out if the company thinks that coming up with new ideas is important or if it wants employees to stick strictly to policy — that type of thing. Here are some of the ways you can dig deeper to find out more about the companies you're interested in:

Talk, Talk, Talk. Take the time to ask your friends and other people you meet if they know anyone who currently works for, or formerly worked for, your target companies (your potential Audience). If the employee is someone your friend knows well, you could even call or e-mail that person to ask them a few questions about the company.

Meet and Greet. If you get the chance to attend an event where you'd be able to meet people who work at one of the companies you've targeted, don't let the opportunity get away! Of course, in that kind of situation, it's critical to keep up a professional image — even if it's a casual event — because you'll be meeting people face-to-face for the first time. If you pick up business cards at these events, make notes on the back about what the person said, what they looked like, and where you met them.

Search the Internet. Thanks to the worldwide web, it's easier than ever to find out a lot about potential employers. The number of online directories has quadrupled in the past ten years. While looking over the company's website is the absolute best first place to start, it still only scratches the surface of what you can find out about a company online. With just a few research skills, you can uncover an enormous amount of great information that you can use to put together a more detailed profile of your target companies.

Try typing the following into your search engine to discover more about a company:

[Company name] [your desired division or department]

[Company name] annual report

[Company name] press release

[Company name] event

[Company name] brochure

[Company name] newsletter

[Company name] e-zine

[Company name] charity

[Company name] values

[Company name] culture

Through these searches, you should be able to collect a lot of information, including:

- How does the company present itself in the media?
- What kinds of documents does the company publish?
- When you read the company's annual reports, brochures, newsletters, and e-zines, what facts and attitudes do they tell you about the company?

You'll be amazed at how much information you can find out about potential employers this way. What other aspects of a company are you interested in? Rev up Google, Yahoo, or YouTube, and see what you can find.

"Ratings" Lists. You can look up companies on a number of traditional "ratings" lists like Standard & Poor's, Dun & Bradstreet, Dow Jones, Moody's Investors Service, and Polk's. These are services that check out companies all around the globe in order to help investors decide if they want to hand over any of their cold hard cash. I know that, as a college grad, you're probably not investing(!), but in the searches that these companies do, they've uncovered a lot of great info that can come in handy for your job search. If you find accessing these lists online means you have to pay a fee, check out your college library to see if they have the printed versions of the lists that you can use for free.

Information that you get from these lists and from the company's website will help you figure out the following:

- Is the company on the stock exchange, or is it owned by individuals? Family-owned?
- Does the company do business locally, across the U.S., or internationally?
- How long has the company been in business? Has it changed owners more than once?
- What other companies are its biggest competitors?
- Has the company grown in recent years, or is it facing tough times?
- What worldwide trends taking place today might have an impact on the company's business?

Articles About the Company. Search for articles about the company on the Internet, too. You'll probably find lots of online articles — even hundreds if it's a large company. If an article is mentioned on the Internet, but you can only read it in print, see if your college library has a hard copy. Articles will most likely help you answer questions like:

- Has the company been in the news lately? If so, why? What are others saying and writing about the company?
- Has the company joined with another company or set up partnerships with any other companies?
- Has the company launched any new products or services?
- Has the company hired new top execs lately?
- What charities has the company supported, and what do these charities say about the company's character and values?

Articles By or About Key People. Find the names of top executives on the company's website, and try another Internet search for articles by or about some of those executives. Since it's often the top management that sets up the company's culture, what an exec says in an interview may tell you as much about the company as it tells you about him or her. Does the exec seem friendly in the article? Does he or she have a sense of humor? Articles like this will give you a good feeling for the company and what it's all about.

You may even find articles that talk about a top manager before he or she joined the company. If this person could be your immediate boss or the head of your division, knowing this background will tell you a lot about the kind of people that the company likes to hire. You might even be able to find direct quotes from some executives about this person to give you an inside look at the kinds of behaviors they like or dislike. Even if this person doesn't end up being your interviewer, by understanding more about a company's execs, you'll end up with a more in-depth profile of the company and its important players.

Articles will also give you a good feeling for the kind of experience the company is looking for. Find out the background of some of a company's current employees, and you might start to see patterns in the types of people the company likes to hire. This kind of probing is definitely worth your time.

Check Out the Company Using Social Media. These days, most companies have their own social media listings on networks like Facebook or Twitter. Search for the company's name on Facebook, and if they have a fan page, definitely become a fan! Some recruiters told me that they will even check to see if potential interviewees signed up on the company's fan page or not. This is a great way to stick out and show your interest in the company as well as to find out all sorts of things about the company's latest news, key players, and culture.

Companies are also releasing news on Twitter. You can search for a company's name or a person at the company on Twitter or one of the many search engines that have been created for Twitter, like Twellow.com. You'll probably find out what other people are saying about the company, too, and you may find someone who works there or who has interviewed with the company. See what kinds of hints they've left there about interviewing and what they learned from the interview, too.

The LinkedIn Advantage

If you're like most college students, you probably know more about Facebook than you know about LinkedIn.com. LinkedIn is a social networking site that's geared toward managing your work life connections and your career. People use it to network with others in their field and to find new jobs.

LinkedIn is growing like a weed! Techcrunchies.com reports that the site had 7.7 million users in June 2008 and a whopping *45 million* by

June 2009. Monthly page views of LinkedIn jumped from 114 million in 2008 to 331 million in the early part of 2009. Now, *that's* growth! So, if you aren't taking advantage of this site to help you with your job search coming out of college, you're missing out.

LinkedIn works off of the idea of "six degrees of separation" — that everyone is only six degrees away from linking with everyone else. In other words, if you set up a profile on LinkedIn and invite others you know into your network, you'll begin to create more and more connections. LinkedIn can search your address book in Microsoft Outlook or your e-mail list and tell you who on your list already has a LinkedIn profile. You may even find out that you already know someone at one of the companies where you want to work! But even if you don't, you may still be able to establish a connection with someone who can help you *make* a connection.

Here's how it works. Let's say someone in your network knows someone in one of the companies you're interested in, and you see the number "2" by the employee's name on LinkedIn. This means that the employee is only one connection away from you — someone in your own network knows that employee directly. LinkedIn then allows you to ask that friend in your network to introduce you to the employee by sending an e-mail to that person through the LinkedIn system — and you're hooked up!

If you see a "3" next to the name of the person you want to meet, it means you're two connections away from that person. So, you would need to request a couple of introductions in order to meet him or her. That means you could ask the friend in your network to set up an introduction with the other person connected to the employee. Then, hopefully, that person would be willing to set up an introduction for you directly with the employee in question. That's a fair amount of work, of course, so you'd want to make sure that the connection will be worth it to you. But if the person works in the specific area at a company you really want to work for, go for it!

If you're only one connection away from someone you want to connect with (a "2"), it should be easy enough to get an introduction, and it's worth giving it a shot. So, don't be shy about making these connections. If someone is unwilling to help you out with information about the company, that's fine, but you may also meet a great ally who could help you get a job that's even better than you'd hoped for.

LinkedIn is also a great source of company information. You may even discover some really great companies that you didn't know about.

For example, LinkedIn hosts hundreds of interest groups, and if you search for groups in your areas of interest, you should be able to find others in your targeted industry who are working for great companies. Let's say your field is graphic design. You can search the "groups directory" on LinkedIn for "graphic design" and join a professional group to meet other designers. You can then ask group members about the companies they work for.

You can search for specific companies, a city you're interested in, or for a specific industry. Make sure to search for old friends and classmates as well to find out if and where they're working. Someone you knew in the fifth grade might be working at the company that's number one on your list! You won't know unless you look, so be sure to try.

When you search for one of your targeted companies on LinkedIn, you'll find lists of its employees who have LinkedIn profiles. Look for people working in the division you're interested in, for example, and check out their details. You'll be amazed at how much information you'll find there. Once you have a list of people on LinkedIn who work at a particular company, you'll be able to see how connected we all truly are to one another. There's a good chance that someone you're linked to knows an employee at your company of interest.

Another great thing about LinkedIn is that people can write testimonials about you and post them directly to your profile. This means that the testimonials are proven to be objective. You can't tamper with them (although you can decide not to add them to your profile if they say something you don't want others to read). These testimonials also give you a chance to see what others are saying about employees at a company you're interested in. Then, you can get a sense of the kind of people the company likes to hire.

When you review the profiles and testimonials, look for *trends* rather than just data about individuals. Does a particular company's employees have things in common that could help you better understand what that company is all about? For example:

- Do the LinkedIn profiles sound similar — such as all conservative and formal or all pretty casual?
- What type and level of education do most of the employees have?
- Can you find profiles of recent college graduates that the company has hired?
- What kinds of things are mentioned most in the testimonials of the company's employees? Do they tend to focus more on

creativity … loyalty … integrity? This will give you an idea of what's important to the company.

Culture is Key

As you sort through all of the information on LinkedIn, Facebook, the rest of the Internet, and elsewhere, see what it tells you about the company's "culture." Every company has one, and as I said before, it's usually driven by its top leaders. So, reading LinkedIn profiles of a company's top execs can be incredibly helpful. Based on how its leaders are presented, you can get a good sense of what's important to the company.

As you think about applying to a company, remember that making sure you fit in with the company's culture is key. First of all, if you don't fit in, you'll definitely have a harder time getting a job there. Second, if there isn't a cultural "fit" once you do get the job, you'll probably end up feeling like a fish out of water. And that's definitely no way to end up in a job you love.

Is Your Audience's Culture Right for YOU™?

Gary Woollacott, CEO of Opus Recruitment, tells the story of a young woman named Angela who was asked through his firm to interview with a bank. Despite Gary and Angela's high hopes, the interviewer didn't like Angela all that much. That very same day, Angela interviewed at a different bank and was hired right away. Angela was just as qualified for the first job as for the second, so what happened?

It turns out that the first bank was very structured, and Angela thrived in a place that gave her a project or task to do and let her run with it. The second bank was the right fit because it was looking for someone who could take charge and be independent, while the first bank wanted someone to follow specific processes without stepping outside of the guidelines. One was clearly right for Angela, and the other was not.

So, do your research on the "culture" of the companies you're interested in. The more you know about the company's culture, the better you'll be able to tell if it's a good fit for YOU™.

The Right Questions

Okay, so now you've done your research, connected with people, and you have an "in" with someone at one or two of your top companies. Suddenly, it's time to talk to this contact on the phone or face-to-face. What questions should you ask?

Here's the very best suggestion I can give you: Ask for advice! Be honest, and let that person know you're interested in working for the company. Ask them what they would suggest you do as first steps to get started finding a job there. You may be surprised by how much someone is willing to help you just because you've asked for their help and guidance.

Here are a few other questions to ask if you get the chance to talk to someone who's already working for a company you're interested in:

- What does the company look for in an employee?
- What do you think are the top five skills the company values most?
- What do you like the most about working there? What do you like the least?
- Is it a training-focused company? If so, does it send employees to outside training programs, or does it hold regular in-house trainings?
- What are three words that best describe the culture of the company?
- How does the company treat its employees in general?
- Does the company hold a lot of events for its employees? If so, what kind? Are employees' families invited to these parties, too?
- On a scale from 1-10, how open to new ideas is the company? What examples can you share with me to show why you give it that score?
- Would you say that the company is more team- or individual-oriented? Can you share with me a few examples of why you think that?

The answers will give you great clues about what to focus on in your resume and interview. If you find out the company values integrity and collaboration skills, you can get some examples ready to share in an interview about situations in school, groups, internships, or part-time jobs where you've been able to show your integrity and how well you work with others.

Of course (and this does happen), in the process of getting answers to your questions, you may find out you no longer want to apply to a particular company. That's actually a good thing! Scratch that company off your list, and focus your energy on getting a job in a different company that's a better fit for your specific likes, dislikes, and talents.

Once you know about the companies where you'd like to work, you can use the same ideas to find out about a specific division, department, or branch office. Most of the time, there's a ton of information out there about the particular area you're interested in.

The Inside Scoop from HR Professionals

Want your initial cover letter to stick out? HR professionals say that it will make a more powerful punch if you mention something specific about the company that you've learned through your research. Of course, you don't want to say something like, "I read that the company appointed a new Chairman of the Board." Anybody could find that out very quickly! Instead, mention something that clearly shows you've done your homework. It might be something like, "I was impressed when I saw that your company doubled its revenues in the past year," or "As an animal lover, I was excited to read about your company's involvement with the Wildlife Conservation Society."

By the way, don't do what one applicant did and mention a story that he'd read about the company's legal problems with unions. He did end up standing out ... but not in a good way!

Find Out About the Interviewer

Sometimes, before an interview, you may actually be told who your interviewer will be. If you're only given the person's title, be quick to ask for the person's name. If you still don't get the name, try an Internet search for the company name and the interviewer's title to see if a name shows up. No matter how you get the name of your interviewer — which is a bit like being handed a golden key — rev up your favorite search engine. Also, look for him or her on social networking sites like LinkedIn, Facebook, and Twitter. Knowledge is power! So, the more you know, the better you can be prepared for your interview. You may not want to talk about any of the information you've discovered in your search — especially if it's something personal like the name of the interviewer's children — but the information you find may tell you a lot about the interviewer's personality. And that can definitely come in handy.

The bottom line is this: The more information you can find out about your interviewer, the more confident you'll feel in your interviews.

✓ What Type of Interviewer Will You Have?

Here's an important thing to keep in mind: Try to find out if you'll be interviewed by a Human Resources professional or by someone who might be your potential boss. Why? Human Resources managers sometimes focus more on what's on your resume than on whether you're a good fit for the company. After all, their main job is to be the "front line," helping the hiring manager screen candidates. Their reputation depends on letting in the right people for that next interview. Think of them as the bouncer at the door of the hottest club in town — the person who decides whether or not you get to go inside. So, HR managers are often more interested in "checking the boxes" to make sure you're qualified. That means they may stick to the basics and spend more time asking questions about your past course work or any experience you've had to see if it fits the requirements of the job.

On the other hand, potential bosses — usually called "line managers" — can be a bit more relaxed when interviewing candidates for their division. That's because they're the ones who know best how well a person would fit into a particular job and within the culture of the company or division. A line manager is more likely to look at everything about you — your personality, look, temperament, etc. — rather than just your skills and education.

Your College Graduate Personal Brand Positioning Statement

Now that you've dug deep and got information about the Audience for your personal brand, it's time to start putting together your College Graduate Personal Brand Positioning Statement.

To help you with your own statement, let's look at a couple of examples. The following College Graduate Personal Brand Positioning Statements are from two students who have different majors, backgrounds, personalities, and job search objectives. As we work through the chapters, we'll follow along and see how these two college students completed each section of their Positioning Statements. Hopefully, these examples will give you lots of ideas and help you understand how the different sections of your own Positioning Statement all fit together. We'll even show you how these two grads went about their own Audience research and what methods they used to find out about one of their main target companies. Let's start with Nicole.

Case Study—Nicole Caviellieri

Nicole had been interested in medicine since she was young, so when she entered her state's university as a freshman, she immediately declared Pre-Med as her major. But halfway through her sophomore year, Nicole was struggling—she just didn't have what it took to get through the science classes necessary to get into med school. So, Nicole switched her major to Business Administration, a move which helped her grades turn around (her Business Administration GPA was a strong 3.68). However, because of poor science grades during her freshman and sophomore years, Nicole's GPA at the end of her senior year was just barely at 3.1. She knew she would have to explain this in her interviews and cover letters.

Even though Business Administration felt like a great direction for Nicole, she still wasn't sure what she wanted to do after she graduated. Then, her uncle suggested she combine her passion for medicine, her business studies, and her outgoing personality and explore becoming a sales rep for a medical supply firm. The idea of selling products that helped make peoples' lives better really excited Nicole. After doing some research into medical sales rep positions, she felt like she finally knew what she would like to do coming out of college.

To create a list of potential employers, Nicole searched Google and LinkedIn for "medical supply company," "medical products company," and "pharmaceutical company." Several company names came up, but after reading through a lot of profiles, the company she was most interested in was a large pharmaceutical firm called Medo-Innovations. Through her research, Nicole learned that almost no one could expect to land a pharmaceutical sales job right out of college. It required about 2-3 years of work in general medical sales first. But Medo-Innovations had a good-sized medical supply division, too, and Nicole felt that working in that division for 2-3 years would be a great way to get started in the field and possibly help her move into pharmaceutical sales later on.

She visited the Medo-Innovations booth at her university's career fair and had a chance to talk with a company rep there. The talk went well, and Nicole found out that Medo-Innovations had plans to expand their sales force in the coming year. The rep took her resume, and then — a week later — Nicole received a call asking her to set up an initial phone interview with a Medo-Innovations in-house HR recruiter.

Nicole prepared carefully for the phone interview (see tips for building your brand through phone interviews on page 207) and felt that her interview went well. It was a basic interview that covered some key questions about why she was interested in the company, why she wanted to sell medical supplies, how she felt about her GPA, and included some verification of other items on her resume. She was told that if the company was interested, she would be called for an in-person interview with the hiring manager. Two weeks later, Nicole was excited to get that call.

Then, it was time to prepare for the interview! Nicole looked up Medo-Innovations on Twitter and read some articles on the Internet, where she found out that the division would soon be releasing a new type of glucose monitor that was one of the key reasons for the expansion of its sales force.

Nicole's College Graduate Personal Brand Positioning Statement

Audience

My Audience is: Medo-Innovations, a large pharmaceutical company with a well-known medical supply division that will soon be launching a new type of glucose monitor.

Company Facts: Currently, the medical supply division of Medo-Innovations has a national sales force of about 150 people. From what I've read on the Internet, it sounds like they're going to add around 15-20 new salespeople, and the rep at the career fair told me they hire new grads pretty regularly. I was told by the career fair rep that you can often stay in your geographic area and that the division may even realign a territory, allowing you to stay close to home.

Nicole looked up the company on Facebook and found a fan page for the medical supply division. There were a lot of photos of people in the division enjoying events together. She joined the fan page, signed up to follow the company's tweets on Twitter, and looked for Medo-Innovations employees on LinkedIn. In the process, she found out that a friend of hers was connected on LinkedIn to someone who knew one of the sales reps of the division. Through this LinkedIn connection, Nicole was able to set up a phone call with the rep and got some inside information that she hadn't asked the rep at the career fair.

Company Culture: Medo-Innovations is all about innovation and new ideas. Every sales rep, even the ones with years of experience, go through a phenomenal training program that's very specific to the company.

> *Division Culture:* The division has a track record of hiring younger employees because top management believes fresh, enthusiastic sales reps represent the spirit of its brand. The division has no problem hiring sales reps right out of college if they have the right personality and intelligence to fit into the culture and do the job well. The CEO of the division is a woman in her late 40s, and the division has a "family" culture that makes it feel like a small company even though it's part of a large corporation. This division isn't as competitive as the pharmaceutical division. Sales reps work out of their homes and have their own territories, as if they're running their own businesses.
>
> *Interviewer:* I'll be interviewing with Kim Mayerson, a 38-year-old hiring manager. She has been with the company for 11 years. From Kim's LinkedIn profile, I can see that she's very well-respected because her testimonials from her boss and three of her direct reports are all excellent. Two people commented about her professionalism and attention to detail. So, even though the culture of the division sounds like a "family," Kim is probably a stickler for details. Medical supplies are serious business, so I can understand why she would be this way.

Case Study – Travis Trent

When Travis was a kid, he loved taking things apart and putting them back together; he was passionate about figuring out how things worked. Travis had also always done well in math classes, so when it came time to declare a major in college, he was naturally attracted to Engineering.

Travis adored all things related to the outdoors, too, and had spent many summers camping with his family and hiking in the mountains. So, during the summer between his junior and senior years, he was happy to land an engineering internship with the state highway department. There, he got to see firsthand how he could work outside in nature while also helping to make an impact on the environment.

Now, as Travis prepared to graduate, he set his objective on getting a full-time job as an Engineering Intern (called "EI" — the typical entry-level engineering position) with a private consulting firm that had an environmental engineering division. He knew that working for a consulting firm meant more work hours and a higher level of stress, but it would also mean higher pay.

The biggest challenge Travis faced in his job search was this: While he had only worked one summer in an engineering internship (his father had needed him to work in their family business during his first two summers at college), a lot of his engineering classmates had held internships every summer during their years in college. Knowing that top-notch engineering companies wanted to hire grads who had more hands-on experience, Travis realized he'd have to work hard to combat this lack of practical summer engineering intern experience and get across to interviewers that he was serious about engineering as a career.

Travis had a few engineering firms in mind where he would like to work, but #1 on his list was PVM Consulting. The most prestigious engineering firm and known for hiring the best and the brightest, PVM had many offices around the world, one of which was near where Travis wanted to live. He knew it might not be easy to get hired there, but he was determined to try his very best.

Travis's College Graduate Personal Brand Positioning Statement

Audience

My Audience is: PVM Consulting, Inc.

Company Facts: PVM is a very well-known company that was founded in the 1920s. It has more than 100 locations around the world and employs more than 5,000 engineers. Everybody in the engineering field knows about this firm and its professional reputation.

The firm's website had a page devoted to its values and mission. So, Travis was able to get some general information about the culture and what was important to the company. He didn't stop there, though. He researched online and at the library, and he found several articles about PVM, including profiles of top engineers and descriptions of some of the firm's most recent projects.

> *Company Culture:* The firm seems to be buttoned down, and seniority appears to matter there. PVM management values teamwork and strives to get repeat business from clients, which I'm sure is one of the reasons they've been around for so long. So, it's clear that they expect a lot from their engineers, whether they're in entry-level EI jobs or whether they've been there for years. In every picture I saw of anyone in the firm, they were dressed in a suit and tie, which confirms the "buttoned down'" type of work environment; they maintain that same kind of professional look in all of their promotional materials, too. Most of the PVM engineers who have profiles on LinkedIn don't have pictures, though. Backgrounds of top PVM engineers on Facebook and LinkedIn show top-notch experience. Even several Engineer Interns had profiles, and the EIs were equally highly qualified. The engineers with testimonials on their profiles were described with words like "reliable" and "detail-oriented."

Through on-campus career services, Travis managed to get an interview with PVM. He was told this first interview would be with a small team of people: One person from HR, the Team Leader who Travis would actually work for if he got the job, and a recently hired EI. He was told the HR rep's name and the Team Leader's name, but he wasn't told who the EI would be. It sounded like they may choose an EI to sit in on the interview at the last minute. Travis asked around and found a professor who knew another student who had been an EI at PVM. This person was able to tell him a little bit about his two interviewers.

> *Interviewer #1:* Joseph Cho is an HR rep at PVM and has been with the company for ten years. Before that, he worked in HR for a smaller, private engineering firm. My contact estimates that he's probably in his early 40s. All of this means that Joseph really knows his stuff. When I Googled Joseph's name, I found that he's a member of a professional HR organization and also a member of The United States Chess Federation. Since I like to play chess, too, I can try to mention this in my interview.

Interviewer #2: Adam Trollar is the Team Leader and, if I get the job, I would report directly to him. My contact says Adam's really into active and outdoor hobbies like skiing, mountain climbing, hang gliding, and scuba diving. He's in his late 30s and very "intense" and "focused" in the words of my contact. I also found a press release about when he was hired, which talked about his prior work with another big engineering firm. In the release, he talked about his commitment to the environment, which is something he and I have in common.

Now, you're ready to complete the Audience portion of your own College Graduate Personal Brand Positioning Statement. If you have more than one target company, you will want to do separate Audience definitions for each target.

YOUR College Graduate Personal Brand Positioning Statement

Audience

My Audience is:

Company Facts:

Company Culture:

Division/Department Culture:

Interviewer/College Recruiter:

Potential Boss/Supervisor:

Define it

Outside ▶ 2 ▶ Need

Step 1

4

Need

College Graduate Personal Brand Positioning Element #2

Before you build a better mousetrap, it helps to know if there are any mice out there.

— Yogi Berra, Professional baseball player and manager

It isn't enough just to know who your Audience is. You also have to know what your Audience *needs*. Good marketers won't build a better mousetrap unless they know there are people out there with a mouse problem who need that mousetrap. If the marketplace doesn't need it, they'll end up with a warehouse full of mousetraps and no one to buy them.

It's the same with personal branding. You want to find the companies that need what you have to offer. Some grads just cast a wide net and apply for jobs at all sorts of companies without any sense of direction. I know someone who applied to 330 jobs and still hasn't been hired. Why? Because sending out generic resumes to anybody and everybody is like trying to teach your great grandmother to text. It's simply a waste of time.

If you don't want to feel like a hamster running inside a wheel that never goes anywhere, then you need to focus and get specific about the companies you're targeting. In fact, if you try to get a job with a company that doesn't need what you have to offer, you're actually slowing down your job search. The outcome? Nothing but frustration and disappointment. If you spend the extra time and energy to really do your homework, you'll get a much better and faster result — a job you know is the best fit for you.

So, the next step in defining your personal brand is to take the information you've uncovered about your Audience and figure out what that Audience *needs*.

Fix the Problem

Whether you know it or not, Needs are an important part of every name brand that exists out there. Whatever your favorite brand is, it exists because it's meeting a Need. What do we mean by that? Well, there are three ways a good marketing team looks at Needs for a brand like Nike or Nestle:

- A problem that requires a solution,
- A problem that current brands aren't meeting well enough right now, and/or
- A new problem we didn't even know existed.

For example, Sprint was the first brand in the U.S. to come out with a cell phone that could also take pictures. What need did it fill? The need for one, convenient device that could make calls *and* take photos. When Apple discovered that consumers needed a more user-friendly computer, it developed the Mac. Viagra was the first drug to solve the problem of erectile dysfunction.

What about a Need that existing brands aren't meeting well enough now? This is an example of Yogi Berra's "better mousetrap." Gillette created a razor that gives you a better shave. iPhone went way beyond Sprint and created the ultimate "life assistant" — one device with a cell phone, camera, MP3 player, and WiFi capability with a multi-touch screen. And while Viagra tackled erectile dysfunction, Levitra did it one better when it proved it could provide erections on demand for a full 24 hours. Cialis then filled yet another Need in the marketplace since it can provide erections for 36 hours, causing the drug to be dubbed "the weekender." How's *that* for a better mousetrap?

Then, there are the Needs we didn't even know we had. Who knew we needed to carry around tiny contraptions that would hold every song we could possibly ever want to hear? Apple did, and so it created the iPod.

Likewise, when a man named Howard Schultz went to Italy to check out several coffee bars, he realized that they offered a lot more to their customers than just coffee. The coffee bars actually gave people a place to meet where they could sit for long periods of time and chat. Customers weren't rushed out the door in order to let someone else have their table; they could relax and hang out together. Schultz saw a Need that most of the world didn't even know existed, and Starbucks was born.

Function and Emotion

In the name-brand world, the Needs of a Target Market can be either functional or emotional. For example, Crest toothpaste fills the *functional* Need of fighting cavities, and Red Bull fills the functional Need of giving you an energy boost. While both of these examples are *physical*, a functional Need can also be something non-physical yet still "touchable," like the Need for a smaller, lighter-weight digital camera.

On the other hand, *emotional* Needs — as you probably figured out — have to do with feelings. Because Scope freshens your breath, it also fills an emotional Need of helping you feel confident when you get close to someone. A Geico car insurance policy gives you peace of mind because you know you won't go broke if you're in an accident. Get the idea?

So, which type of Need is most important — functional or emotional? The answer is: *both!* The best brands are designed to hit both of those types of Needs smack on the head. That powerful combination is what builds the most successful brands. Here are some examples:

- Bubble Wrap

    Functional Need: *Makes sure things won't break during shipment.*

    Emotional Need: *Gives you 100% assurance that your cousin Mary's wedding vase will arrive at the church in one piece — not ten.*

- YouTube.com

    Functional Need: *Gives people a forum for sharing videos online.*

    Emotional Need: *Allows people to connect with others and express their creativity.*

- Starbucks

    Functional Need: *A better tasting cup of coffee.*

    Emotional Need: *A rewarding coffee experience — a place where you can take a break during the day, have a tasty reward on a comfy couch, and hang out with your friends.*

Starbucks' emotional need is the key to its success. Think about it: If Starbucks had stopped at only meeting its Audience's functional Need of a better tasting cup of coffee, it might never have been such a huge success. After all, there are lots of great cups of coffee out there, right?

So, just as these name brands make sure they fill both the functional and emotional Needs of their Target Markets, it's your job as the Brand Manager of YOU™ to make sure that you meet both the functional and emotional Needs of your Audience when it comes to your job search. But how exactly does this tried-and-true branding model apply to YOU™? And how can you use it to focus on — and land — a great new job?

Functional Needs for Job Seekers

First, like any good Brand Manager, you'll want to figure out what your Audience's functional Needs are. In personal branding, functional Needs can usually be described by the roles you play — the services you could provide in your new job. Think of it as a combo of the list of work activities you would find in a job description and the job title itself: tax accountant, sales rep, bank teller, computer programmer, etc. In other words, when thinking of functional Needs, ask yourself what you would be hired to *do*. If you're an assistant office manager, you'd probably take care of your Audience's Need to keep the office running smoothly, make sure the office machines are working, keep the supply cabinet full, etc.

Functional Needs are also related to your skills and your knowledge. If you're hired as a graphic designer, it's automatically expected that you're going to be creative. If your job title is bank teller, it just goes without saying that you should be good with numbers.

Emotional Needs for Job Seekers

But how do you apply *emotional* Needs to the job-seeking YOU™? Let's look at name brands again. When you're loyal to a particular brand year after year, you've gone beyond just the functional or physical Needs that brand fills for you. At that point, you've entered "Brand Land" — the place where a brand has made a true emotional connection with you. A while back, a participant in one of my Personal Branding workshops admitted that she couldn't live without her Extra chewing gum. "Somebody will have to fight me to get it out of my hands!" she cried. Now, *that's* a strong emotional brand connection.

Take me as another example: I've been using the same brand of toothpaste every single day for more than 20 years now. *Twenty years!* Just to give that some perspective, I've only been married to my husband for twelve years … so, if you think about it, you might say I'd be more likely to cheat on my husband than switch toothpaste brands! (Of course, I wouldn't do that, but I do admit that changing my brand of toothpaste would probably feel a bit like a divorce.) The point is: Some people would rather trade their boyfriend or girlfriend than switch to a different brand of cereal. When you make that kind of emotional connection with your Audience, you've created true brand loyalty.

Okay, so you aren't a brand of cereal, but that's exactly why it's easier for your Audience — the potential bosses you want to work for — to connect with YOU™ emotionally. Have you ever been in a job or a group where someone kept coming back to you, asking you to do more work for them? I guarantee you it's because you met that person's emotional Need by building a relationship of reliability and trust. The functional Need you met was delivering whatever work you did, but more than that, this person knew you were going to deliver quality work on time, again and again. Just like with my favorite toothpaste, *that's* powerful branding.

What Do Your Potential Employers Need?

So, how do you determine the functional and emotional Needs of the companies you've targeted in your job search? First, let's start with functional needs. To sniff out the functional Needs a company is looking for you to meet, check out job descriptions on Internet job sites like Monster.com, CareerBuilder.com, or on the company's website. Most job descriptions only mention a part of what's actually required for the job, but they can give you a good overview of what the company is looking for, especially from a functional standpoint.

There are a number of ways you can find out about a company's functional Needs. Maybe a friend of yours knows an employee in the company, or maybe you can connect with a current employer through LinkedIn just like we talked about in the Audience chapter. If that's the case, try to get the inside scoop on what the job requires. Here are some questions you can ask:

- What skills and talents are needed to do this job well?
- What kind of person is the company looking for to fill this job?
- Who had this job last, and why is the job open now? Did that person get promoted, fired, or leave the company to take a job elsewhere?
- What was it that made that person either a good or not-so-good fit for the job?

Of course, you want to be careful not to come across as too much of a snoop, especially if you don't know the employee all that well. Just ask some general questions about the position, and see if the person just naturally offers more information.

Play the "Analyst"

When you get your hands on a job description, take off your Brand Manager hat for a minute, and put on your Analyst hat. Size up the job description for both functional and emotional Needs. Let's take a look at an example from a recent job posting:

CONTRACT SPECIALIST

Work with a team and contribute to a dynamic agency with an opportunity for advancement. New graduates receive practical training and development in all aspects of the agency's acquisitions operations and all types of contracts.

Position Requirements:
- A bachelor's degree in business or a related field.
- A cumulative GPA of 3.0 or higher.
- Strong analytic and problem-solving skills.
- Exceptional customer service skills.
- Ability and willingness to attend to some administrative duties with attention to detail.

Ideal candidate will have a GPA in business-related courses of 3.5 or higher, as well as excellent communication skills—both written and oral.

Based on this description, the functional Needs of the company are pretty obvious, which is a good thing! You know the company's functional Needs include a bachelor's degree in a business field and a GPA of at least 3.0. You know that they want analytic and problem-solving skills, as well as skills in customer service, communication, and administration.

So, if you were to interview for this Contract Specialist job, you would want to share specific stories and examples of how you solved problems at school, in groups — wherever. You might talk about an experience in a class where you analyzed and solved a complicated problem. You might share another story where you managed a tough customer service situation and had to deal with people and win them over.

But what about the *emotional* Needs of this job? If you look at the job posting again, the company uses the words "ability" and "willingness" in the description, which means they need someone who doesn't mind doing the "little" jobs now and then and who can pay attention to detail. They need someone who can take care of some tasks independently, without being supervised. When you sit back and look at this posting this way, "reliability" and "responsibility" (willingness) come to mind as the emotional Needs of this company.

So, if you were applying for this Contract Specialist job, you would also want to share some examples of where you've shown how reliable you are. Maybe you were in a retail sales job and held the employee record for never being late to work. It could be that you were involved in volunteer work when a member of your team called in sick. You were able to drop everything and fill in for her, taking care of your responsibilities as well as hers for the day. There you go — just the kind of story that will show the interviewer you can fill the company's Needs.

Here's an important point to keep in mind when it comes to stories. There's no need to feel embarrassed about any kind of job you've held in the past. All of these jobs were learning experiences for you. Cindy Godel, former recruiter for Motorola, says, "*Any* past experience can exhibit skills or behaviors that companies look for like teamwork, accountability, leadership, adaptability, and the ability to learn quickly." It's just up to you to figure out what you learned and how to talk about it in an interview in order to show what you can do. For example, a job at McDonald's absolutely qualifies because it involves customer service.

Even if you have little job experience, take some time to dig deep into your past experiences. I'll bet you have plenty of stories you can share that showcase your skills in all of these areas. One human resources manager I interviewed told me: "Past tangible experiences that a candidate can relate back to my company mean more to me than anything on a resume." And this is true even if those experiences aren't related to a past job. *Anything* that you've done related to the skills you need for the job are important to mention in an interview — personal, volunteer work, group involvement — you name it. That's how you fill an emotional Need.

Are YOU™ the "Ideal" Candidate?

When you're wearing your Analyst hat and reading through a job description, see if you can find a description of the "ideal candidate." In our Contract Specialist example, it gives you a lot of ideas about what could give you the edge over other applicants. For example, if your business course GPA is 3.5 or higher, you're in the "ideal" category. If your written and oral communication skills are excellent, you also automatically have an edge. The more you're able to fill the shoes of the "ideal" candidate, the better chance you'll have of getting the job.

But what if you don't exactly fit the profile of the "ideal"? If you have most of what the company is looking for, don't let very specific requirements stop you from applying for a job you really want. It may be that the ideal candidate never shows up for an interview, or the interviewer may have a better feeling about you and your personal brand than someone who looks fabulous on paper. If you have "most but not all" of the qualifications they're looking for, don't hesitate — go for it! What do you have to lose?

What Needs Can You Fill?

Here is a list of possible emotional Needs that your Audience may have. What other emotional Needs could you add to the list?

Trust	Honesty	Sincerity
Resourcefulness	Empathy	Encouragement
Creativity	Self-reliance	Diligence
Enthusiasm	Responsibility	Assertiveness
Reliability	Energy	Sense of Humor
Flexibility	Resourcefulness	Dedication
Objectivity	Tenacity	Thoroughness
Optimism	Patience	Conscientiousness
Imagination	Versatility	Determination

Tolerance	Intensity	Cooperation
Eagerness	Persuasiveness	Decisiveness
Loyalty	Dependability	Commitment

Once you have a full list, think about which of these Needs you think each target company most requires from you. Based on what you've found out about each company, make your most intelligent guesses. Then, narrow your list down to the top two or three that you believe will best fill the Needs of each company.

Now, ask yourself: What past experiences could I share with a job interviewer that would show how I can fill these most critical emotional Needs? Don't underestimate the importance of this. Recruiters and interviewers remember *stories* far more than statistics, previous experience, or what's on your resume. And sharing good, applicable stories are also one of the best ways you can build an emotional connection with your interviewer.

Again, think about everything you've done. Did you work at a summer camp as a counselor for kids? Did you volunteer to help make new freshmen feel at ease during orientation? One college recruiter I talked with told me that being involved in team sports shows that a candidate is competitive, while working on a farm shows willingness to do hard work without complaining about the "little things." So, any or all of the skills and experiences you've gained in your life can be meaningful to a potential employer. Remember: It's not so much *what* you did — it's what you did *with it* that matters.

When you actually show the interviewer what you can do to make life easier for your potential employer — even in the short time span of a job interview — you are definitely pulling on emotional cords and building a strong and memorable personal brand that will help you stand out from the pack of others applying for the same position.

Your College Graduate Personal Brand Positioning Statement

So, what does *your* Audience Need? Let's check in with Nicole and Travis to see how they completed the Needs section of their College Graduate Personal Brand Positioning Statements. You'll see they've each identified the main functional and emotional Needs of a key company where they want to work. Use their statements as examples to help you complete the Needs section of your own Positioning Statement.

Nicole's College Graduate Personal Brand Positioning Statement

Needs

Functional:

- Strong sales skills and customer relations ability.
- Comfortable selling to a highly intelligent, professional customer base.
- Ability to self-manage and get results.

Emotional:

- Outgoing personality; not afraid to embrace new challenges.
- Enthusiasm and passion for science and medicine.

Travis's College Graduate Personal Brand Positioning Statement

Needs

Functional:

- Entry-level engineering skills/ability to apply engineering education to the real world.
- Great attention to detail and to "getting it right the first time."
- Strong at problem-solving.

Emotional:

- Collaborative team player.
- Commitment to preserving the environment.

What are *your* Audience's Needs for your own College Graduate Personal Brand Positioning Statement?

YOUR College Graduate Personal Brand Positioning Statement

Needs

Functional:

Emotional:

> *It's your job as the Brand Manager of YOU™ to make sure that you meet both the functional and emotional Needs of your Audience.*

Define it

O
u
t
s
i
d
e
▶ 3 ▶ Comparison

Step 1

5

Comparison

College Graduate Personal Brand Positioning Element #3

Sometimes you can't see yourself clearly until you see yourself through the eyes of others.
— Ellen DeGeneres, Comedian and TV show host

Now that you have defined the Audience and Needs for your college grad personal brand, you're ready to move on to Comparison — the third key piece of the puzzle that defines what your brand is all about.

Remember what we said about personal branding for job hunters? It's the way you want potential employers to perceive, think, and feel about you "as compared to other candidates." The Comparison element is where the "as compared to other candidates" part comes into play.

For marketers who manage big name brands, this element is called the "Competitive Framework." That's because name brands *compete* with one another for a share of the market. There are only so many buyers of shampoo in the world, for example, so Pantene and Herbal Essences each will grab a certain share of the "shampoo pie." (How's that for a tasty-sounding treat?) The manufacturers of each brand will always look for new ways to drive their share up and take a larger piece of the pie from other brands.

But in personal branding, there is no "market share," so this is where personal brands and name brands are definitely different. I guess you might say this is one of those times when YOU™ *aren't* like shampoo!

When You Are *Not* Like Shampoo

As a personal brand, if you have a piece of the pie, it doesn't mean you've taken someone else's portion, even if you're the one chosen for a specific job and they're not. Why? Well, as humans, we're simply more multi-dimensional than name brands. You are a unique individual, and it's up to you to determine your own specific personal brand and what role it will play in the workplace.

To show you what I mean, let's think again about celebrities. Yes, it's possible that two actors like Matthew McConaughey and Ben Affleck could compete for the same part in a movie, but each of them would bring something entirely different to a role, wouldn't they? So, you can see why personal branding is not so much about competing as it is about *comparing*.

All that said, your personal brand as a job-seeking college grad exists in relation to other applicants for a job, so no matter what you do, Comparison *is* a key part of how you define it. Then, how do you succeed at the Comparison game?

Playing the Comparison Game

Remember that we said interviewers hire people they like? Well, here's another truth about interviewing that you may not know but that can make a huge difference to your job search success: The candidate who can best fill the Audience's *emotional* Need is more likely to get hired than the "best qualified" candidate. For example, if two entry-level accountants are equally as good at filling the functional Need (they can both post accounting entries, reconcile accounts, and prepare financial reports equally well), your Audience is likely to choose the one who fills the *emotional* Need best. That might be the accountant who, during an interview, can relay good stories from past experiences that prove reliability, for example. Or it might be the one who presents the best "can-do" personality when meeting with the interviewer. This is the kind of Comparison that can win you the job you want even when somebody else looks better on paper.

Wear an Interviewer's Shoes

If you're trying to decide if it makes sense to apply for a particular job, try walking a mile in the interviewer's shoes. Again, it's about the Audience and their Needs, right? We all have room for improvement, so be honest with yourself: How would an interviewer see you as compared to other candidates?

- Have you never worked, even in a part-time job?
- Have you participated in very few extracurricular activities?
- Is your GPA on the low side?

I'm not emphasizing negatives here — not at all, I promise — but a great Brand Manager needs to know the honest truth about what's good and what can be improved when it comes to the brand they're marketing. The same is true of personal branding. If you don't know what to improve, you really can't move up in the world. So, make a realistic list of how an interviewer might view you and your experiences as compared to others — and, yes, be sure to include both the good *and* the bad!

Once you have a better sense of how your interviewer might perceive YOU™, your college courses, and your past work experience, you have a golden opportunity to offset your interviewer's fears by pointing out your most positive attributes. If you've made mistakes, be honest about them. But even more importantly, immediately share with the interviewer what you learned from those mistakes. Then, explain how you are now a better person — and will be a better employee — as a result. This really shows your character, and it will speak loudly that you're someone interested in learning, growing, and constantly improving.

Remember, you also already have an edge simply because you've put in the energy and laptop time to learn as much as you can about the company. As we mentioned before, recruiters and interviewers complain time and time again that most graduates who arrive for an interview know very little about the company. They get lazy. Brigid McMahon of IBM says, "It boggles my mind how many candidates don't do their homework. It's a sure fire way to eliminate yourself from the competition."

Don't let that be YOU™! Powerful personal brand builders stay the course and do the same amount of interview preparation for each and every opportunity. This alone will help you to stand out.

So, what else can you do to give yourself a "comparative" edge?

Your Job Search Comparison

If I asked you, "What is Bud Light?" you'd answer, "It's a beer," right? When it comes to name brands, the "average" marketer thinks of their brands that way. For example:

- Dell is a ... computer.
- Listerine is a ... mouthwash.
- Harley-Davidson is a ... motorcycle.

So, in personal branding, it would be easy to fall into the trap of seeing yourself as only the job title or the job description. Are you looking for a job as a:

- Public Relations Assistant?
- Elementary Education Teacher?
- Financial Analyst?
- Research Assistant?

Those titles don't tell you very much. And they definitely don't tell you much about who you might be compared with for a job. No, the job title is just the tip of the iceberg.

When YOU™ Are More Than You

Have you ever seen those plain white-labeled generic cans that just say, "Soup" on them? Imagine a plain bottle with just the word "Beer" on it. It doesn't make you want to drink it, does it? The same holds true with people. What could be more boring than just a job title as a label? Computer programming is exciting work, but if you just call yourself a "Computer Programmer," it doesn't necessarily make you stand out from any other Computer Programmer applicant.

That's why you need to create what I call a "Desired Label." Your Desired Label will allow you to go beyond just that standard average job title. It's all about getting creative about how you think of yourself and how you want to be seen when you're compared with other candidates applying for the same job. Great brand managers do this with the brands they manage. If Bud Light only positioned itself as "a beer," it probably wouldn't sell very well. If Mac made just any old computer, why would anyone choose it over another brand?

Richard Czerniawski and Mike Maloney, marketing colleagues of mine and partners at Brand Development Network International, call this creating a "Perceptual Competitive Framework" of a brand. Here are some great name-brand examples of Perceptual Competitive Framework that Mike and Richard share:

Starbucks isn't just a coffee restaurant ... it's a *rewarding coffee experience.*

Gatorade isn't just a thirst quencher ... it's *the ultimate liquid athletic equipment.*

Snickers isn't just a candy bar ... it's a *between-meal hunger satisfier.*

McDonald's isn't just a fast food restaurant ... it's a *fun family food destination.*

Expand Your Thinking

Let's look at this another way and stretch our minds a bit using an exercise called:

When is an apple not just an apple?

If you looked at an apple as only an apple, then you would automatically think of it as a fruit, right? In this case, that apple would be compared to other fruits like grapes, bananas, or oranges.

But what if you looked at an apple as "a portable, ready-to-eat snack?" (And it is, of course!) If you did that, the apple could then be compared to other snacks like cookies, protein bars, and potato chips.

Now, let's think of an apple as "a daily health maintenance provider." (Once again, it's that, too.) If you thought of an apple in that way, it could then be compared to taking vitamins, exercising, and getting plenty of sleep.

But wait! You could also think of an apple as "a beautiful tabletop decoration." (Yep, it is! Doesn't your Mom or your Grandma put apples in a basket in the middle of the table?) So, that means you could also compare an apple to candles and flowers. Get the idea?

If you can get your Audience to think about YOU™ in that same expanded way, you can potentially fill all sorts of Needs you hadn't even thought about yet. And that's what can help you land the job you're dreaming of, even if someone else in the line waiting to see the college recruiter has a higher GPA or did an internship in the field. How's *that* for a "comparative" edge?

Never Get Typecast

Think about how you want to be viewed, and let your imagination go. How can you change the perception of YOU™ from simply, say, an "Assistant Manager" applicant to the "Take-Charge Guru"? If an interviewer thought of you that way, and a "take-charge attitude" was an important emotional Need of the company, you'd have a better chance of being a shoo-in for that job. The "Take-Charge Guru" would become the Desired Label of your personal brand.

Below are a few more examples of potential Desired Labels. How do you make sure you communicate your Desired Label? Once again, the key is to offer stories during your interviews from your past experiences in jobs, school, volunteer organizations, clubs, etc. that clearly show how you were the "Dynamo" or the "Innovator." You wouldn't necessarily talk about these titles in an interview (you want to come across as confident, but not *over*confident). But it definitely helps to think of yourself this way. It gives you a focus for your college grad personal brand that's fun, and it's a great way to really stand out and get excited about what you can offer a potential boss.

By the way, if you're a natural storyteller, this part will come easily to you. If you're not necessarily good at telling stories, practice your stories ahead of time. Try them out on a friend or family member before you actually get into an interview situation. The more you practice your stories, the more they will flow naturally and highlight the key points you want to make in an interview.

What examples can you share which would demonstrate that you are:

> **The "Get It Done Guy or Gal"** — When your fraternity/sorority was up against a challenge, people turned to you as the "closer." You were the person they relied on to finish the job. Offer a specific example from your past experience. Maybe you took charge of a problem project at school, in the community, or at a part-time job and came up with a solution that meant the project could be completed on time and within budget.

> **The "Connector"** — You have nearly 1,000 friends on Facebook, so you know the perfect person to call for every task. Everyone at school always knew to "just give you five minutes to check your contact list," and they would instantly have a valuable person to call.

Offer a story that shows how your widespread connections helped a group at school or a former employer. Maybe your company's printer couldn't do a job at the last minute, so you sent an instant message to your Facebook friend whose family is in the printing business, saving the day just in time.

The "Tension Breaker" — Your dorm mates always counted on you when the tension was high to tell a joke and bring a smile to everyone's face once again. Of course, if you tell stories about breaking the tension, make sure you show exactly how it helped everyone around you. The interviewer shouldn't get the impression that you're someone who cracks jokes all day and gets nothing done. But a clear story about that time in an internship or during a school project where you found a way to bring humor to a situation when everyone was tense, maybe even preventing an argument, can go a long way in the eyes of an interviewer.

The "Innovator" — When a new idea was needed, everyone always knew to come to you for your imagination and creativity. This Desired Label is easy to convey in an interview. Be ready to share several new ideas that you came up with and how you were successful in putting them into practice. That's powerful!

The "Dynamo" — When energy and persistence were called for, you were the first person who came to mind at school, in your dorm, or in campus clubs. You kept everyone motivated and on target until the job was done. While this might be a bit harder to show in an interview, share situations where you helped others to keep their eyes on the task at hand and get the job done despite roadblocks.

"Mr. or Ms. Precise" — When something had to be done right the first time down to the last detail, everyone knew your work would be meticulous and thorough. Pinpoint and be ready to share examples of when people came to you because of your strong attention to detail. If you can show some proof, arrive at your interview armed with the numbers.

These are just a few possible Desired Labels. What other Desired Labels can you think of that can spotlight your specific talents?

Have Fun With Your Brand!

When Korey began to interview for film production assistant jobs after graduation, she chose a Desired Label of "The Juggler." She liked this Desired Label a lot, and she thought it was the kind of thing she could actually tell her potential employers. So, she used the label in interviews, telling them that she was the person who could take on loads of responsibilities and use her resourcefulness to get a lot done at once. She told a couple of stories from school and work experiences about how she juggled everything successfully at the same time — 18 hours of course work, a paid part-time job off-campus, and a position as editor-in-chief of the college newspaper.

Korey's Desired Label really stood out and made her memorable to interviewers. It also showed potential employers that she was willing to work hard and make a significant contribution to any company. Within a very short time, she landed a great job with a higher salary than she expected because her Desired Label gave her a unique personal brand that was much more exciting than just "Film Production Assistant."

The moral of this story? Whether or not you think it makes sense to actually tell your interviewers your Desired Label, enjoy being creative as you come up with ways YOU™ can be more than just you. That's how you succeed at the Comparison game.

There's More to YOU™ Than Meets the Eye

Smart job seekers will come up with a Desired Label that will help them in their job hunt, so it's time to be imaginative and look beyond the obvious. What more can YOU™ be? Brainstorm until you come up with many possibilities, and let your mind run wild without over-thinking it. You never know when a gem may come out of something that at first seems pretty crazy.

Try to brainstorm lots of possible Desired Labels that a potential employer might find powerful based on what you've learned about the companies where you want to work. Don't feel like you have to think of all of the possibilities in one sitting, though. You can always come back with fresh eyes at a later time to find new ideas, some of which may just pop into your head during the next few days. And don't hold back! Ask your friends to brainstorm with you. It can be a lot of fun.

Example:

I'm not just a Film Production Assistant; I'm The Juggler.

Now, you try it:

I'm not just a _____; I'm a _____.

How many Desired Labels can you think of?

Who Do YOU™ Most Want to Be?

Now that you've got your imagination going, how do you decide which Desired Label to use for your job-seeker personal brand — the brand that will help land you a job you really love? One way to choose is to go back to the Needs section of your College Graduate Personal Brand Positioning Statement. Ask yourself which one of your potential Desired Labels will best fill your Audience's Needs. And, most importantly, which Desired Label is most in line with who YOU™ really are and how you really want to kick off your career?

Remember: When you make your choices, they don't have to be set in stone. As you work through the parts of your College Graduate Personal Brand Positioning Statement, you may find that you have two or three Desired Labels that could apply and that you could communicate easily. You might even want to use one Desired Label for one specific target company and another for a different company. If so, that's completely fine.

For now, go ahead and make some choices based on the companies where you'd most like to work. This will keep you moving forward in building your Positioning Statement.

Your College Graduate Personal Brand Positioning Statement

So, how did Nicole and Travis apply these ideas to their statements? Take a look below.

Nicole's College Graduate Personal Brand Positioning Statement

Comparison

Job Title: Sales Representative – Medo-Innovations Medical Supply Division

Desired Label: I *want* to be the brand of *(the way I would like to be perceived):* "**Company Champion**" who passionately promotes and sells the company's innovative products so that they can improve the lives of customers' patients.

Travis's College Graduate Personal Brand Positioning Statement

Comparison

Job Title: Engineering Intern (EI)

Desired Label: I *want* to be the brand of *(the way I would like to be perceived):* "**Collaborative Problem-Solver**" who bounces ideas off others to come up with great solutions.

Now, you're ready to take what you've learned and apply it to your own College Graduate Personal Brand Positioning Statement. I hope this chapter brings new creative spark to your job search and helps you see how you can definitely win at the Comparison game — and have fun doing it, too!

YOUR College Graduate Personal Brand Positioning Statement

Comparison

Job Title:

Desired Identity: I *want* to be the brand of *(the way I would like to be perceived)*:

> *" Your Desired Label gives you a focus for your college grad personal brand that's fun, and it's a great way to really stand out. "*

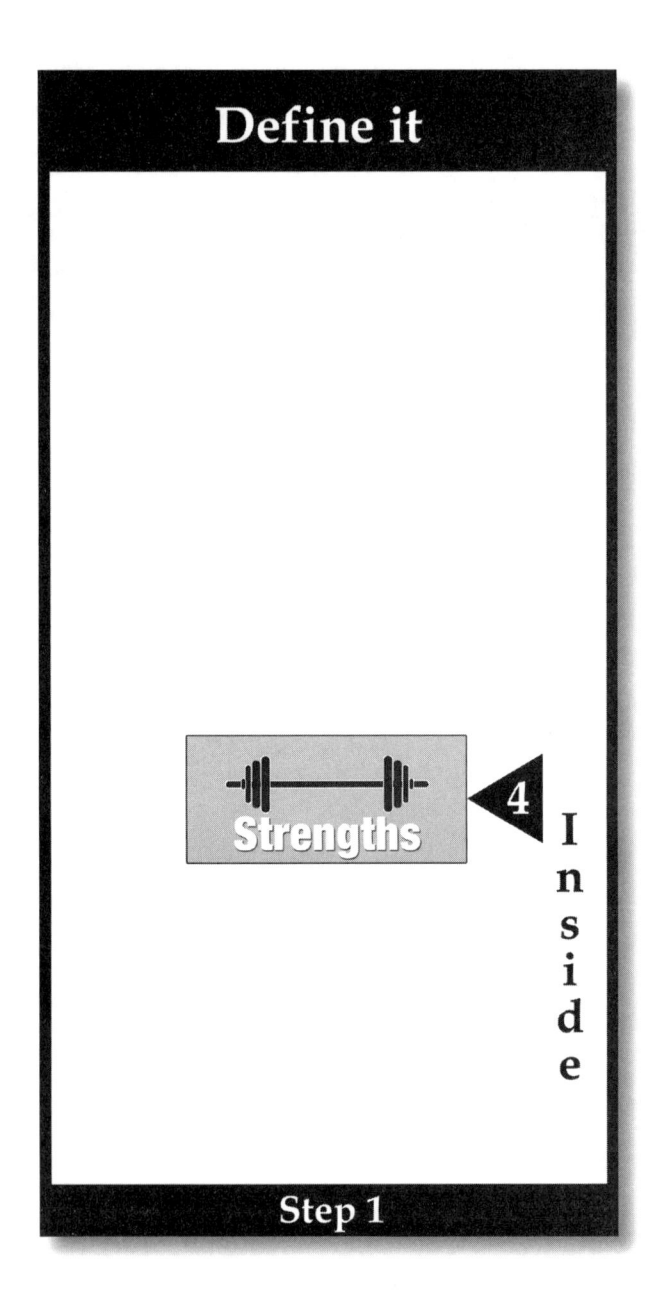

Define it

Strengths 4 Inside

Step 1

6

Unique Strengths

College Graduate Personal Brand Positioning Element #4

> *Every person born into this world represents something new, something that never existed before, something original and unique. It is the duty of every person ... to know and consider ... that there has never been anyone like him ..., for if there had been someone like him, there would have been no need for him to be in the world.*
>
> — Martin Buber, 20th century philosopher and author

If someone who knows you well was stopped in the middle of the street and asked — "What does _____ [insert your name here] stand for?" — what would this person say about you? What would they share that is specific to who you are and what you can do? These are your Unique Strengths. They are the nuts and bolts of your college graduate personal brand — where the rubber hits the road when it comes to branding yourself.

In the world of name brands, Unique Strengths are called the "Benefits" that a brand offers — the most meaningful promise that a brand can, and wants to, own in the mind of its Target Market. Let's take a brand you probably know as an example. When most people hear the name Ford Trucks, the word "tough" comes to mind. People tend to think of Ford Trucks as tougher than any other truck brand on the market — tougher than Chrysler, Toyota ... you name it. Ford has done such a good job with its brand image that a lot of people perceive it as one of the toughest trucks on the market.

How does this apply to personal branding? Well, for a name brand, the Benefits answer the Target Market's question: "What's in it for me?" For personal branding during a job hunt, your Unique Strengths answer your Audience's question: "What's in it for the company?" They tell your potential employer what you can offer their organization if you're hired.

When I speak or conduct a training about personal branding, it's not unusual for an audience member to come up to me and say, "The truth is, Brenda, I'm not really that unique. I don't think what I have to offer is very different from anybody else." And, often, no matter how hard I try, nothing I can say seems to change their minds. As a new or soon-to-be college grad, you may feel like you have nothing all your own to offer. But let me try to change your mind about that!

Not that long ago, I bought a new Toshiba laptop that illustrates how unique each one of us truly is. That's because my new computer comes with a very cool feature — "biosensor fingerprint identification." That means the computer has software that records and recognizes my fingerprint. It then uses my fingerprint as the "password" for accessing my keyboard, hard drive, bookmarked log-in pages, etc. No other fingerprint will do! It has to be my right index finger and mine alone.

I'm infatuated with this new "toy" of mine. But besides that, I'm also excited by this constant reminder that each one of us is so incredibly unique. Every time I start my computer with my unique fingerprint, I think to myself: "No one else on the face of the planet can do that." I'm the only individual out of the six billion+ people who call this earth home who can simply "swish" a finger over the top of that biosensor and unlock this computer. My husband has tried, my assistant has tried, my family members have tried ... but, nope — it's my fingerprint, or it just won't work. How powerful is that?

Okay, so you already know that you have a different physical makeup from everybody else. But it makes sense that if your fingerprints and DNA are so unique, then so is the exact make-up of your talents and personality. It's an absolute impossibility that anyone else can contribute to a company in exactly the same way as you. It doesn't matter if you've never had a full-time job before or you have little experience yet in your field. Recognizing what you truly have to offer and making sure that your potential employers see it during your job search is what your job-seeker personal brand is all about.

It's a matter of defining clearly what truly differentiates you (beyond your fingerprints) and helps you stand out. That's the key to successfully branding yourself. Your very individual combination of values, passions, and talents is what unlocks the real YOU™ — just like my fingerprint unlocks my computer. It's up to you to discover and celebrate your uniqueness. Then, you will know exactly what you can offer to a new company that no one else can.

Unearthing Your Strengths

So, how do you figure out what your Unique Strengths are? There are a lot of ways you can nail them down. Allow yourself some good quality time to think about what you have to offer, and try these ideas to begin uncovering the Unique Strengths you already have:

Pay Attention. Simply listen to what people say when they talk about you. When you're introduced to someone, what words are used to describe you? How do your friends introduce you to someone new? Have you ever given a presentation or received an award? If so, what Unique Strengths were highlighted when you were introduced? If you haven't been formally introduced anywhere, do you have any programs or materials from past events at school or elsewhere that would have a description of you written by someone else?

Performance Reviews. If you've had a part-time or full-time job while in school, were you given performance reviews? If so, you're probably like most people, and you focus on what you need to "fix" when reading these evaluations. But if you take a second look at reviews you've had on the job, you'll probably also see Unique Strengths that are consistent throughout. What is written there that reveals your specific talents? Read between the lines to learn what qualities truly help you to stand out from others. If you don't have any personnel reviews from the past, did you receive compliments from your supervisors or co-workers? What types of work did you do best, and what types of jobs did you like the most?

Take Personality Profiles and Tests. There are several personality tests like Myers-Briggs (www.myersbriggs.org) that can give you insight into your Unique Strengths. You may uncover some new things about yourself by taking these tests. If you purchase the book,

Now, Discover Your Strengths, you can access the computerized quiz at www.StrengthsFinder.com to find out your top five Strengths.

There are lots of personality tests out there, and we've checked out a few for you. Look for our recommended list in Appendix B at the back of the book, and try them out.

List Your Values. Take stock of what values are most important to you. If being trustworthy really matters to you, for example, this may be a Unique Strength you want to apply to your college grad personal brand. If loyalty is most important to you, maybe that's the Strength you most want employers to think of when they consider you. Your list of values will help you to figure out which of your Strengths hold the most meaning for you. If you truly care about the Unique Strengths that are the basis of your job-seeker personal brand, you'll be even more passionate about what you do.

One thing to watch out for as you create your list is to make sure you don't borrow someone else's values. Sometimes, the values of your parents or friends can get mixed up with your own. Keep a watch out for this, and make sure the foundation of your personal brand is authentically yours.

List Your Passions. People often do best at the activities they love to do the most, so your Unique Strengths are directly related to what excites you. If you're passionate about your Unique Strengths, that passion will move you forward and help you do well, and you'll enjoy every minute of it. Yet, we often become so involved in the "shoulds" of life that we forget about our passions.

My passion is brands. I love them, I study them, I know them, and I teach them. When people who know me hear the name "Brenda Bence," they think "branding." So, make a list of the things you like doing that make you feel enthusiastic and joyful, and don't limit the list to activities that are only related to work. You may find something unexpected among the passions in other areas of your life.

Ask Your Friends and Colleagues. You can't uncover your Unique Strengths only by searching within. Ask your friends and co-workers to tell you what they think your Unique Strengths are. Ask them to tell you what they believe is exceptional, rare, and special about you. Be sure to ask these questions of people who know you well, and let them know you want honest answers from them. If you feel comfortable, you can even ask some of your professors this question.

I know that asking for feedback can be awkward, but without it, you'll end up with a very limited picture of your Strengths. Nine times out of ten, others judge you less harshly than you judge yourself, and they will notice positive aspects about YOU™ that you may have overlooked entirely. So, don't be afraid to ask for feedback — it's a key way to discover the perfect Unique Strengths for your personal brand. Only then can you be sure that you won't undersell or oversell yourself in the job search process.

Here are some questions you could ask others in order to uncover more Strengths, but feel free to add to the list:

- When you think of me, what are the first positive traits that come to your mind?
- What special talents do you think I have?
- What attributes do I have that stand out from others?
- What, if anything, is exceptional or rare about me?
- What would you consider my very best qualities?
- What would you recommend to others about me or my work?
- If you were trying to convince someone to hire me, what would you say?

Now, make a list of your Unique Strengths. Have you discovered any that you didn't know you had?

Your Audience Needs YOU™

Here's a fundamental fact when it comes to branding whether it's for name brands or for personal branding:

Your Unique Strengths must respond to your Audience's Needs.

And, if you remember, Needs come in two forms — functional and emotional. So, in keeping with that, your Unique Strengths also need to be both functional and emotional.

Let's look at Ford trucks again. The functional need that a Ford truck fills is being so tough, sturdy, and solid that you know it's going to last a long time. But driving a Ford truck also fills an important emotional Need, too. What is that? Peace of mind. The toughness helps you to feel safe and less likely to be injured in an accident. Ford trucks could also fill an emotional Need related to Brand Character if the driver relates to the character of "toughness." That person might think, "My Ford truck is tough like me!"

In personal branding, a functional Unique Strength might be something like your ability to write a report that's very detailed. You might call this "accuracy." An emotional Unique Strength could be the fact that you provide those reports on time every time. You might call this one "reliability." Get the idea?

Your Functional Unique Strengths

First, let's consider the functional Needs of your Audience. Which of the Unique Strengths on your list will best match those Needs? Be honest and realistic about how well your Unique Strengths actually meet your Audience's Needs.

It's okay if you don't have a Strength to match every one of your Audience's Needs. This will tell you where you want to focus and develop new Unique Strengths to help improve your job-seeker personal brand for the future. These will become what we'll call your "Future Unique Strengths." The strengths you can already provide will be called your "Existing Unique Strengths."

Here's a scale to help you rate how well your functional Unique Strengths actually meet your Audience's functional Needs. Go through each of your Audience's Needs and choose from 1 through 6:

1 = *I can't respond to this Need at all.*

2 = *I can respond slightly to this Need but below average.*

3 = *I can respond to this Need at an average level.*

4 = *I can respond to this Need well.*

5 = *I can respond to this Need to a large degree.*

6 = *I am outstanding at responding to this Need.*

Here's an example:

Functional Need of Your Audience: Accurate Financial Analysis
Your Functional Unique Strength: Precision
Your Rating from 1-6: 5

Once you're done, sit back and look at what you've written. How did your functional Unique Strengths rate?

Your Emotional Unique Strengths

Now, let's consider your Audience's *emotional* Needs. Which of your Unique Strengths would best meet the top emotional Needs of your Audience?

Rate how well your emotional Unique Strengths meet your Audience's emotional Needs using our scale:

1 = I can't respond to this Need at all.

2 = I can respond slightly to this Need but below average.

3 = I can respond to this Need at an average level.

4 = I can respond to this Need well.

5 = I can respond to this Need to a large degree.

6 = I am outstanding at responding to this Need.

Here's an example:

Emotional Need of Your Audience: Turning financial reports in on time
Your Emotional Unique Strength: Reliability
Your Rating from 1-6: 4

If you find that your Strengths don't respond to your Audience's Needs as much as you'd like, don't worry! Unless you can't respond to *any* of a company's Needs, you may still be a candidate for an entry-level job. As a college graduate, you often aren't expected to respond to every one of your Audience's Needs right away. In your interviews, you will focus on the Needs that you can meet. Then, as you work toward advancing in your career, you will develop Future Unique Strengths that will help you do even better in later positions.

Listening to Your Passions

Once, after giving a speech about international marketing and branding, I was approached by a college grad named Mark who said he wanted to do what I do. He told me that he was willing to work hard and asked to take me to lunch in exchange for some career advice. I admired him for being so outgoing, so I said yes.

At lunch, Mark talked about how he'd been studying Spanish and German and told me that he wanted to go into international business. Then, he asked me what I'd do if I were just starting out. "Well," I said, "if it were me, and I wanted to get into international business, I'd move to China and learn Mandarin."

His face sunk. Here he'd been studying Spanish and German, and I was suggesting moving to a new continent and learning an entirely different language with a completely foreign alphabet. So, I changed course and said, "Mark, tell me what you're passionate about. What do you *love*?" That's when Mark lit up like a spark, and he told me about his undying passion for soccer. But because he didn't feel he had the talent to be a soccer player, he hadn't done anything with this passion.

"What if you could combine your interest in international business with your love of soccer?" I asked. "What would *that* feel like?" His entire demeanor changed, and he excitedly admitted that his dream job would be to work with FIFA, the international soccer federation.

"So, then, why not set your sights on that?" I said. Right then and there, a dream was seeded...

Six months later, I got an email from Mark ... *from China!* He had actually moved there and gotten a job (ironically, using both his German and his Spanish skills!). His dream of working in international business was already on its way to becoming a reality, and he was actively learning Mandarin.

Shortly thereafter, however, I was at a resort in Malaysia with my husband, and we met a guy from Hong Kong who worked for — yes — FIFA. We started to talk, and he told me that

> the organization was looking to hire some bright young people. So, I managed to connect this guy to Mark, and Mark ended up landing a job with FIFA in China! Eventually, Mark worked on the 2008 Olympics in Beijing and later moved to Switzerland where he still works for FIFA and uses his German, Spanish, and Mandarin skills while traveling the world to promote soccer. There you have it: International business and soccer combined. Mark's passionate dream had become reality.
>
> So, what's the lesson here? Don't sell your passions short. Listen to what you really want to do, and figure out how to make your dreams come true. Use Nicole and Travis as examples, too, who are both pursuing their passions. In Nicole's case, she wanted to be a doctor but discovered another way to use both her love for medicine and her love for meeting people. How can you incorporate your passions into *your* work?

If you struggle with determining what your passions are, try the Passion Profiler™ Tool at www.thepurposelink.com/passionprofdef.htm. It will help you assess your passions and sense of purpose and how you can express that through your work.

Streamlining Your Strengths

You've scored yourself against your Audience's Needs, you've uncovered your Unique Strengths, and you have a good long list of both. Now, it's time to make choices. You have to choose which of your Unique Strengths will be the truly important Strengths you want to stand for — i.e., the heart of your job-seeker personal brand. Of course, keep in mind: The Unique Strengths you choose should also respond well to your Audience's Needs.

Choosing isn't always easy, but imagine what would happen if a brand tried to stand for too many things. Let's look at Ford trucks again as an example. It's easy to remember that the brand stands for toughness but, if the brand also tried to stand for beauty, innovative style, and unusual extras, it wouldn't end up standing for anything, right?

That's why most name brands try to own no more than one or two specific benefits. Pantene owns healthy and shiny hair. Head & Shoulders owns beautiful, dandruff-free hair. It isn't that these are the only benefits these brands offer. They may also have a nice fragrance, contain moisturizing ingredients, and help repair split ends. But good marketers make choices, and that means sticking to just one or two Strengths that the brand truly wants to — and can — own.

So it is with personal branding. As the Brand Manager of YOU™, it's your job to choose two to three — four maximum — of your top Existing Unique Strengths that you can, and want to, own.

Many people resist this. They say, "Wait a minute, Brenda! There's more to me than just 1-2 aspects. I have a lot of Unique Strengths, and I want to use them all in my job search as well as in my future job." And, of course, you should use all of them, and you will. Choosing now doesn't mean you won't work on additional Future Unique Strengths that you want to develop later on. But which are the Unique Strengths you want most to be associated with your job-seeker personal brand right now? You need your Audience to be able to remember what you stand for (whether or not they will ever verbalize it). Your Audience can only remember so much, and you will need to be focused and consistent in order to be known for your Unique Strengths and remembered by interviewers.

As you reflect on your Unique Strengths, think once again about how you'd like potential employers to perceive, think, and feel about YOU™. What are the three or four key qualities that you want to pop into the minds of interviewers when they remember YOU™? Which Strengths are the most meaningful and will help you to stand out the most? And how do these particular Unique Strengths respond to your potential employer's greatest Needs?

As you're looking for that great new job, it may be that one of your target companies has different Needs than another. You might decide that you want to focus on one of your Unique Strengths with one company and another Unique Strength with a different company. This is absolutely fine if you think it makes sense. But do try whenever possible to focus your personal brand on the three or four Unique Strengths that show you off the most and that you want to use most in your future job. That kind of consistency always pays off in the end.

Your College Graduate Personal Brand Positioning Statement

Spend some time with your list of Unique Strengths until you feel comfortable with (and excited about) the two or three most important ones. In the meantime, take a look at the Unique Strengths of Nicole and Travis.

Nicole's College Graduate Personal Brand Positioning Statement

Unique Strengths

My Existing Unique Strengths are:

Functional:

- Demonstrated sales results and customer relations abilities.
- Ability to self-manage and get results.

Emotional:

- Outgoing personality; not afraid to embrace new challenges.
- Enthusiasm and passion for science and medicine.

The Future Unique Strengths That I Want to Work on Are:
- Gain more medical knowledge to make me more comfortable selling to a highly intelligent, professional customer base.

> ### Travis's College Graduate Personal Brand Positioning Statement
>
> #### Unique Strengths
>
> *My Existing Unique Strengths are:*
>
> *Functional:*
> - Entry-level engineering skills/ability to apply engineering education to the real world.
> - Strong at problem-solving.
>
> *Emotional:*
> - Collaborative team player.
> - Commitment to preserving the environment.
>
> *The Future Unique Strengths That I Want to Work on Are:*
> - Great attention to detail and to "getting it right the first time." In the past, I've made some mistakes because I rush, so I need to focus on slowing down and paying more attention.

When you've narrowed down your Unique Strengths to those you want to apply to your personal brand, add them to the Unique Strengths part of your College Graduate Personal Brand Positioning Statement, dividing them between Existing and Future Unique Strengths. This will tell you which strengths you can apply immediately to your personal brand and which ones you need to work on.

YOUR College Graduate Personal Brand Positioning Statement

Unique Strengths

My Existing Unique Strengths are:

The Future Unique Strengths That I Want to Work on Are:

"That picture portrays his desired Unique Strengths!"

Define it

? Why ◀ 5 Inside

Step 1

7

Reasons Why

College Graduate Personal Brand Positioning Element #5

To be persuasive we must be believable; to be believable we must be credible...

— Edward R. Murrow, U.S. broadcaster and journalist

You're getting close to finalizing the definition of your college graduate personal brand! We're moving on to personal brand positioning element #5 — your Reasons Why. This is about the reasons why your Audience should believe you can deliver your specific Unique Strengths. It's all about credibility, and it's absolutely fundamental when it comes to looking for a new job. Your Reasons Why give potential bosses reasons to trust that you can do what you say you can do. Now, I know that as a new college graduate, you may not find it easy to prove that you can do what you know you can do. But you may be surprised to find out that you have a lot more "Reasons Why" than you realized.

Returning to name brands again, they also have Reasons Why that come in many different forms. Here's a list of some popular brands and the Reasons Why you and I believe those brands can deliver what they promise.

Brand	The Reason(s) Why	Type of Reason(s) Why
Dove	1/4 Moisturizing Cream	Ingredient
Neutrogena	#1 Dermatologist Recommended	Endorsement
Google	PigeonRank™ Search Technology	Design
Corona Extra	U.S.'s #1 Imported Beer	Market Experience
Evian	Water from Source Cachat	Source

In *personal* branding—especially when it comes to using your personal brand to get your foot in the door of a new company—your Reasons Why mainly come in three forms:

Education. This is where your years at college do their job of showing that you've learned your stuff. You may even have other education, too, from seminars or special training courses outside of your college classes.

Experience. Your past work, internship, or volunteer experience can be a powerful Reason Why. Think about all of the experiences you've had that might show what you can do. These could include working as a cashier, working on projects for school competitions, fund raising efforts at your university, or serving as president of your sorority. Don't discount anything that you might use as a Reason Why!

Endorsements. Someone who knows you well may offer a reference that gives your Audience a good reason to believe you can do what you promise. In the hiring process, references—which are a form of endorsement—can be incredibly important. When someone with a good reputation sings your praises, it's a powerful Reason Why someone would choose to give you the job versus someone else applying for the same position. One human resources manager

I interviewed said: "Never underestimate the power of a good testimonial or reference. What someone else has to say about you makes a big difference to potential employers."

Whatever the form of your Reasons Why, they need to be as strong as possible so that your Audience believes you can deliver what you say you can in a way that uniquely responds to their Needs.

Your interviewer has no personal experience of you on the job, so you have to make your Reasons Why as dynamic and believable as you can. Every time a company hires someone new, it's a risk, and the person doing the hiring is trying to reduce that risk as much as possible. So, it's your job as the Brand Manager of YOU™ to convince your potential employer that you can deliver your Unique Strengths.

The Reasons Behind Your Strengths

A Unique Strength without a Reason Why is like an airplane without wings — it will never hold up. Think about it: If a brand of shampoo simply said it was the best shampoo on the market, would you believe it? No, you'd want some form of proof that this shampoo is better than the rest. You'd feel better knowing it has some kind of new patented ingredient that adds shine to your hair or that it's been formulated with a specific vitamin known for keeping your hair healthy. So, it's very important that each one of your Unique Strengths also has at least one Reason Why in order to justify your Audience's trust in you.

How many reasons can you think of that would prove to your Audience that you can deliver each of your Unique Strengths? Think about them in terms of the three types we talked about earlier: education, experience, and endorsements. Which category or categories do your Reasons Why fall into?

Here's an example:

Unique Strength:

Creates innovative software programs

Reasons Why:

- *Experience:* Participation in the development of a new software program that won a state award for best application developed by a college team.
- *Education:* A degree in computer technology from New York University.

Review each of the Unique Strengths you chose from the last chapter. Think hard about all of your courses and any experience you've had at work, internships, clubs, community involvement, athletics, volunteer work, etc. Where did you show each Unique Strength? Then, write down your Reasons Why for each Unique Strength on your list.

Could Your Existing Reasons Why Be Even Better?

If you have time before you start looking for a job, is there more you can do to create new Reasons Why? If you're reading this before graduation, for example, you might be able to do some additional volunteer work or take a training course that will give you another Reason Why to support your Unique Strengths. If not, don't worry. Just use what you have. As a new graduate, you're not expected to have extensive experience.

Another way to develop more Reasons Why is to work for free. Once you have more experience, I wouldn't recommend offering your talents for free, but when you're just starting to build your brand, it's a great way to prove your Unique Strengths. That's what internships are all about, right? But if an internship isn't possible, you can still offer your talents to a company or individual.

Creating a Reason Why

Tiffany was an exercise science major who wanted to become a physical therapist ("PT") after graduation. But her undergraduate grades weren't quite good enough to get into a PT graduate program — it's a field that's extremely competitive and in demand. To complicate things, without PT experience, she couldn't get a job. So, she decided to volunteer at a local physical therapy clinic instead. She really threw herself into the position and became known as the "go-to" person at the clinic, taking care of anything that needed to be done.

Of course, without training and a PT license, Tiffany couldn't actually advise or work on patients. But she was still taught how to do ultrasound procedures and was allowed to work with patients in that way. Even more valuable, she was able to watch and interact with trained physical therapists as they worked. So, she learned a lot about the field.

What happened with Tiffany? Well, the clinic liked her so much that they eventually offered her a part-time job. While she was making money at that job, she took some additional math and science classes to get ready for reapplying to physical therapy school. With better grades from those key math and science classes, she later was able to use these great Reasons Why (improved grades and part-time work at the PT clinic) to prove her Unique Strengths. This eventually landed her a spot in a great physical therapy graduate program.

The moral of the story? Offering to work for free can be a great way to create a Reason Why when you're just starting out. Remember that not all volunteering has to be for a non-profit organization. Even if you aren't getting paid, you can gain priceless experience that you can often use to make money later.

Narrowing It Down

How many Reasons Why should you have in your College Graduate Personal Brand Positioning Statement? The answer depends on how many your Audience will find meaningful. In other words, how many Reasons Why do you need to truly differentiate YOU™ from other candidates? Perhaps even more importantly, how many can your Audience honestly remember? It's better to keep your Reasons Why to a minimum, so focus on quality, not quantity. The Reasons Why won't matter much if your Audience can't remember them at the very moment they're considering choosing YOU™ over someone else for the job you want!

If you aren't certain which Reasons Why to focus on, think back again to the knowledge you have about your Audience:

- What have you learned about the companies you're targeting that can offer you clues about the types of Reasons Why they would value most?

- Have you found out anything from your research or contacts about whether the company focuses more on education or if they're very interested in volunteer work/internship experience?

Just a little bit of research can help you learn what each company considers to be powerful Reasons Why. Knowing that, you can emphasize your own related Reasons Why in your resume and during interviews.

"Your resumé is outstanding, but somehow we don't feel you're quite right for this firm!"

Your College Graduate Personal Brand Positioning Statement

Let's check in with fellow students, Nicole and Travis, to see how they have applied their Reasons Why in their Personal Brand Positioning Statements.

Nicole's College Graduate Personal Brand Positioning Statement

Reasons Why

My Existing Reasons Why are:

- *Endorsements:* I have existing letters of recommendation from:
  - My current boss at my part-time department store shoe sales job. He talks about my sales and customer relations experience. He also talks about my self-management abilities in setting stretch sales targets and reaching them.
  - My faculty advisor and mentor, who talks about my enthusiasm and passion for science and medicine.
- *Education:* Bachelor's degree in business with a sales and marketing focus, as well as my early interest in medicine (evident by my freshman and sophomore pre-med science courses).
- *Experience:*
  - Rated one of the top part-time sellers in my retail job at the local department store's shoe department.
  - To show I'm not afraid to face new challenges, share the story about taking over management of the Red Cross campus blood drive when the coordinator got sick. I saw it through to completion even though I hadn't been that involved.

The Future Reasons Why That I Want to Work on Are:

- *Education:* Before my job interview, I will take time to learn about medical supply competitors and about existing glucose monitors from Medo-Innovations, as well as key competitors.
- *Experience:* I will meet with two local pharmacists, asking their opinions about what makes a good medical sales rep and what aspect of medical sales reps they *don't* care for. During the interview, use that data to share what I learned.

Travis's College Graduate Personal Brand Positioning Statement

Reasons Why

My Existing Reasons Why are:

- *Endorsements:*
  - Letter of recommendation from my summer internship supervisor talking about my problem-solving skills and how I worked as a team player to identify problems and helped to fix them.
  - Letter from my faculty advisor who supervised my senior design project; in it, he talks about how I applied my engineering education to real-life problems.
- *Education:* B.S. degree in Civil Engineering, *magna cum laude*.
- *Experience:*
  - Summer internship for the state highway department, working outdoors; gained hands-on experience applying engineering concepts to an actual highway project. Also demonstrates my commitment to helping the environment.
  - Senior design class project during which I applied engineering theory to an actual case that our team worked on for an outside company.

The Future Reasons Why That I Want to Work on Are:

- *Experience:* Continue to work on improving my attention to detail, particularly when it comes to doing something new that I'm not familiar with. I will practice slowing down and focusing to reduce my error rate.

YOUR College Graduate Personal Brand Positioning Statement

Reasons Why

My Existing Reasons Why (why my Audience should believe I can deliver my Unique Strengths) **are:**

The Future Reasons Why That I Want to Work on Are:

> *A Unique Strength without a Reason Why is like an airplane without wings — it will never hold up.*

Define it

Character

Inside 6

Step 1

8

Brand Character

College Graduate Personal Brand Positioning Element #6

Attitude is a little thing that makes a big difference.
— Winston Churchill, Former British Prime Minister

The remaining positioning element in Step 1 of our system — Brand Character — may be last, but it definitely isn't the least. Your personal Brand Character is incredibly important as you look for a job out of college. Why? Because being crystal clear about your Brand Character can help YOU™ stand out from other candidates applying for the job you want. Throughout the whole job search process, Brand Character is something that can and will separate you from other applicants.

But What Exactly Is Brand Character?

When it comes to name brands, you may not have heard of "Brand Character" before. But it definitely exists. And many of the most successful brands out there use Brand Character to separate themselves from other similar products — Pepsi and Coke, for example. Let's be honest: Both Pepsi and Coke are made up of the same basic ingredients — carbonated water, sugar, and flavoring, right? Yet, absolutely everyone seems to have a do-or-die preference for one over the other. I've even seen people get into heated debates over which cola is "the best!"

With products like Pepsi and Coke that are so similar in ingredients, you can thank their distinctive Brand Characters for the strong brand loyalty people have for them. And the players behind those Brand Characters? The smart Brand Managers who develop and manage those brands. Let's face it: The functional Needs that Pepsi and Coke fill are pretty much the same. They quench your thirst and satisfy your taste buds. But the Brand Character of each of them creates a unique emotional connection that has taken both brands to the top. A brand's Character may be harder to pinpoint than the Needs it fulfills, but smart Brand Managers take this element of a brand very seriously. It can literally make or break a brand's success.

What are some other brands that are mainly differentiated by Character? Think perfume, clothing, and alcohol just to name a few. Take some time to notice some ads for these types of brands. For example, what about an ad for Skyy Vodka compared with Jose Cuervo Tequila? The Character of Skyy is chic and sophisticated while Jose Cuervo is youthful and focuses on partying with friends. It's actually a lot of fun to discover the Brand Characters that come out in ads and commercials. Keep a watchful eye out for them, and you'll clearly see that Brand Character is a critical element that separates one brand from another.

From Pepsi and Vodka to YOU™

So, how does Brand Character apply to you and your personal brand? Your Brand Character is the one element in our six elements that has as much to do with *who* you are as what you do. Think of your personal Brand Character as the "personality" of your brand. While your Unique Strengths are what you offer to your Audience, your personal Brand Character is more about the *way* you offer those Unique Strengths — your attitude and your prevailing temperament.

How do you talk about personal Brand Character? It's most often described with adjectives — the same way you would describe a person. Watch out, though — don't get it confused with a Unique Strength. A Unique Strength is a noun — it's *what* you can offer. To use a brand name example, Duracell Battery's Strength might be "longer-lasting," but the Character of the battery brand would be "persistent" or "never gives up."

Are You a Character?

The first task we need to tackle is to figure out your personal Brand Character as it stands right now. In other words, what Brand Character are you currently presenting to others, whether at school or in your job interviews?

One of the best ways to figure out these Character traits is simply to ask classmates, friends, fraternity brothers, or sorority sisters what they think your Brand Character is. You might ask people you know from situations like volunteer work, athletics, community involvement, or church. Their answers will give you a better idea of your personal Brand Character. As always, you want to make sure you ask people you trust. Here are some questions you might ask:

- What are the first words you think of to describe me?
- What do you consider to be the most positive aspects of my personality?
- What do you consider to be less positive aspects of my personality?
- If you were trying to sell my Character to someone, what would you tell them?
- If you were writing my obituary, what would you say about me?

Describing Your Character

What adjectives describe your personal Brand Character? Include those you heard from the people you asked, and add in your own words that you think best describe your Brand Character. At first, think about your overall personality rather than just the Character traits that might come through at work. The key is to be as specific as possible, and try to think of traits that aren't the same as everyone else's. Look up words on dictionary.com or thesaurus.com if you need help coming up with more adjectives.

Here are some examples:

Irreverent	Calm	Dedicated
Fun-loving	Earnest	Even-tempered
Street-wise	Sparkling	Decisive
Authentic	Soulful	Vivacious
Maverick	Eloquent	Generous
Professional	Soft-spoken	Chic
Focused	Outgoing	Spiritual
Gracious	Grounded	Considerate
Altruistic	Industrious	Sociable
Fair-minded	Courageous	Visionary
Colorful	Approachable	Daring
Magnetic	Original	Ethical
Inspirational	Direct	Compassionate
Engaging	Wise	Encouraging
Influential	Persuasive	Passionate

As you think about this list, consider which of these Character traits are most important to you—the most true to the authentic YOU™. How many of your Character traits have you expressed openly and comfortably up to this point in your life? Do you regularly communicate these traits at school and at any jobs you've held so far?

Another Option: Short Narrative

Another way to describe your personal Brand Character is to develop a short narrative that describes your Character. Using a name brand example, the Brand Character of the colossal Tide laundry detergent brand could be something like: "The perfectionist who doesn't stop until the job gets done." Switching back to personal branding, YOU™ might be: "The invaluable can-do person you can always count on to take care of what needs to be done." What might be a short narrative descriptor for YOU™?

Let's Get Creative!

You may have hidden some of your personality's strongest characteristics, even though these traits could help you get a better job if they were communicated as part of your college grad personal brand. Thinking along those lines, let's dig deeper and uncover even more aspects of your Character that can help you in the job search process.

Keep in mind that your Brand Character usually stays pretty consistent throughout your life — it's a fundamental part of who you are. But you can also develop certain aspects of your Brand Character if you really set your mind to it. For example, take Connor, who was a business major. In the fall of his senior year, he knew exactly which company he wanted to work for when he graduated because two of his friends who were a year ahead of him had gotten jobs there and loved it. The challenge was that the company preferred grads who were outgoing and who were good at giving presentations. This was a problem for Connor who was more introverted by nature, and he worried that it might hold him back from getting the job he wanted. So, he decided to do something about it.

There was a speakers club at his college, so Connor decided to join it, even though the idea made him nervous. He set a goal of working on the Brand Character trait of being "persuasive." The other members of the speaking club and the club's professor/sponsor all helped him a lot, and Connor gradually got more comfortable giving speeches in front of people. After practicing and gaining some confidence, Connor was able to give a speech in front of 60 people. Also, as part of some volunteer work Connor was doing as a dorm rep, he made a proposal to the university's student board to change some signs on campus that were confusing new students. He won over the board and got the signs changed. This gave Connor much more confidence that he could communicate a "persuasive" Brand Character in interviews. Of course, it also gave him some good experiences he could talk about when meeting with company recruiters. Thanks to his proactivity and knowing exactly what Brand Character he wanted to communicate, it worked! Connor got the job with the company he wanted.

Creative Comparisons

Sometimes, thinking about the character traits of others can give you a good idea of some qualities you might want to focus on or develop in yourself, too. Here are three ways to open up your imagination to other possible words you could use to describe your own personal Brand Character.

1. **Compare yourself to a celebrity.** For example:

    Madonna is ... *daring and original* ... and so am I.

    Lance Armstrong is ... *forward-looking and determined* ... and so am I.

    Oprah Winfrey is ... *charitable and influential* ... and so am I.

    Who could you compare yourself to? Try to think of more than one:

    _____ is _____ and so am I.

2. **Compare yourself to a popular name brand.** For example:

    The clothing brand I'm most like is Nike because ... *I'm sporty and adventurous.*

    The car brand I'm most like is Lamborghini because ... *I'm cutting-edge and state-of-the-art.*

    The bookseller brand I'm most like is Amazon.com because ... *I'm fast and have everything at my fingertips.*

    What name brands are you most like?

    The _____ brand I am most like is _____ because I'm _____.

3. **Compare yourself to a role model.** Think of someone you admire from your university or from your local community, like a favorite professor, Scout leader when you were a child, a college advisor, or the mayor of your city.

    - How would you describe this person? As a leader? An honorable person?

    - What characteristics of this person do you want to develop in yourself?

    - Is there another role model in your community that you admire? If so, ask yourself the same questions about that person.

Narrowing It Down

Does your current personal Brand Character seem to "fit" with the wants, needs, and attitudes of the employers you're targeting? Will it connect with them? If not, which of your other Character traits can you emphasize in upcoming job interviews that will appeal even more to your Audience?

Note that I used the word "appeal." Remember: Personal Brand Character is about the personality, dominant attitude, and temperament that your Character communicates to others. Will your Audience be *attracted* to your personal Brand Character? This is key when it comes to building a connection with a potential employer and finally finding yourself in that job you've been wanting. If your Brand Character doesn't match what your target companies are looking for, you need to either choose different potential employers or think about adding Brand Character traits that are more desirable. Remember, though: YOU™ must be true to who you are. Don't try to turn yourself into someone you're not.

"How's **this** for portraying my desired Personal Brand Character?"

> **Corporate Brand/Personal Brand—Make the Connection**
>
> This may be surprising to hear, but businesses have a Brand Character just like people. Remember how we've talked about a company's "culture?" If you've worked in more than one place, you already know that there are definite cultural differences between companies, just like there are cultural differences between countries. So, be sure to think about the Brand Character of the companies you're targeting. Do they fit with your own personal Brand Character, or are they out of sync? If your Brand Character is very different from a company's Brand Character, you probably won't feel comfortable there. Since your Brand Character has a lot to do with who you are on a fundamental level, it simply won't work to try and change who you are just to fit in somewhere. So, think hard about whether a company's brand is too far away from your own.
>
> Wesley Thorne, an Assistant Director for Business & Employer Relations at Northwestern University, says, "Some candidates try to adapt or change things about themselves—their resume, qualifications, skills, etc.—in order to 'fit' the job requirements. This usually prevents [them] from presenting their true and authentic selves to the employer and, in most cases, leads to more problems down the road." So, try to make a connection between the company's brand and your personal brand, and choose companies where you think you might "fit."

Reality Check

So, you've done the research on your target companies, and you've evaluated the corporate culture of each. Sit down and look at your list of Brand Character traits, and see which ones are a good fit for your target companies. What have you discovered about each company's "Character" in your research? Are they a good match with your own Brand Character? This is the last piece that can help you decide which of these companies would be a good fit for you.

What happens if you discover that there's a disconnect between your own Brand Character and the Character of a company you've targeted for a job? Well, you may need to sit back and think about whether a real connection with this potential employer (your Audience) is ever truly going to happen. If you would say that your fundamental personal Brand Character traits are "outgoing, entrepreneurial, innovative, and energetic," for example, but your Audience is looking for someone who is "stable, sticks to status quo, and follows established procedures," what would you have to do to make an emotional connection with this Audience? And do you really want to make those changes in your personal Brand Character in order to create that connection, or would it be better for you to spend your energy looking for a job in a company where you know you'd feel more comfortable?

If that's the case, you may have some soul-searching to do in terms of how you've been thinking about your job search. You may want to rethink your target companies and look for others that offer more of a "cultural connection" with your own individual Brand Character.

Sometimes, no matter how great a company looks from the outside, your Brand Character may just not be right for it — or the company's Brand Character may just not be right for "YOU™."

Bigger Isn't Always Better

A trend I've noticed with a lot of soon-to-be-college graduates is that they say they want to work for big firms. You know what I mean — the companies with the big names, the big budgets, and the big prestige. But the truth is that many of those companies' Characters don't fit at all with the grads who say they want to work for them. I see this over and over again.

The truth is: Over 90% of all companies in the world are small or medium-sized. That means the majority of people working in the world are in firms that have a smaller number of people working there. So, even though it may not seem like it, there are actually not all that many truly large companies out there. The bulk of jobs available are within smaller firms. And that means the bulk of the biggest *opportunities* are in smaller firms, too.

Still, I meet a lot of college seniors who tell me they think they should "tough it out" and do the "big company thing" for a while as a resume builder. One of the recruiters I interviewed had the following to say about that: "Most of these people would be happier and do better in their careers if they just found the 'right' company for them instead of worrying about size or name." You can spend a lot of unhappy time trying to prepare for happiness in the future. In fact, as Jim Rohn, motivational speaker, said: "Happiness is not something you postpone for the future; it is something you design for the present."

So, remember: Great jobs often come in small packages! Don't overlook smaller companies as excellent places to begin to build your career.

Your College Graduate Personal Brand Positioning Statement

As you get ready to fill in the personal Brand Character section of your College Graduate Personal Brand Positioning Statement, our fellow job seekers—Nicole and Travis—have completed theirs as well. Read their personal Brand Character sections, and choose five to six of the most important qualities, attitudes, and character descriptors you have discovered to describe YOU™. Then, add them to your Positioning Statement. These should be the qualities you consider to be your best, as well as the ones you want to develop and grow in order to leapfrog you to "You're hired!"

Nicole's College Graduate Personal Brand Positioning Statement

Brand Character

My Personal Brand Character (how I want my personal Brand Character to be perceived, including my overriding attitude, temperament, and personality) **is:**

Outgoing, passionate, results-oriented. A confident self-manager.

Travis's College Graduate Personal Brand Positioning Statement

Brand Character

My Personal Brand Character (how I want my personal Brand Character to be perceived, including my overriding attitude, temperament, and personality) is:

Committed, collaborative, real-world engineer who won't stop until client's problems are solved.

What Character do you want to bring to your personal brand? Fill it in to complete the last element of your own Personal Brand Positioning Statement.

YOUR College Graduate Personal Brand Positioning Statement

Brand Character

My Personal Brand Character (how I want my personal Brand Character to be perceived, including my overriding attitude, temperament, and personality) is:

So, now you've completed Step 1 and defined all six elements of your personal brand. It's time to pull all of the elements together and create a big-picture portrait of your College Graduate Personal Brand Positioning Statement.

Step 1
Define it

Outside
1. Audience
2. Need
3. Comparison

Inside
4. Strengths
5. Why
6. Character

9

Pulling It All Together

Your Complete College Graduate Personal Brand Positioning Statement

Details create the big picture.
— Sanford I. Weill, Banker, financier, and philanthropist

Congratulations! You've defined all six elements of your personal brand and filled in all of the boxes in your College Graduate Personal Brand Positioning Statement. Now, it's time to pull it all together into a clear and consistent "big picture."

Before we do, though, let's take a look at the completed Personal Brand Positioning Statements of Nicole and Travis. Take some time to read these with an overall sense of each of their college grad personal brands.

Nicole's College Graduate Personal Brand Positioning Statement

Audience

My Audience is: Medo-Innovations, a large pharmaceutical company with a well-known medical supply division that will soon be launching a new type of glucose monitor.

Company Facts: Currently, the medical supply division of Medo-Innovations has a national sales force of about 150 people. From what I've read on the Internet, it sounds like they're going to add around 15-20 new salespeople, and the rep at the career fair told me they hire new grads pretty regularly. I was told by the career fair rep that you can often stay in your geographic area and that the division may even realign a territory, allowing you to stay close to home.

Company Culture: Medo-Innovations is all about innovation and new ideas. Every sales rep, even the ones with years of experience, go through a phenomenal training program that's very specific to the company.

Division Culture: The division has a track record of hiring younger employees because top management believes fresh, enthusiastic sales reps represent the spirit of its brand. The division has no problem hiring sales reps right out of college if they have the right personality and intelligence to fit into the culture and do the job well. The CEO of the division is a woman in her late 40s, and the division has a "family" culture that makes it feel like a small company even though it's part of a large corporation. This division isn't as competitive as the pharmaceutical division. Sales reps work out of their homes and have their own territories, as if they're running their own businesses.

Interviewer: I'll be interviewing with Kim Mayerson, a 38-year-old hiring manager. She has been with the company for 11 years.

From Kim's LinkedIn profile, I can see that she's very well-respected because her testimonials from her boss and three of her direct reports are all excellent. Two people commented about her professionalism and attention to detail. So, even though the culture of the division sounds like a "family," Kim is probably a stickler for details. Medical supplies are serious business, so I can understand why she would be this way.

Needs

Functional:

- Strong sales skills and customer relations ability.
- Comfortable selling to a highly intelligent, professional customer base.
- Ability to self-manage and get results.

Emotional:

- Outgoing personality; not afraid to embrace new challenges.
- Enthusiasm and passion for science and medicine.

Comparison

Job Title: Sales Representative – Medo-Innovations Medical Supply Division

Desired Label: I *want* to be the brand of *(the way I would like to be perceived):* **"Company Champion"** who passionately promotes and sells the company's innovative products so that they can improve the lives of customers' patients.

Unique Strengths

My Existing Unique Strengths are:

Functional:
- Demonstrated sales results and customer relations abilities.
- Ability to self-manage and get results.

Emotional:
- Outgoing personality; not afraid to embrace new challenges.
- Enthusiasm and passion for science and medicine.

The Future Unique Strengths That I Want to Work on Are:
- Gain more medical knowledge to make me more comfortable selling to a highly intelligent, professional customer base.

Reasons Why

My Existing Reasons Why are:

- *Endorsements:* I have existing letters of recommendation from:
  - My current boss at my part-time department store shoe sales job. He talks about my sales and customer relations experience. He also talks about my self-management abilities in setting stretch sales targets and reaching them.
  - My faculty advisor and mentor, who talks about my enthusiasm and passion for science and medicine.
- *Education:* Bachelor's degree in business with a sales and marketing focus, as well as my early interest in medicine (evident by my freshman and sophomore pre-med science courses).

- *Experience:*
  - Rated one of the top part-time sellers in my retail job at the local department store's shoe department.
  - To show I'm not afraid to face new challenges, share the story about taking over management of the Red Cross campus blood drive when the coordinator got sick. I saw it through to completion even though I hadn't been that involved.

The Future Reasons Why That I Want to Work on Are:

- *Education:* Before my job interview, I will take time to learn about medical supply competitors and about existing glucose monitors from Medo-Innovations, as well as key competitors.
- *Experience:* I will meet with two local pharmacists, asking their opinions about what makes a good medical sales rep and what aspect of medical sales reps they *don't* care for. During the interview, use the data to share what I learned.

Brand Character

My Personal Brand Character (how I want my personal Brand Character to be perceived, including my overriding attitude, temperament, and personality) is:

Outgoing, passionate, results-oriented. A confident self-manager.

Travis's College Graduate Personal Brand Positioning Statement

Audience

My Audience is: PVM Consulting, Inc.

Company Facts: PVM is a very well-known company that was founded in the 1920s. It has more than 100 locations around the world and employs more than 5,000 engineers. Everybody in the engineering field knows about this firm and its professional reputation.

Company Culture: The firm seems to be buttoned down, and seniority appears to matter there. PVM management values teamwork and strives to get repeat business from clients, which I'm sure is one of the reasons they've been around for so long. So, it's clear that they expect a lot from their engineers, whether they're in entry-level EI jobs or whether they've been there for years. In every picture I saw of anyone in the firm, they were dressed in a suit and tie, which confirms the "buttoned down'" type of work environment; they maintain that same kind of professional look in all of their promotional materials, too. Most of the PVM engineers who have profiles on LinkedIn don't have pictures, though. Backgrounds of top PVM engineers on Facebook and LinkedIn show top-notch experience. Even several Engineer Interns had profiles, and the EIs were equally highly qualified. The engineers with testimonials on their profiles were described with words like "reliable" and "detail-oriented."

Interviewer #1: Joseph Cho is an HR rep at PVM and has been with the company for ten years. Before that, he worked in HR for a smaller, private engineering firm. My contact estimates that he's probably in his early 40s. All of this means that Joseph really knows his stuff. When I Googled Joseph's name, I found that he's a member of a professional HR organization and also a member of The United States Chess Federation. Since I like to play chess, too, I can try to mention this in my interview.

Interviewer #2: Adam Trollar is the Team Leader and, if I get the job, I would report directly to him. My contact says Adam's really into active and outdoor hobbies like skiing, mountain climbing, hang gliding, and scuba diving. He's in his late 30s and very "intense" and "focused" in the words of my contact. I also found a press release about when he was hired, which talked about his prior work with another big engineering firm. In the release, he talked about his commitment to the environment, which is something he and I have in common.

Needs

Functional:

- Entry-level engineering skills/ability to apply engineering education to the real world.
- Great attention to detail and to "getting it right the first time."
- Strong at problem-solving.

Emotional:

- Collaborative team player.
- Commitment to preserving the environment.

Comparison

Job Title: Engineering Intern (EI)

Desired Label: I *want* to be the brand of *(the way I would like to be perceived)*: **"Collaborative Problem-Solver"** who bounces ideas off others to come up with great solutions.

Unique Strengths

My Existing Unique Strengths are:

Functional:
- Entry-level engineering skills/ability to apply engineering education to the real world.
- Strong at problem-solving.

Emotional:
- Collaborative team player.
- Commitment to preserving the environment.

The Future Unique Strengths That I Want to Work on Are:
- Great attention to detail and to "getting it right the first time." In the past, I've made some mistakes because I rush, so I need to focus on slowing down and paying more attention.

Reasons Why

My Existing Reasons Why are:

- *Endorsements:*
  - Letter of recommendation from my summer internship supervisor talking about my problem-solving skills and how I worked as a team player to identify problems and helped to fix them.
  - Letter from my faculty advisor who supervised my senior design project; in it, he talks about how I applied my engineering education to real-life problems.
- *Education:* B.S. degree in Civil Engineering, *magna cum laude*.
- *Experience:*
  - Summer internship for the state highway department, working outdoors; gained hands-on experience applying engineering concepts to an actual highway project. Also demonstrates my commitment to helping the environment.

- Senior design class project during which I applied engineering theory to an actual case that our team worked on for an outside company.

The Future Reasons Why That I Want to Work on Are:

- *Experience:* Continue to work on improving my attention to detail, particularly when it comes to doing something new that I'm not familiar with. I will practice slowing down and focusing to reduce my error rate.

Brand Character

My Personal Brand Character (how I want my personal Brand Character to be perceived, including my overriding attitude, temperament, and personality) is:

Committed, collaborative, real-world engineer who won't stop until client's problems are solved.

"Pay attention! You're my target Audience!"

Reading through their examples, do you see how the elements of Nicole's and Travis's statements all fit together? Do you think their statements could be improved? If you were sitting at a coffee shop with either of these two college students, and they asked you for feedback, what would you say?

Now, one more time, read through your own completed College Graduate Personal Brand Positioning Statement. As you review it, try to look at it objectively. If you were an outsider reading through it for the first time, what advice or recommendations would you give to YOU™?

YOUR College Graduate Personal Brand Positioning Statement

Audience

My Audience is:

Company Facts:

Company Culture:

Division/Department Culture:

Interviewer/ College Recruiter:

Potential Boss/Supervisor:

Needs

Functional:

Emotional:

Comparison

Job Title:

Desired Label: I *want* to be the brand of *(the way I would like to be perceived):*

Unique Strengths

My Existing Unique Strengths are:

The Future Unique Strengths That I Want to Work on Are:

Reasons Why

My Existing Reasons Why (why my Audience should believe I can deliver my Unique Strengths) **are:**

The Future Reasons Why That I Want to Work on Are:

Brand Character

My Personal Brand Character (how I want my personal Brand Character to be perceived, including my overriding attitude, temperament, and personality) **is:**

Is Your Statement Complete?

As you sit back and look at the work you've done, be sure to double-check that your Positioning Statement has all of the information it needs:

1. **Audience**
   - Does your statement have all of the elements of a well-defined Audience? When you read it, do you really feel you "know" what your target companies are all about?

2. **Needs**
   - Are the Needs listed the ones you honestly believe to be the most important ones for this potential employer?
   - Did you list both functional and emotional Needs of your Audience?

3. **Comparison**
   - Is your Desired Label clearly defined?
   - Is it unique and different enough that it can help you stand out from other job applicants?

4. **Unique Strengths**
   - Do you have 1-4 clear Unique Strengths that you know you want to — and can — own? If you have more than four, are they truly the most important Strengths for YOU™?
   - Do your Unique Strengths respond to both the functional and emotional Needs of your Audience?

5. **Reasons Why**
   - Are your Reasons Why strong enough to be convincing to your Audience? Will they really help to prove you can deliver the Unique Strengths you've outlined for yourself?

6. **Personal Brand Character**
   - Is your personal Brand Character in sync with what you've found out about the culture and the values of the companies you're targeting?
   - Based on what you know about your target companies, is your stated Brand Character going to appeal to that Audience?

How Does It Look?

So, all in all, how do you feel about your personal brand now that you can sit back and see the big picture? Does it feel "right" to you? Is your statement on target, and does it accurately tell your story? On a scale from 1 to 10, how well does your statement really communicate who YOU™ are and who YOU™ want to be? If you don't think you can score your statement at least at an 8 or 9, take some more time to think about the various elements to see how you might improve your personal brand definition. It's important to get this part right, so be sure to take the time you need to feel as good about your college grad personal brand as possible.

Get Feedback

Before you sign off on your Positioning Statement, get some objective opinions.

- Show your College Graduate Personal Brand Positioning Statement to others you trust, and ask for their feedback. If you know any recruiters or HR professionals personally, they can help by commenting on your statement. Do they agree it presents a great personal brand for you, knowing what they know about you? Do they think your brand is strong enough to help you get the type of job and salary you're looking for?

- Feeling a bit daring? If so, you could even e-mail or call a person who interviewed you in the past but didn't offer you a job, and ask that person for a few minutes of friendly feedback. You could tell that person how you had hoped to come across in your interviews as hardworking, loyal, and good-natured (or whatever brand characteristics are appropriate to YOU™) and ask how well you succeeded at that. By the way, I don't recommend you share your entire Positioning Statement with this person, but just tell them how you had hoped to come across in the interview. This will help you do better the next time.

- Visit www.BrendaBence.com and, for a small fee, you can download a helpful "E-Audit" form that will ask you more questions to consider as you finalize and review your College Graduate Personal Brand Positioning Statement. We also offer one-on-one coaching sessions by phone to discuss your Personal Brand Positioning Statement. Visit the site to find out more.

Now, we're getting ready to move on to Step 2 of our system where you'll discover what you need to do to best communicate your personal brand before, during, and after job interviews. This is where you will really start to see how you can put your personal brand into action to get you a job you'll love.

> *So, all in all, how do you feel about your personal brand now that you can sit back and see the big picture? Does it feel 'right' to you?"*

"Hire the college grad in there selling maps!"

10

Taking YOU™ On Interviews

The more work I do, the more important it is to work with people I like.
— Frank Oz, Film director, actor, and puppeteer

Remember what we said earlier in the book about interviewers hiring the candidates they like and connect with? It's true! In fact:

The best, most qualified candidate doesn't always get the job. It's the best interviewee who almost always gets the job.

No matter how great your resume, if you don't communicate your personal brand well in your job interviews, there's a good chance you'll be out of luck — and, unfortunately, miss out on getting a job you might have loved.

This happens time and again. A great college grad on paper may have trouble getting a job because he or she just isn't all that good at interviewing. It can be incredibly frustrating to candidates who aren't chosen when they know their qualifications are perfect for the job. But if they've spent more time perfecting their resume than focusing on the great personal brand they want to communicate in their interviews, their qualifications may simply not be enough.

The Likeability Factor

Here's another stark reality: Interviewers hire people they like. In fact, as I mentioned earlier, some recruiters estimate that as much as 40% of the hiring decision is based on whether or not you were liked in your interview.

If you think about it, this is also the case with name brands. After all, you buy name brands you like, right? The same holds true on the job. Wouldn't you prefer to work with people you like?

It's no different with potential employers. They hire people they believe they will like working with, and YOU™ are no exception. The truth is: Interviewers will hire you because you've made a connection with them.

This is where Step 2 of our college graduate personal branding system comes in. It will show you how to intelligently and effectively communicate your unique brand in interviews. It will teach you how to be a great interviewee and to really connect with recruiters. That's what personal branding is all about—communicating who YOU™ really are.

Bring On the Heavy Interview Artillery

I know interviews are stressful, but there's an entire arsenal of things you can do to feel more confident and master the interview process. The upcoming chapters will lay out for you the five core activities that are designed to help you have non-stop successful interview experiences and—yes—walk away from interviewers knowing that you were "liked." This is how to make sure the best parts of YOU™ are communicated in the strongest way possible to potential employers. And that, of course, leads to your ultimate objective: an inspiring, exciting new job that you love.

> *That's what personal branding is all about — communicating who YOU™ really are.*

Step 2
Communicate it

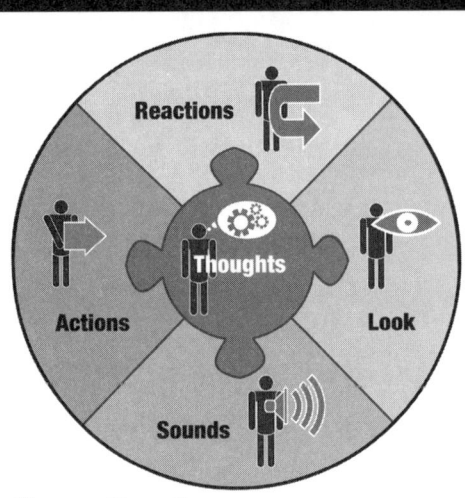

Reactions

Thoughts

Actions

Look

Sounds

College Graduate
Personal Brand Marketing Plan

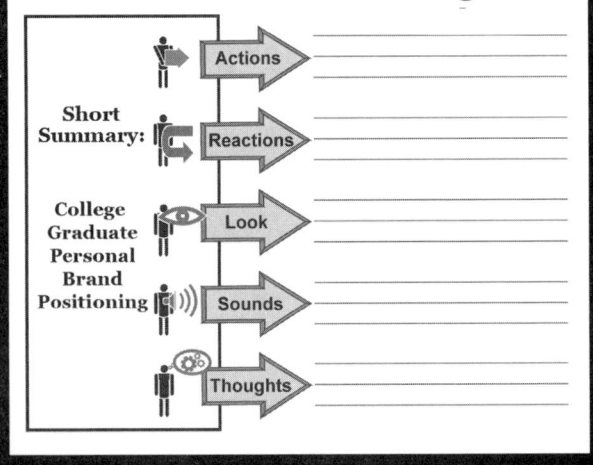

Short Summary:

College Graduate Personal Brand Positioning

- Actions _____
- Reactions _____
- Look _____
- Sounds _____
- Thoughts _____

11

Launching Your College Graduate Personal Brand

The way we communicate with others and with ourselves ultimately determines the quality of our lives.
— Anthony Robbins, Author and motivational speaker

No matter how brilliant the personal brand is that you've defined for yourself, it won't serve any purpose unless you communicate it well to the people who are making the hiring decisions. And that means from the moment your resume crosses their desk, to your first interview, as well as throughout all follow-up communications. The bottom line is: How you communicate your personal brand is how you control the way potential employers perceive, think, and feel about YOU™.

The key to success is being *consistent*. The more consistently you communicate your college grad personal brand throughout your job search, the faster you will be able to turn your personal brand from a concept in *your* mind to a perception in the mind of your Audience — your potential employers. Then, you and "YOU™" will be the same before, during, and after your job interviews. This is what helps you take control of your career and land a job you will really love.

Your Personal Brand Out in the World

Your personal brand should come out into the open so that it can do what you want it to do—get you the job you want. So, the question is: How do you communicate the college grad personal brand you've worked so hard to define?

Think about the ways that successful name brands communicate their brands to their Target Market. Sit back for a minute, and consider a brand you feel really strongly about—a brand that you use regularly and that you have a powerful connection with. How has this particular brand communicated to you what it stands for? How has it made clear to you what *its* Positioning Statement is all about? How has this brand found its way through your wallet and into your life?

Maybe you're loyal to Colgate toothpaste because you like the way it tastes and because you haven't had a bad dentist visit in five years. Do you go to Taco Bell because they stay open late and offer great food to take care of your late-night cravings? Or is it Wendy's signature chili and Frosty that keep you coming back for more, again and again?

What these examples show is that a big name-brand communicates its positioning to you via what it *does*, not by what it says it is. Think about it: You've never seen Wendy's Brand Positioning Statement, right? And the brand manager at Colgate isn't likely to invite you to dinner in order to show you the definition of Colgate's Brand Character. That would be crazy! The *experience* you have with a specific brand is what most communicates its positioning statement.

As I said before, the true key to success for any brand is how *consistent* it is in communicating what it does. For example, Nike wouldn't support an online computer game contest targeted at couch-potato teens, but it *would* support a charity marathon. No, to be consistent in its communications, Nike will regularly communicate its "Just Do It" attitude to its sports-loving audience. This kind of consistency is the Holy Grail when it comes to positioning a brand in the marketplace.

It's the same with personal brands. I can show you my Personal Brand Positioning Statement, and I can tell you that's what I stand for. But you'll decide what my personal brand stands for in your mind based on what I do, not on what I say.

The Five Activities That Communicate Your College Graduate Personal Brand

Now you know that your personal brand is communicated by what you do. But "what you do" covers a lot of territory. I have interviewed hundreds of people in companies around the world, and I've spoken with dozens of recruiters and human resources professionals, asking them how grads like you can best communicate their personal brands. As a result, I firmly believe that there are five core activities you do before, during, and after every job interview that most communicate your personal brand as a job-seeking college grad:

> Your ... **Actions**
> Your ... **Reactions**
> Your ... **Look**
> Your ... **Sound**
> Your ... **Thoughts**

I really believe that these five activities are responsible for 99% of how a potential employer perceives, thinks, and feels about YOU™. These five activities are critical to success in the interviewing process. They're how you will showcase your unique brand to a company where you want to work.

All That—In the Short Span of an Interview?

Now, you may be thinking that a job interview only lasts for a short time. How can you communicate your personal brand in less than a half hour? No matter how much time you have with an interviewer, I will show you how you can use all five of these activities to get across your personal brand in a short time. You can absolutely, positively communicate your personal brand in the span of just a few short minutes. In fact, you'll see that you begin communicating your brand as soon as your resume and cover letter leave your e-mail outbox or as soon as they arrive in the company's mail!

But let's not get ahead of ourselves. We're going to devote the next five chapters to each of these five activities, so you'll have plenty of time to learn how to master each one. No marketing plan would be complete, though, without a clear positioning summary to start us off.

Your College Graduate Personal Brand Marketing Plan

Remember the College Graduate Personal Brand Marketing Plan I mentioned at the beginning of the book? Just like successful name brands have full-blown marketing plans to make sure they communicate their messages consistently in TV commercials, magazine ads, sponsored events, their website, the brand's packaging, public relations efforts, etc., so the five activities we're going to talk about are your own "media" of sorts when it comes to your own Personal Brand Marketing Plan. These five activities are how you communicate to a potential employer who YOU™ really are — whether it's during a phone conversation or in a face-to-face meeting.

If you're serious about how you want a potential company to perceive, think, and feel about you, keep these five activities top of mind every single day throughout your job search to make sure you're absolutely consistent in conveying the personal brand you want. Plus, you never know when you might meet someone who could help you get the job you'll love. So, it's important to be consistent all the time — not just during your interviews. Keep the five activities in mind in every situation.

The College Graduate Personal Brand Marketing Plan Format

Let's look at the College Graduate Personal Brand Marketing Plan format. On the left side, you'll put a brief summary of your Personal Brand Positioning Statement. On the right, you'll decide which elements of the five activities you need to work on in order to better communicate your personal brand throughout your pre- and post-graduation job search process.

First, you'll want to develop an overall positioning summary of your personal brand. What's that? Well, think of your personal brand positioning summary as a tag line or "slogan" of sorts that you'll keep to yourself — a short statement that pulls together the core of what YOU™ want to stand for.

How do you write this? Look again at the different parts of your College Graduate Personal Brand Positioning Statement, and come up with what you think is the heart of the personal brand you want to communicate.

Your summary statement might come from your Brand Character, your Unique Strengths, your Desired Label, your Reasons Why — or maybe a combination of one or more of these.

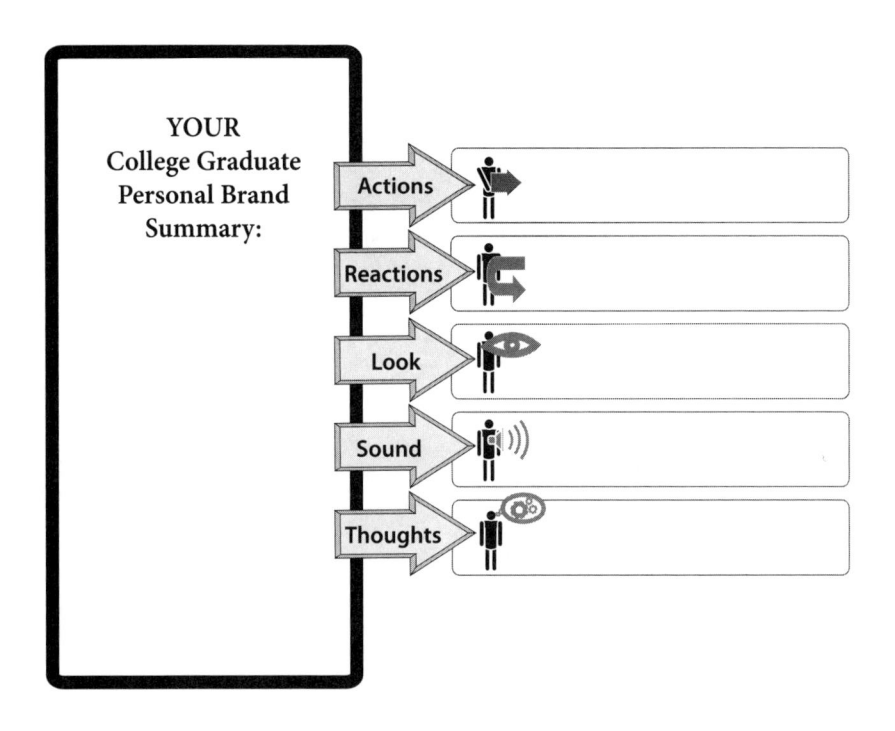

YOUR College Graduate Personal Brand Summary:
- Actions
- Reactions
- Look
- Sound
- Thoughts

On the next page, you'll see what fellow college students Nicole and Travis have chosen for their own personal brand positioning summaries. This can help you get a sense of how the summary looks and sounds.

> *Your personal brand should come out into the open so that it can do what you want it to do — get you the job you want.*

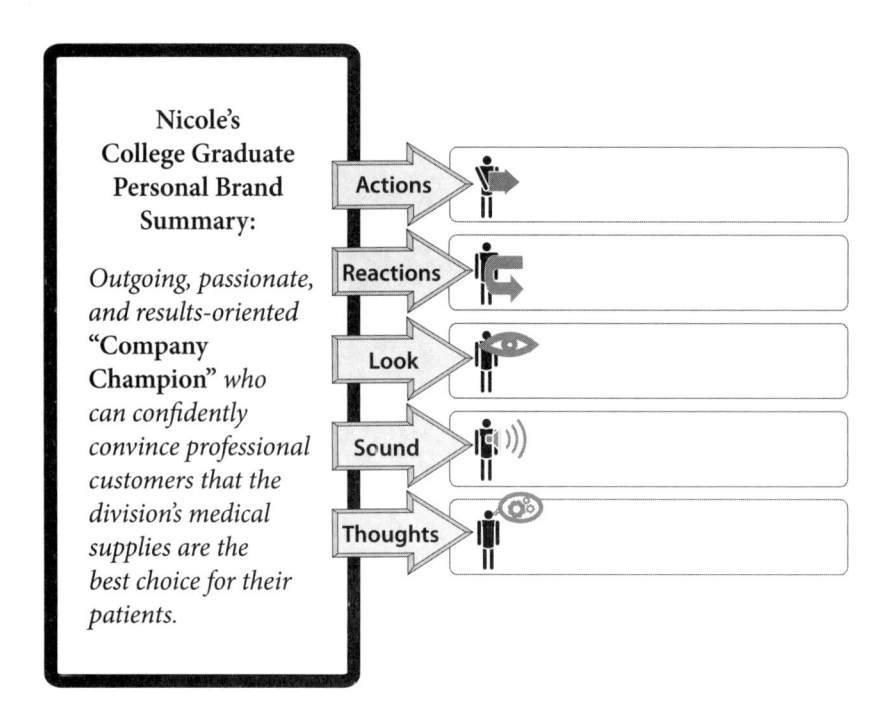

Nicole's College Graduate Personal Brand Summary:

Outgoing, passionate, and results-oriented **"Company Champion"** *who can confidently convince professional customers that the division's medical supplies are the best choice for their patients.*

- Actions
- Reactions
- Look
- Sound
- Thoughts

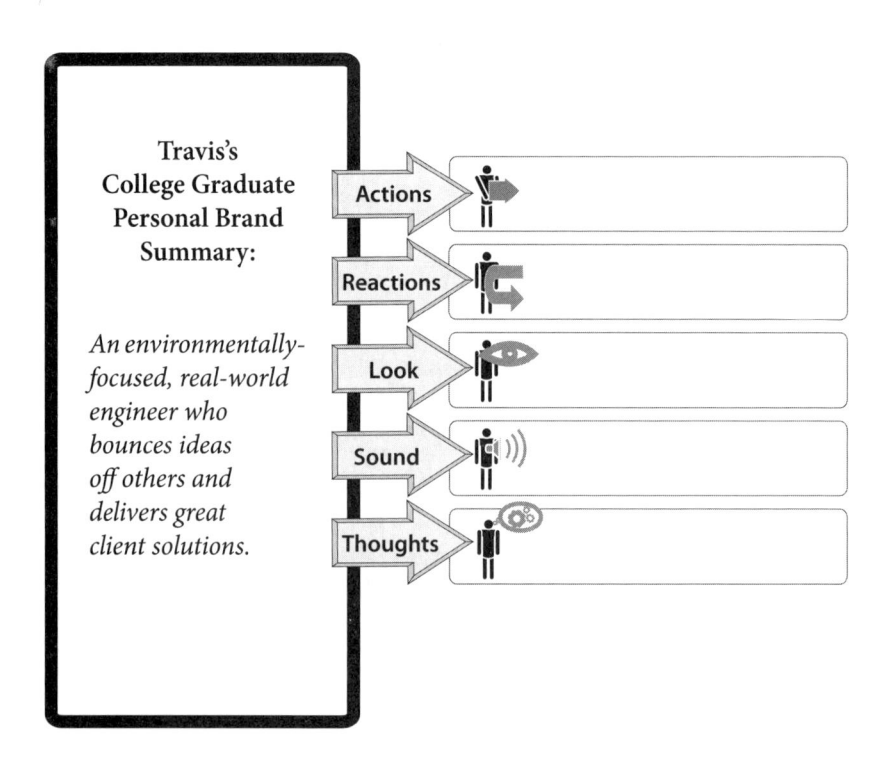

Travis's College Graduate Personal Brand Summary:

An environmentally-focused, real-world engineer who bounces ideas off others and delivers great client solutions.

- Actions
- Reactions
- Look
- Sound
- Thoughts

Hopefully, you can see how the summaries of Nicole and Travis briefly and simply state what they want their personal brands as job-seeking grads to stand for. Now, go ahead and add your own personal brand summary to the left of your College Graduate Personal Brand Marketing Plan. At the end of each of the next five chapters, you'll be able to add your own ideas about how you plan to use the five Marketing Plan activities during your job search.

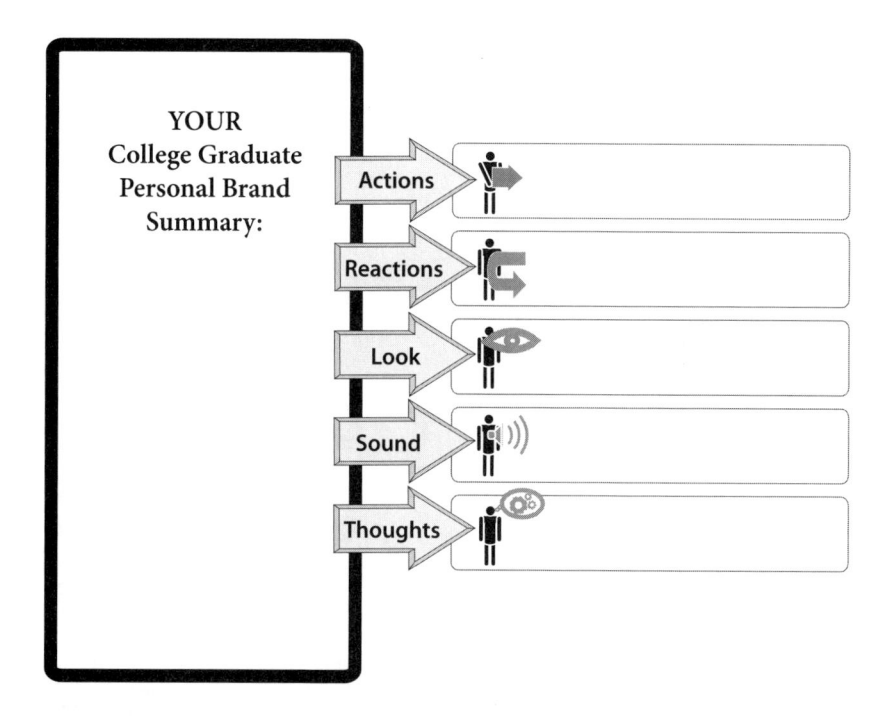

YOUR College Graduate Personal Brand Summary:

- Actions
- Reactions
- Look
- Sound
- Thoughts

Communicate it

Actions

Step 2

12

Actions

College Graduate Personal Brand Marketing Plan Activity #1

An idea not coupled with action will never get any bigger than the brain cell it occupied.

— Arnold Glasow, American humorist

The first activity in your College Graduate Personal Brand Marketing Plan is your Actions. You may think that all five of the activities that make up your Personal Brand Marketing Plan are "actions," but in this case, what I mean by Actions are behaviors others can see that can impact the way your personal brand is communicated. Think of it as how you conduct yourself — your overall manner. This includes how you handle yourself on the phone, in e-mails or letters, during an interview, etc.

You may not even be aware of some of your Actions, but they can make a big difference in how a potential employer perceives, thinks, and feels about YOU™.

No matter how great your GPA, your personal brand will take a hit if your Actions turn off an interviewer. Think for a second about people you've met. Have you ever had a phone conversation, and the other person hung up without saying goodbye? What did you think of that person? Maybe you know someone who's really smart and capable but never looks you in the eye. It can come across as a lack of interest or lack of confidence. These kinds of Actions influence the way your college grad personal brand is perceived by that key person or group of people who are considering you for a job.

The Actions we're talking about can be either social or directly related to the job you're after. When you think about it, interviewing for a job is kind of a combination of the two, right? It's definitely a work-related meeting, but it's also somewhat of a "social" meeting, too, where you and the interviewer get to know each other as people. That's why your Actions are judged in an interview both in terms of how right you are for the job, as well as how much the interviewer likes you and gets along with you.

Actions are an important part of a successful job search and an important way to communicate your college grad personal brand in an interview, but how can you take control of your Actions — especially if you're not even aware of them?

Seeing Yourself Through the Eyes of an Employer

It's important to try to see yourself the way a potential employer sees you, but that isn't always easy. You're inside yourself, so it's hard to know how your Actions "read" to others on the outside. But figuring out which of your Actions might be helping your personal brand — and which ones might be hurting it — is an important part of a successful job search.

The first step to seeing yourself through the eyes of someone who might hire you is to really know your Audience. The work you've already done to understand your Audience and what they need will be incredibly helpful at this stage. Since you've already completed the Audience portion of your College Graduate Personal Brand Positioning Statement, you should have a pretty good idea of the Actions your target companies would look for in a candidate.

In fact, take time now to go back and review the Audience section of your Positioning Statement. Think about what Actions your target companies would value most. What work behaviors and what social behaviors? For example, if you know a company values reliability, the Actions you will want to focus on in your interview would be always showing up on time, calling back exactly at the time you've been asked, following up as promised with the interviewer about any unanswered questions from the interview, etc.

But your Actions don't just affect how your college grad personal brand is perceived while you're sitting across from the interviewer.

There are Actions you can take before and after your interview, too, that will have an impact on your job search.

Your Actions *Before* the Interview

The Actions you need to focus on before an interview are: (1) communicating with a target company through phone calls, e-mails, your cover letter, and your resume, and (2) preparing for the moment you step into the company's offices. You'll want to take each of these into account before every one of your interviews.

But how do you get the interview in the first place? Besides career fairs and your college placement office, try these Actions:

> **Network, Network, Network.** How many times have you heard about the importance of networking when it comes to looking for a job … dozens? hundreds? Well, there's a reason. Hiring experts estimate that as many as 60% to 75% of all jobs are found through networking as opposed to job postings. Without a doubt, networking is one of the most effective ways to find a job.
>
> What does this mean for YOU™? Pick up the phone, make connections with anyone and everyone you can, and let them know what kind of job you're interested in after you graduate. E-mail family, e-mail friends, and e-mail friends of friends (where appropriate). This can be a challenge if you tend to be on the shy side, but it's important to take a deep breath, swallow your fears, and get the word out.
>
> **Throw the Net Wide.** Think of all the people you could contact: former coworkers at part-time jobs/internships, former bosses, classmates, friends, family, acquaintances, and people you know from your community. Brainstorm as many contacts as you can. Make connections through Facebook, MySpace, Twitter, LinkedIn, and other online networks.
>
> But don't forget to be careful with your social networking! If you have photos of your spring break antics on your Facebook or MySpace pages, you might want to think twice about friending professional contacts. If you *do* choose to friend potential employers, or even employees at potential employers, stop yourself before you post the news about a drunken night at a local club, your break-up with your boyfriend, or even the nasty video that you found on YouTube that's *so* funny. Share it with your close friends in an e-mail instead. The same

goes for Twitter. Interviewers can look up your name on Twitter and find out what you've been tweeting about. And if they follow you, it can be damaging if you're tweeting about things that you don't want someone in a professional context to know about you. Do you really want a potential employer to see your "How Sexy Are You?" rating?

In other words, social networks are social, but they're out there on the Internet where the information can be found by most anybody. Facebook has settings that allow you to restrict what certain friends can see on your profile and wall. But again, be careful! Some of these settings are not foolproof. For example, when you take a quiz on Facebook, that quiz was created by someone outside of Facebook. So, the results of that quiz may be available to anyone, and you may have no control over who can read them on your wall.

So, be sensible about social networks when you're creating your professional personal brand. It isn't worth it if something you've posted ruins your chances of getting the job you want.

Send Resumes to Your Favorite Companies. Apply directly to the target employers you've identified through your sleuthing and networking. Yes, networking is a great way to find a job, but the U.S. Census Bureau reports that applying directly to employers is one of the best ways to find a new job. It doesn't matter if the company hasn't placed a job listing anywhere yet.

Once you get the interview process rolling, how can you keep track of where you've been and where you're going? Here are some important tips to remember:

Stay Organized. As Nora Bammann, Assistant Human Resources Manager of The Kroger Company, says: "One of the most important parts of any job search is to adopt an organized approach." This means that you need to keep track of all of the companies you're applying to, all of your appointments, and all of your interviews. It's a lot to remember, so you simply have to create a plan for recording the information in order to find it fast when you need it.

Here are more ways to help you stay on top of your job search:

- Keep all of your appointments in your cell phone or Blackberry with the time of your appointment, address of the company, name of the person you're meeting, and directions to the company's location.

- Keep notes — in a binder or on your computer — about each company that you target, all of the people you meet and their job titles, each job, and each interview.
- Make a separate folder for each company. Include the time and date when you spoke with each individual, a summary of what was said, and what "next steps" were indicated, if any.
- Keep a list of the right way to spell names, including the receptionist and any assistants you meet (so that you can call them by name when you arrive for an interview or if you need to follow up with them). Include job titles on your list, too.

This may seem like a lot of work, but trust me — it works. Take Kaylyn, a grad who was offered not one, but *three* teaching jobs! "If I hadn't written down the specifics of what took place during my interviews, I wouldn't have gotten as many offers as I did," she says. "I had to meet with so many different people throughout the interview process, I had first, second, and third interviews, and I also visited with various administrators from different schools. Keeping track was crazy! They always smiled when I was able to bring up something from the last meeting I had with them, so I'm sure it had a lot to do with why I got so many offers."

Your Cover Letter and Resume. If you're like most people, you've probably put in a lot of work trying to develop the "perfect" cover letter. And you've dotted every "i" and crossed every "t" of your resume, right? But how do you really know these documents are perfect for YOU™?

Here's a great exercise to help you see how others might view your cover letter or resume: Print out a copy of what you think is your very best cover letter, attach your resume, fold it up, put it in an envelope, and mail it to yourself. When it arrives in your mailbox a couple of days later, pretend you've never laid eyes on either one before. Open them up, and look at them objectively. What's your initial impression? Go back to your personal brand summary and remind yourself of how you want a potential employer to perceive, think, and feel about you. Are your cover letter and resume truly "working" for YOU™?

Here is a tip for your resume and cover letter: Recruiters and HR people don't have a lot of time to read all of the details of all of the resumes and cover letters they receive. So, they need you to get to the point. Put the most important information you want the recruiter to know on the top half of your resume because there's a good chance that if you don't capture the interest of the recruiter right away, they may not read your whole resume or cover letter.

What's the most important information on a college graduate's resume? It's usually your education, followed by any internships or work experience that you've had. And make that information *easy* to read, too. Kristi Oltman, Manager of Talent Acquisition at National Research Corporation, says that bullet points are "easier to read and to get through." Make it easy for the person reading your resume and cover letter to see *immediately* why you're the best person for the job.

Put Yourself in the Shoes of a Potential Employer. What would you think of someone who sends you an impersonal form cover letter that has obviously been sent to lots of other companies, too? It might even be addressed to "Dear Sir or Madam" instead of your name. Or how about receiving a resume with almost nothing on it — no evidence that the grad has made efforts to achieve anything or get involved on campus or in the community? What about someone who presents you with a ridiculously long and wordy resume, going on and on and bragging about accomplishments that don't sound possible for a college grad?

Wouldn't these be very different brand images compared to someone who simply presents you with a brief cover letter that talks about the specific position the grad wants and offers knowledgeable details about the target company? What about a resume that looks very neat and organized and shows that the grad has really worked on learning and developing himself/herself through being involved in campus activities and the community? All of these people may have the same desired personal brand of "the go-to person" but the Actions that these grads take with their cover letters and resumes will have a big impact on how their job-seeker personal brands are communicated.

Norman Saale, Chief Operating Officer at a multi-office accounting firm, recruits candidates on college campuses. He says, "College students applying for jobs need to show that they've spent time developing themselves." This might include part- or full-time work, internships, volunteer work, or involvement in campus government or athletics, for example. "Show that you have commitment — that you are working toward something and have thought out a longer-term plan," he says. So, for example, if accounting is your major, what can you do to show that you have a long-term commitment to your field? You can volunteer to do the accounting for a community organization, join an accounting organization, take professional training courses in the field (outside of college), or become active in your campus accounting club.

Practice Great E-mail Etiquette. An important Action to keep top of mind in the pre-interview part of your job search is good e-mail etiquette. In these days of phone texting and quick "one-liner" e-mails, it's easy to forget that e-mail is actually a replacement for the old-fashioned physical letter. If you were sending a letter in an envelope via the post office to a potential employer, how would it look, and what would you say? Do your e-mails read the same? For example, try to include the name and title of your interviewer in your e-mails, and make sure you spell the name right. Begin every e-mail just like you would a cover letter with "Dear _____." End each e-mail with "Sincerely" or "Best regards." Remember: Every piece of communication you have with a potential employer plays a role in how that employer will perceive, think, and feel about your job-seeker personal brand.

Anticipate Questions. Sit down and brainstorm every possible question you think an interviewer might ask you, and prepare your answers. Well thought-out responses will show you've spent time thinking about your accomplishments and capabilities — and that builds a strong personal brand image. Even if an interviewer asks a question you didn't think of beforehand, you'll feel more confident if you're ready with answers to every question you've brainstormed. As Tim Wilson, CPA and Partner at BKD, LLP, says, "There is no excuse for not having excellent questions ready for each interview."

Be sure to check out Appendix A at the end of this book for a list of questions you should be prepared to answer in any interview. As Penn State football coach Joe Paterno put it, "The will to win is important, but the will to prepare is vital."

Make Lists for Each Interview. Prior to each of your interviews, make three separate lists:

1. List the key points you want to get across in the interview about your experience, your education, and how you "fit" with the job you're going for. You can base this on what you've learned in your research about the company's expectations, values, and Needs.

2. Develop a second list that outlines all of the info about the job or the company that you don't currently know. Split this list into two: (a) the information you feel you *need* to know in order to decide if the job is right for you, and (b) the information you feel you would *like* to know but that isn't absolutely necessary to know. (Remember not to ask questions about salary, time off, hours, perks, transfers, or vacation time until much later in the interview process!)

3. Based on your lists of what you need to know or would like to know, make a final list of the questions you want to ask during your upcoming interview about the job and/or the company. Here, prioritizing is key because you may only be given enough time to ask one question. With that in mind, if you really do get to ask only one question about the job or the company, which one will it be? If you have time to ask just two questions, which two are the most important? Again, remember that they may be the only questions you have time to ask in the interview, so make them the most critical ones.

Appendix A's list of key questions to consider when in an interview can really help you, too. While you're putting together your three lists, take a look at those questions to give you some ideas.

Practice, Practice, Practice. Now that you know how you would answer just about every imaginable question, it's really critical to practice. Get a friend or family member to help, and write each question on a piece of paper. If you can find someone who actually conducts interviews regularly, you'll receive the best possible feedback. Have your friend ask you each of the questions one right after the other at a fast pace. Then, ask your friend for honest feedback and insights about how well you answered each question. Did you answer the questions in a way that communicated your personal brand well?

Make a Video of Yourself in a Mock Interview. Get another friend to play interviewer, and make a video while your friend asks you the same questions you think you'll be asked. (The career development center at your college might do this for you, too. Be sure to ask!) Then, sit back and watch yourself. This is one of the best ways to learn how you're coming across in a potential interview, and it can be a real eye-opener. In all honesty, it may not be much fun (does anybody really like watching themselves on video?), but it will show you what you need to work on in order to improve the way you're perceived by an interviewer.

Get Truly Objective Feedback. Once you've recorded your mock interview, get a critique from your career development center, or ask someone who doesn't know you very well to watch the video and give you feedback about what they perceive, think, and feel about YOU™ based on the video. This is such a good learning experience, and it will be your strongest clue about whether or not you're communicating the personal brand you want through your Actions.

Communicate Your Personal Brand to Everyone. Don't forget: Your personal brand needs to be communicated to everyone you meet during the interview process, from your first phone call or e-mail, to the moment you walk in the door of the company, to your last phone call or e-mail. This includes any recruiters/employment agents as well. Think about it: These agencies represent you, so if they don't get a clear sense of your brand, how can they help you find the job you want? Recruiters and employment agencies want to keep up their own reputation with their client companies, so they won't be enthusiastic to sell you if they don't feel they know YOU™. This means that your Actions need to demonstrate to these people exactly how you will come across in an interview. Your meeting with them isn't a time to relax and be laid back.

What Signals Do You Send? Become as aware as you can of the signals your Actions send. Of course, remember that different people interpret Actions in different ways. For example, let's say Jessica has talked to a few people who actually know her prospective boss. Through these inside talks, she has found out that one of her potential boss's core Needs is for an employee who is precise. For her interview, Jessica has been asked to bring a portfolio showing her work as a civil engineering summer intern complete with case studies of projects she worked on.

- If Jessica arrives with her portfolio in an attractive folder with the case studies printed out and well-organized, that's a very different "precise" brand than...

- If Jessica arrives with the requested case studies, but they are in a random pile of papers out of order. That's yet a very different "precise" brand than...

- If Jessica shows up with some handwritten notes and no real portfolio ... well, that's not really a "precise" brand at all.

Make sure that everything you present supports your desired brand image!

Stick Extra Copies of Your Resume in Your Briefcase. Good personal branders are ready for anything, and that means having extra copies of your resume handy during an interview. In fact, Kate Cancro of Hilton says she finds it "important to ask students if they have a copy of their resume just to test if they are prepared for the interview." Don't be caught.

Never Forget Your Personal Brand. Right before arriving for the interview, remember who YOU™ are by keeping your Personal Brand Positioning Summary top of mind. Go back over your personal brand key attributes and the definitions you've developed in your College Graduate Personal Brand Positioning Statement. You might even type up a small reminder, print it, and stick it in your pocket so that you can review it immediately before walking into the interviewer's office.

Your Actions *During* the Interview

Let's say your hard work and pre-interview Actions have paid off, and you've received a call to set up a meeting with the HR Department of a company where you really want a job. Now, it's the day of the interview. You arrive at the interview location, and it's the moment of truth. It's critical to make sure your Actions communicate your personal brand from the minute you step into the company's offices to the moment you walk away from the building. What will be your first Action? It might be introducing yourself to the security guard or the receptionist. Maybe it will be a handshake with one of these people. Here are some ways that you can make sure YOU™ perform like the strong brand you want.

Always Be Polite. Let's face it: "Nice" works! Are you pleasant to *everyone* you speak with from the minute you walk in the door? Don't treat the receptionist or the security guard with impatience either on the phone or in person. That kind of Action could very easily get back to your potential employer and spoil your chances of being hired.

If you enter a room with a smile and your hand extended for a warm handshake, it communicates that you're happy to be there. Even if you're nervous, walking in with a friendly attitude will help you relax, especially since others will probably be friendly back and help put you at ease.

Always Be Professional. Do you say, "Hello. It's nice to meet you"? Or do you say, "Hey there, how's it goin'?" When you greet anyone in the company — no matter who it is (even if it's someone you already know) — are you professional? An interview is a time to be friendly, but not overly casual.

Be Personable at All Times. Don't stay silent if you walk with the interviewer toward the office where you'll sit down for the interview! Use that time as an opportunity for small talk. You might comment on something positive that you observed in the office or while you were waiting in the reception area. But avoid a "don't speak until you're spoken to" attitude. Present your personal brand right away. If you suddenly "turn it on" when you sit down for the interview, you'll come across as phony.

Kristi Oltman says, "I love it when an interviewee has been talking with someone in the waiting room. That shows they understand the importance of building relationships." So, even before you meet with the interviewer, look for opportunities to start conversations — with the receptionist or with others in the waiting area. (Of course, don't distract the receptionist with a conversation if he or she looks too busy.)

How's Your Handshake? Don't underestimate the importance of your handshake! In most interview situations, before you even open your mouth or hand over your resume, you're making a first impression with your grip. Trust me: Your interviewer is going to judge your level of confidence based on your handshake. With that in mind, is your handshake "interview-ready?"

I've had the most amazingly burly men offer me handshakes that were so "wimpy" they completely destroyed my impression of their initial personal brand image. Maggie Yontz, College Recruiting Manager at ConAgra Foods says, "I can't stand limp, sweaty handshakes!" No matter how you look, if you don't offer a handshake that comes across as confident, you run the risk of hurting your personal brand from the start.

On the other hand, is your handshake just the opposite of wimpy? I've had some people crush my hand so badly with a forceful handshake that my ring engraved itself into my finger in a matter of seconds. What kind of personal brand message do you think that person just communicated to me? A bully? Someone who must have their way by force? In either case, it's someone I would never want to work with!

I don't know of any schools that offer a "Handshake 101" course, so unfortunately, most of us are never taught the best way to shake hands. So, it's important to practice your handshake if you aren't sure about it. Maggie Yontz concurs: "Another Personal Brand Buster® in my mind is not practicing and perfecting one's handshake prior to interviewing." A handshake should be firm and link thumb-to-thumb with the other person. If you're afraid of being too forceful or not sure if you're squeezing too hard, ask someone you trust to let you shake their hand. Then, ask them to tell you honestly what kind of signal your handshake is communicating.

Also, if you have a tendency to get sweaty palms, keep a handkerchief or tissue in your pocket to wipe your hands right before the interview. Maybe you have poor circulation, and your hands are always cold? If so, place your hand in your pocket to warm it up before you go into an interview, or go to the nearest restroom and run warm water over your hands. Whatever you do, make sure your handshake is communicating your personal brand well, or it could put YOU™ at a disadvantage from the very start of your interview.

Don't Forget to Breathe! Let's be honest: Interviews can be nerve-wracking experiences, and it's a medical fact that when you're nervous, your breathing becomes shallower. The solution? Take subtle deep breaths to help calm you down. You don't want it to be obvious that you're breathing deeply, but it's important to make sure you don't hold your breath or breathe shallowly and rapidly due to being nervous. The last thing you want is not to get enough oxygen to your brain where you've stored all those great answers to potential interview questions! If you find that your breathing is not deep enough because of nerves, pause for a second, and take a subtle but deep breath.

If you tend to have excess nervous energy in interviews, practice calming yourself down before you walk into the interviewer's office. Do some deep breathing to get your heart rate down, and keep your hands clasped together on your lap if they tend to fidget. Concentrate on keeping your feet flat on the floor, and help ease your anxiety by turning your attention to what the interviewer is saying.

Watch Out for Nervous Body Language. You may have some body language habits that go against the brand you want to communicate. Say, for example, you're in an interview, and you suddenly hear a repetitive tapping sound. Look around—it might be you tapping your foot or a pen against a table! Just like a leg that bounces up and down uncontrollably, most people are completely unaware of the unconscious signals they send to others simply by how they move. If you exhibit nervous Actions that you're not even aware of, begin to notice them to gain control of your excitement. The body language you communicate may actually come across to your interviewer as a lack of self-confidence.

Do you:

- Bite your nails?
- Drum your fingers?
- Swing your leg?
- Blink rapidly?
- Grip the arms of your chair?

These are all Actions that will make you appear nervous. Here are some additional typical nervous body language habits to watch out for:

- Avoid fidgeting. Stay as still as you can (without becoming too stiff, of course), or you may risk coming across as impatient.
- Try not to use your hands more than necessary when you speak. According to body language experts, confident people don't feel the need to prove their points by gesturing too much.

- Don't let your eyes wander while the interviewer is speaking. If your eyes *do* wander, the interviewer may get the idea that you're not interested in what he or she is saying, and that may give the impression that you're not very interested in the job.

Maintain "Open" Body Language. In interview situations, good personal brand builders practice body language that makes them appear "open" and friendly. Here are some "open" body language tips:

- Avoid folding your arms across your chest because it communicates that you're closing yourself off to other people.
- Avoid putting your hands in your pockets during the interview because you might look like you're trying to protect yourself out of fear or shyness.
- If you want your interviewer to know you're interested in what he or she is saying, lean forward slightly.
- If you want to show sincerity when making a point, touch your palm to your chest as you speak.
- Men, when you first walk into an interview, have your suit jacket buttoned, but feel free to unbutton it when you sit down. Not only will this keep your jacket from bunching up, but it will communicate YOU™ as someone who is receptive.
- What about when you're sitting? Experts say it's fine to cross your legs knee over knee.
- Don't lean back in your chair, however, or clasp your hands behind your head. This conveys an attitude that's too casual and may even come across as *over*confident, making you potentially less likeable to an interviewer.
- If you're sitting at a table, resting your elbows on the table with the fingertips of both your hands touching is considered an expression of self-confidence.

Observe the body language of people you feel drawn to. What are they doing that makes them so likeable? On the other hand, what Actions do you see in people who are not that likeable or approachable? Once again, this is why recording yourself on video before interviews can be so valuable. You may notice yourself unconsciously doing something that you've seen unapproachable people do. By discovering it now, you can fix it before it loses you the chance at an important job.

Take Notes. Almost all of the company recruiters I spoke to said that candidates should bring a notebook and a pen to interviews.

Then, be sure to take notes throughout the interview. It communicates a conscientious personal brand and also helps you remember key points you covered during the interview. You don't want to write down every single word that's said, but it's perfectly fine to write down a few brief notes. Be sure to write down names and titles of key people who are mentioned during your interview. You can use those later, and your personal brand will come across positively as a result.

To show you're engaged, make sure the notebook contains prepared questions to ask your interviewer.

One interviewer I spoke with estimates that nearly half of the candidates she meets arrive *without* a notebook. So, set yourself apart with a nice pen and a neat and professional looking notebook (one without any tears or scribbling on it). One more tip: Take an extra pen with you in case your first one runs out of ink.

Leave the Interviewer Impressed with YOU™. When you walk out of an interview, make sure you leave a lasting impression. Stand up, offer your goodbye handshake, look the interviewer respectfully in the eye, and smile. We'll talk later about what to say when you're leaving, but your Actions — your body language — at the end of an interview will play a key role in what the interviewer remembers about you long after you've left.

Your Actions *After* the Interview

Strong personal brand builders know that they must keep up with their Actions as much *after* interviews as before and during interviews. That's key to communicating a job-seeker personal brand well. Here are some tips to remember after an interview is over.

Summarize Immediately. As soon as an interview is finished, find a quiet place to sit down, and write your summary of the meeting. Don't expect that you'll remember enough to write it later. You'll inevitably forget some important points even if you wait just an hour or two after the interview. Trust me — after several meetings with a number of companies, the interviews will start to blend together in your mind unless you take good notes right away. When your job search is in full swing, you'll be glad you made the time to summarize immediately.

As you think back and jot down notes, ask yourself: What were the key topics you and the interviewer discussed? What were the names of the critical decision-makers who were mentioned? What did you notice about the company environment? Did people look content or unhappy? Were you treated well? Did you get a "good feeling" while you were there? Writing down notes after the interview will help you refer to important points in follow-up e-mails and also refresh your memory when it comes time for a second interview. Believe me — remembering your first interview well will communicate a great "conscientious" personal brand, and you can't go wrong with that kind of brand image.

Follow Up. Don't take it personally if you don't hear back quickly from your interviewer. HR representatives are often so busy that, even though the hiring process is important, they're sometimes forced to put it on the back burner. In fact, some companies have fairly complex processes to follow before anyone can be hired, including asking other employees for input. So, don't sweat it if you don't hear back right away.

All that said, you should definitely follow up immediately with a thank you e-mail. We'll address this more in the Sound chapter, but this is a critical Action that will help you stand out from the crowd. Write the thank you within 24 hours after your interview at the latest. The interviewer may be conducting one interview after another, so get that thank you to him or her while YOU™ are still fresh in the interviewer's mind! Just make sure that your thank you is well-written. If it's filled with typos or it doesn't say anything particularly noteworthy, you've just put yourself out of the running for the job. As Norman Saale puts it, "A thank you note can provide an opportunity for someone to make a mistake, and bad mistakes can change the recruiter's mind! If you're not a great writer, it can work against you." So, write your thank you, but get help if you need it.

> ### How Much Can Typos Hurt You?
>
> Accountemps conducted a survey of 150 senior executives and published the results in *USA Today*. They asked the executives how many typos it would take for them to decide against a candidate for a job. 40% of them said it would only take *one typo*, 36% said it would take two, and 14% said it would take three before they'd discount someone. So, proofreading is very, very important! What's one of the most common typos? "Dear Sir or Madman." Ouch!

The Waiting Game. Haven't heard back from your interviewer, and it's been about a week or more since your interview? It's okay to call and leave a voicemail message or send a follow-up e-mail to let the interviewer know you're still interested. The key is to ask the question politely and just let him or her know that you'd still like to work for the company. If you have a chance to actually get someone on the phone, you can mention something about the interview that you've been thinking about and, once again, how well you believe you would fit with the job and the company.

If you've been told, for example, that the decision will be made about the job within two weeks of your interview, send a follow-up e-mail a few days before that deadline. If you still hear nothing from the interviewer, follow up in another week or two, depending on how quickly the interviewer told you the job would be filled. After two or three follow-ups, you can probably assume that you didn't get the job if you don't hear anything from the interviewer.

A Second Interview. If you're called for a second or third interview, don't change your strategy, but keep building on it! You've made it this far because of who YOU™ are, so continue to do what you did in the first interview by keeping your Audience and their

Needs top of mind. And don't forget that you're communicating your personal brand every minute. In second or third interviews, for example, you might be taken for a walking tour around the company. If this happens, remember that your Actions, Reactions, Look, Sound, and Thoughts will all be observed even during this less formal time.

Your College Graduate Personal Brand Marketing Plan

Reflecting on all of the Actions outlined in this chapter, which ones do you believe you should work on most or improve as you think about how to effectively communicate your personal brand as a college grad looking for a job? With those in mind, it's time to pull together your College Graduate Personal Brand Marketing Plan. To help you, Nicole and Travis have completed the Actions part of their individual Personal Brand Marketing Plans.

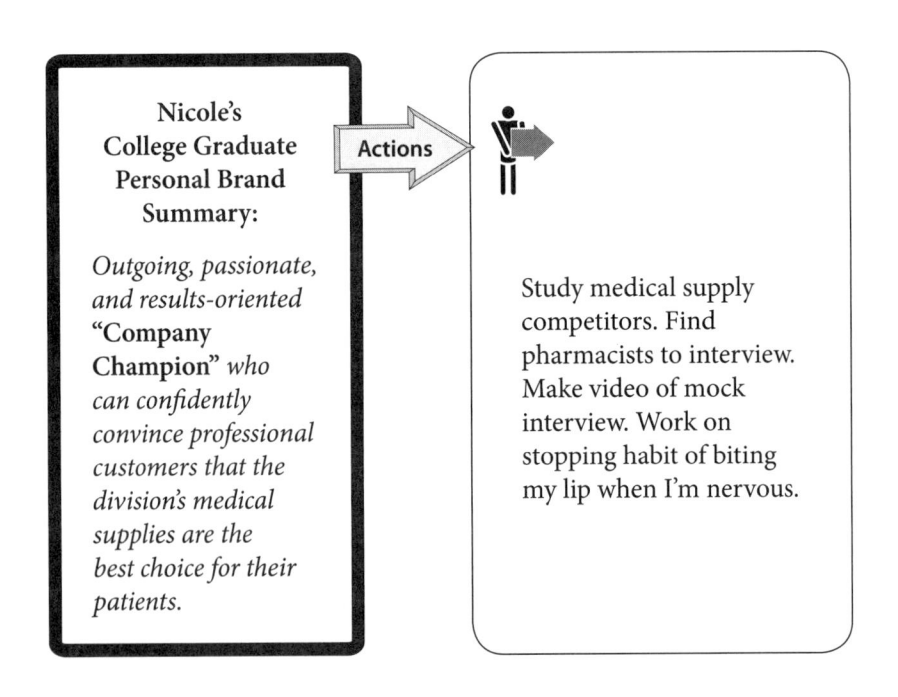

Nicole's College Graduate Personal Brand Summary:

Outgoing, passionate, and results-oriented **"Company Champion"** *who can confidently convince professional customers that the division's medical supplies are the best choice for their patients.*

Actions

Study medical supply competitors. Find pharmacists to interview. Make video of mock interview. Work on stopping habit of biting my lip when I'm nervous.

Travis's College Graduate Personal Brand Summary:

An environmentally-focused, real-world engineer who bounces ideas off others and delivers great client solutions.

Actions

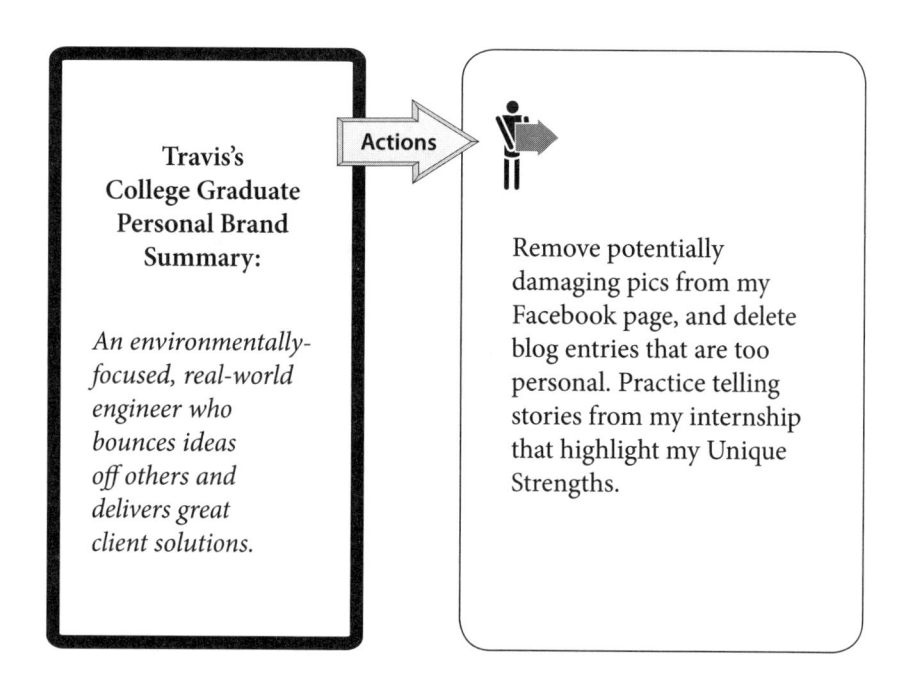

Remove potentially damaging pics from my Facebook page, and delete blog entries that are too personal. Practice telling stories from my internship that highlight my Unique Strengths.

Now that you've seen how Nicole and Travis will use their Actions to market their personal brands, you should have an idea of what Actions you can take to communicate YOU™. What Actions do you need to work on in order to make your personal brand a reality in the minds of your Audience?

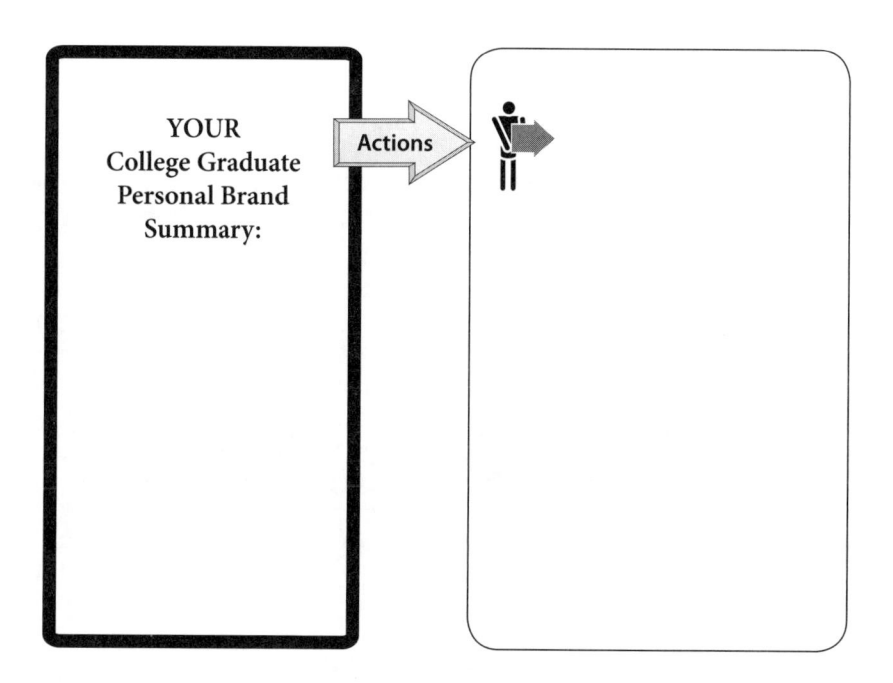

YOUR College Graduate Personal Brand Summary:

Actions

Communicate it

Reactions

Step 2

13

Reactions

College Graduate Personal Brand Marketing Plan Activity #2

It's not the situation. It's your reaction to the situation.
— Robert Conklin, Author

Back in 1998, former U.S. President Bill Clinton was proven to have lied under oath. When he was accused of sexual misconduct in the White House, at first he strongly denied what was later confirmed to be true. A few years after that, when President Clinton published his memoir, he told the truth, explaining it as a mistake. So, his first Reaction when faced with a tough challenge was to lie. His second Reaction was to explain it as a personal failure. Ultimately, he recovered well from the entire affair (every pun intended!), but it's a great lesson about how important Reactions can be and the kind of impact your Reactions can have on your personal brand.

Most of us face our biggest personal brand Reaction challenges when we're nervous or under the gun. If you want to see someone's true personal brand, watch them react to a difficult situation. Does that sound like an interview to you? A tough interview situation can cause self-control to fall apart, and — if you're not careful — all the work you've done to communicate your personal brand can be erased in one fell swoop. Let's face it: When things are going great, it's easy to stay consistent with your personal brand. It's when you're nervous and things *aren't* going very well that you find it hard to hold onto the personal brand you want to communicate.

Maybe you're one of the lucky few who don't see an interview as a challenging situation, but most college grads in job search mode find interviews stressful enough to cause them to occasionally lose control of their Reactions. How you react to what happens in a job search situation can make or break your personal brand during the job search process. If something happens in the interview that causes you to have a negative knee-jerk Reaction, you could seriously hurt your brand, preventing you from landing the job you really want.

The Reactions I'm talking about here are Reactions you can see, read, or hear — how YOU™ might respond to an unexpected challenge or an interviewer's Actions. (Your Reactions can also take the form of negative *Thought* Reactions, but that's not the focus of this particular chapter. We'll get to that subject later on.) The Reactions YOU™ make — that can be seen, read, or heard — will definitely influence the way potential employers perceive, think, and feel about you as an applicant.

The bottom line is this: The way you react will serve as a real "torture test" for sticking to and communicating your personal brand, especially in interviews and throughout the entire process of searching for a job.

Whose Emotions Are These Anyway?

Have you ever heard the phrase, "You can't always control what happens to you, but you can control how you react to it?" I'm not sure who originally came up with this phrase, but I couldn't agree more. We often say, "He made me feel bad about my resume," or "Her comments about my cover letter made me so angry!" The truth is that someone else's Actions may push a button that influences your emotions, but only *you* are responsible for how you react. No one can "make" you feel anything. You are in charge, so you can actually take over and learn to transform your Reactions into something else. It's really about mastering self-control.

Think about how you would typically react to something you weren't prepared for or to something nasty that happens to you. Maybe you found out about a change of appointment time two minutes before you were leaving for an interview, or an interviewer made a snarky remark about something on your resume. If you're like most people, your automatic Reaction probably comes from your "gut" without any conscious thought.

An automatic Reaction like that may actually be based on a habit you've developed over time. Sometimes, without even realizing it, a comment someone makes can bring up a negative situation from years ago and send you into emotional overdrive. Or maybe you've conditioned yourself to react in a certain way because that's the way you saw your parents respond when bad things happened. You might have had a professor who went on a tirade every time you didn't do something exactly right, and now you're overly-sensitive when someone suggests you made a mistake. So, your negative Reactions may just be bad habits in disguise.

Taking Control

Learning to get rid of old Reaction habits and replacing them with new, more positive habits can be difficult. In fact, learning to control your emotions is generally a lifetime lesson. But the truth is that knee-jerk Reactions almost always lead to conflict, and they probably won't help you get the job you want. In other words, knee-jerk Reactions during your job search will probably just make things worse for you in the long run.

Here's an example: Matthew had a job interview coming up at one of his top targeted companies, and he was really nervous about it. He knew from the job listing that they wanted someone with a higher GPA than his, and he didn't know how to handle that. (Actually, Matthew's lower GPA made his job search tougher in general because he knew he would have to explain it in every single interview.)

When Matthew arrived for the interview, he was prepared for the question about his GPA, but what he *wasn't* prepared for was an interviewer who practically accused him of being lazy. Matthew was still able to give his prepared answer (he had started with a major in his freshman year that clearly wasn't right for him, and his grades in the last three years in his major were good). The interviewer wasn't buying it, though, and Matthew found himself having a knee-jerk Reaction and getting defensive about his grades. Even though he answered the question, he knew that he came across as "angry" about it. If he had been able to respond calmly, he would have come across as confident. As it was, it sounded like he was just making excuses for his less than stellar GPA. Needless to say, he didn't get the job.

So, when you practice, prepare yourself for interviewers who may challenge you — especially about the things in your history that aren't so great. The more you practice and prepare yourself for a situation like this, the calmer you'll be able to stay, and the better you can manage your Reactions.

Avoid Regrets

If you're like me, you can think of times in your life that you wish you could relive, reacting in a different way that wouldn't make you cringe later. One way to gain better control over your Reactions is to think about how you want to remember interview experiences in the future. You don't want to have regrets, so how could you react in a way that you would actually be proud to remember later on?

Do remember, too, that time heals. Is there something that happened to you when you were younger that you thought you'd never recover from? Maybe you've already had a terrible interview experience where you reacted in a way that haunted you for a long time afterwards. We all have experiences like this, and most of the time, they're not as bad when we think back on them as they were at the time we experienced them.

When I'm on the verge of reacting negatively, I've found it helpful to take a moment and ask myself: "Is this really as bad as I think it is?" Once the initial flood of emotion passes, I find it easier to separate my emotions from the situation and see things more clearly. So, overreacting will most likely just lead to regret, especially if it seriously undermines your personal brand during the job search process. Why add to your list of unpleasant memories?

Just as we mentioned in the Actions chapter, your Reactions can impact your job search before, during, and after your interviews. So, what can you do to make sure your Reactions promote and support your job-seeking college graduate personal brand throughout your entire job search?

Your Reactions *Before* the Interview

It's important to be ready with your Reactions before a tough interview situation comes up. But how do you do that?

> **Be Prepared.** As we said in the Actions chapter, you'll want to have an answer ready for every question you can possibly think of that might come up in an interview. And if you're like Peter with something in your history that might be hard to talk about with an interviewer, be sure to prepare your answers carefully in advance, keeping in mind what your usual Reactions might be to a negative question.

Take Samantha as an example. During an interview she had with a company recruiter, the interviewer challenged her about the fact that she didn't work part-time until her senior year in college. She was prepared for this and was very honest, saying, "Actually, my parents divorced during my freshman year, and I lost my motivation and focus during my first two years. The summer after my sophomore year, though, I really turned things around, and, by the fall, I joined some campus activities and got involved with a non-profit working with kids. That following summer, I became an unpaid camp counselor. My senior year, I started working and really gained a lot of great experience at that company. Can I tell you more about it?" Notice that in this answer, Samantha didn't make excuses for herself. She just told it like it was. And it worked for her—the interviewer liked her objective perspective and invited her back for a second interview.

Of course, you want to present YOU™ in the best possible light, but honesty about a mistake or shortcoming can actually be a great job-seeker personal brand "booster!"

How Would YOU™ React? Keep your college grad personal brand summary in mind, and think about how someone with that brand would respond during an interview. Consider many different scenarios and Reactions based on how you want an interviewer to see YOU™. This exercise can be a great "tool chest" for dealing with a whole range of possibilities that could come up in a job interview.

By doing this, you'll be able to move beyond your "gut" Reaction to a place where you can just automatically think: "This is the type of situation where someone with my personal brand would respond by focusing on my Unique Strengths instead of what's going wrong." Working through an entire range of possible personal brand Reactions will give you confidence that you know how to react when something unexpected comes your way.

Facial Reactions. Do you wear your heart on your sleeve ... or, rather, your face? If you're someone who tends to bare your feelings and thoughts on your face for all to see, try practicing your "poker face" in the mirror before your interviews. The more you practice, the better you'll be able to keep your cool when you're sitting across from an interviewer. Ask some close friends to help you practice by having them say unexpected and upsetting things to you. Then, see how calm you can keep your face without reflecting what you're really thinking and feeling.

Telephone and E-mail. Never respond on the phone or in an e-mail in a way that you wouldn't respond if you were face-to-face. If a secretary or receptionist is rude to you on the phone or in an e-mail, don't react negatively! Take a deep breath, and count to ten in your head — whatever it takes. While this person may not be the interviewer or your potential boss, he or she could easily make negative remarks about you to the person with hiring power. It simply isn't worth it to have a knee-jerk response to someone who may just be having a bad day. Remember the personal brand you're working to communicate, and pick your battles. The satisfaction of telling someone off for a petty comment is much less than the satisfaction of getting a job you love in a terrific company.

Your Reactions *During* the Interview

Of course, your Reactions during the interview are of primary importance, but it's fundamental when you're face-to-face with an interviewer to focus on more than just controlling your nerves. Why? Well, the Reactions we're talking about are ones your interviewer can plainly see or hear.

Verbal Control. Do you tend to become easily angry or defensive in the face of an unexpected situation? If so, be sure to take a breath before responding, and give yourself a moment to calm down. In fact, sometimes, the less said, the better. Often, the best Reaction to this kind of unexpected situation might just be to remain quiet. Holding back a verbal Reaction can communicate strength and conviction. So, learn to be comfortable with silence when it makes sense, and it might actually work in your favor.

Take Your Time. When asked a question by the interviewer, take a few seconds to think about what you want to say before you answer. That's how you can guard against bursting out with any response that pops into your head. If you're really stumped about how to respond, you might even say, "That's a good question; let me take a moment to think about that." It shows that you're really putting thought into your answer. It's better to have a few seconds of silence to gather your thoughts than to rush and stumble on your words (which, let's face it, we often do when we're nervous).

> ### ✓ Speaking of Silence
>
> Some interviewers have been known to stay quiet for several seconds just to see how you'll handle it. If an interviewer becomes quiet for an unusually long time, wait a few seconds, then ask if he or she would like any clarification about the last answer you provided.
>
> But don't feel you have to rush to fill the silence with just anything that comes to mind. This is the kind of Reaction that might cause you to babble or share something by mistake that the interviewer might interpret as negative. In some cases, your interviewer may just be having a bad day and struggling to stay focused. Just naturally continue the conversation by asking what else he or she would like to know about you, or ask questions about the company and/or the job.

Don't Fake It. If you truly don't know the answer to a question, absolutely, positively avoid making something up! How's that going to help the "authentic" YOU™? Tell the interviewer you're not sure of the answer, and say that you'll get back to him or her as soon as possible with a response. Explain that you'd rather do the research and make sure you're answering correctly than to answer in a way that might be misleading. Most interviewers won't see this as a negative; they may even see it as a sign of integrity.

Let's say that an interviewer asks you about your "non-major" GPA (the GPA for courses you took outside of your major), and the question takes you by surprise. You're not sure of the answer ... what do you do? *Be honest.* Tell the interviewer you'll send him or her an e-mail with your GPA calculation within 24 hours. Then, as soon as you return to your dorm, do the calculation and send that important follow-up e-mail. The outcome? You've probably just turned a potential negative into a positive by showing that you're reliable and will stick to your word. In the interviewer's mind, you've just become someone the company can count on to do exactly what you say you'll do.

Another mistake to avoid when it comes to "faking it" is to pretend you understand a question when you really don't. You shouldn't feel badly about asking the interviewer to repeat a particular question or explain it more clearly. You might think you'll look "stupid" by doing so, but the truth is you'll only look stupid if you answer the question in a way that doesn't make sense. The interviewer might even think you aren't a good listener if you answer the wrong question!

React to Your Reactions. If your nerves cause you to get a bit tongue-tied during an interview, don't be afraid to acknowledge it, make a joke, and move on. You could simply say something like, "Wow! I guess my nerves got the better of me there for a second!" There's nothing wrong with being honest about feeling some nervousness in an interview situation — everyone does (even people who have been working for many years). As long as your nerves don't prevent you from communicating your personal brand the way you want to, a small acknowledgement here or there won't do YOU™ any serious damage.

Your Reactions *After* the Interview

Write It Down. As I mentioned in the Actions chapter, immediately after the interview — while the experience is fresh — find a quiet space and "unload your mind," writing down all you can remember from the interview. Just write and write and write. Don't think about how well the interview went until you have all of what you remember written down on paper. Then, and only then, ask yourself: How well did I manage my Reactions? How well did I answer difficult questions? Did I keep my cool? What Reactions can I work on improving for my next interview? This is how you continue to improve your Reactions over time.

Use Every Experience to Improve. If things didn't go exactly as you planned, don't be too hard on yourself. Just focus on what you did well and what you can do better in the future. Remember: Nobody's perfect. The key is to learn from your mistakes, figure out what you would do better the next time, and add it to your Marketing Plan as something to work on.

Don't Let a Rejection Get You Down. If you get a "no" response after an interview, that's okay. In fact, look at it as a way to save you time and money. Why? Because you can now focus on other target companies or jobs where you have more potential. Nora Bammann of The Kroger Company says: "Rejections are tough but (a) you got interview practice, and (b) you can use the experience to further refine your job search criteria."

When a "no" happens, take the time to evaluate what you would have liked the most and the least about the job you didn't get. You can then use that information to help you choose the best companies and jobs for YOU™. It can also help you to come up with better questions to ask in future interviews. Retired professional basketball player Michael Jordan said: "I've missed over 9,000 shots in my career. I've lost almost 300 games. Twenty-six times, I've been trusted to take the game-winning shot ... and missed. I've failed over and over and over again in my life. And that is why I succeed." The truth is that we learn the most, and uncover what we need to improve upon, mainly through failing.

A "No" Can Still Be a Connection. Don't get rid of any information you have about your interviewer! You never know what can happen from the connections you make during an interview. You may be called in for a different job with that same company at a later date, or the interviewer may get a new position elsewhere and remember you.

Here's a personal example of how important this is: When I was looking for my very first job right out of college, I interviewed with a company that was offering a position I really wanted. After a couple of (what I thought were good) interviews, I was told the crushing news: I didn't get the job. I was crushed, but I resigned myself to the bad news and wrote a thank you note anyway to the person who would have been my boss. In that note, I said I was very interested in the company and asked him to please consider me for any future openings. One month later, the person who had just been hired for that original job was fired. One phone call and one more interview later, I was working! I learned firsthand that a "no" doesn't have to be forever. So, hold on to your interviewers' information — you never know when it might come in handy again.

Ask for Feedback. If you receive a "no," use it as an opportunity to figure out how you could increase your chances the next time. If you feel comfortable with it, ask your interviewer politely if he or she could share a reason or two why you were turned down. You can explain, of course, that this will help you to improve in your next interview. Would they consider you for any other jobs? This is a great example of how you can succeed by failing—just like Michael Jordan.

Don't Relax Too Much in a Second Interview. If you get called back for a second or third interview, it's easy to get lulled into believing you're just a signature away from "You're hired!" But this can be dangerous. Most HR experts agree that it's actually in follow-up interviews that a large number of college grads fall out of the hiring pool. Remember: Be watchful about communicating your personal brand in *every* interview, not just the first or second one. Once you have the formal hiring letter and you've signed it and sent it in, consider yourself hired; until then, it's important to keep a steady course and never stop communicating YOU™.

Putting Your Reactions Into Action

Now, let's check in on Nicole and Travis to see what Reaction plans they will use in their College Graduate Personal Brand Marketing Plans.

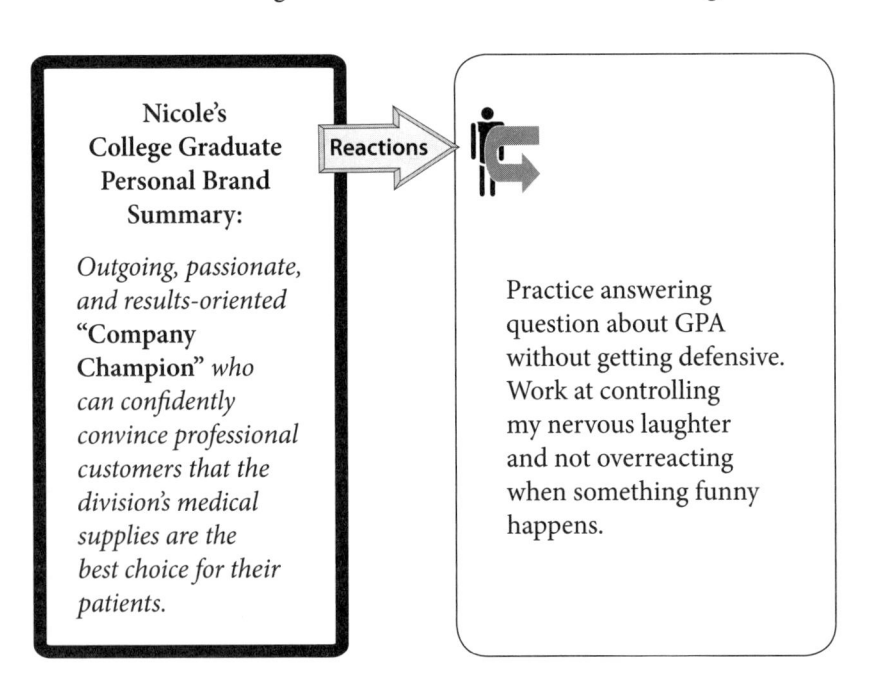

Nicole's College Graduate Personal Brand Summary:

Outgoing, passionate, and results-oriented **"Company Champion"** *who can confidently convince professional customers that the division's medical supplies are the best choice for their patients.*

→ Reactions →

Practice answering question about GPA without getting defensive. Work at controlling my nervous laughter and not overreacting when something funny happens.

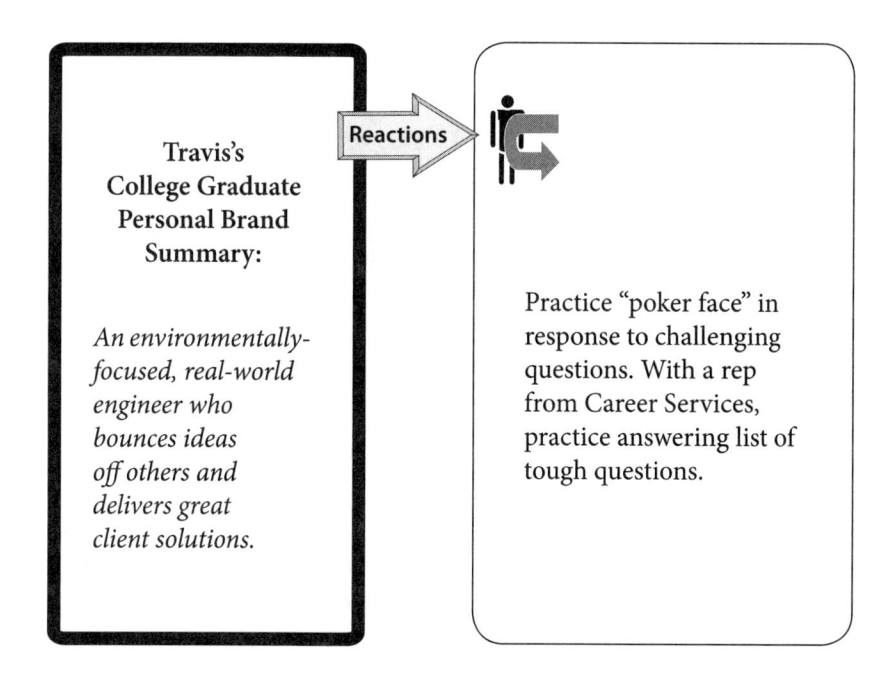

Activity #2: Reactions

Travis's College Graduate Personal Brand Summary:

An environmentally-focused, real-world engineer who bounces ideas off others and delivers great client solutions.

→ Reactions →

Practice "poker face" in response to challenging questions. With a rep from Career Services, practice answering list of tough questions.

What Reactions do you need to work on to make your job-seeking college graduate personal brand more powerful?

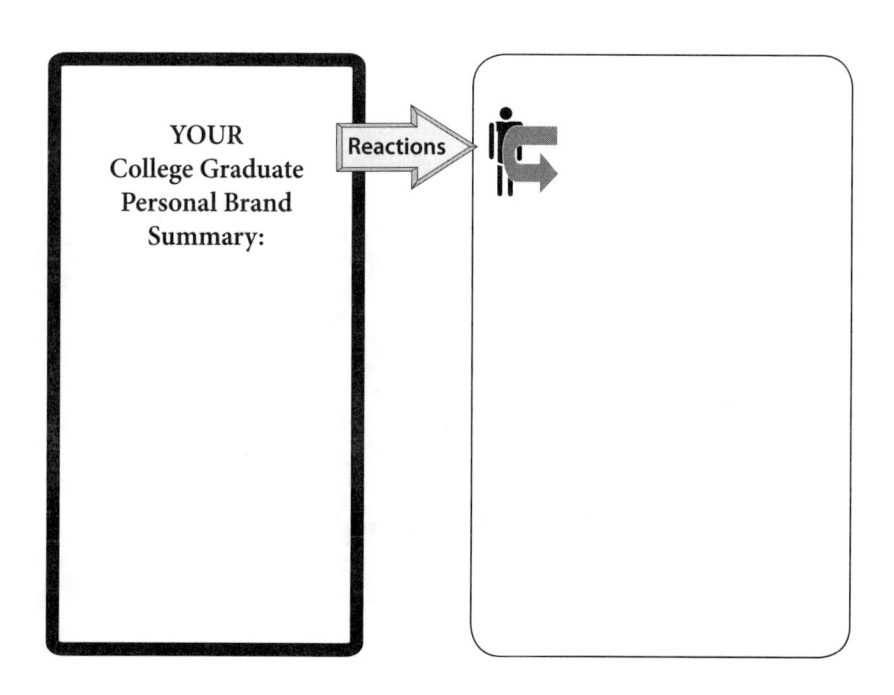

YOUR College Graduate Personal Brand Summary:

→ Reactions →

Communicate it

Look

Step 2

14

Look

College Graduate Personal Brand Marketing Plan Activity #3

Never trust a skinny chef.
— Anonymous

If there is ever a time when first impressions matter, it's in a job interview. Study after study tells us that interviewers form an opinion about a candidate as quickly as 15 to 20 seconds after the start of the interview. Since there clearly hasn't been much said in that short time, the cold, hard reality is: The opinion the interviewer has about you has been based primarily on how you look.

I can hear you out there saying, "Give me a break! I wasn't born with a movie star face or body ... what can I do about that?" Listen, I'm no beauty queen myself, and no one expects you to be either. It's not about being gorgeous; it's about presenting the best possible Look for the college graduate personal brand you want to communicate.

You may have heard the old adage: "You never get a second chance to make a first impression." Unfortunately, it really is true. Now, that doesn't mean you won't necessarily get a chance to make a *second* impression that could change the first impression someone has of you. But no matter how you slice it, that first image is a tough one to undo. It takes hard work to make someone change their first impression of you since that first personal brand image happens so quickly — and unconsciously. Creating the best Look for your college grad personal brand will help you come across as the YOU™ that you want your Audience to see.

The Packaged YOU™

Think of your Look as your "packaging." Just like a bottle that holds shampoo has been designed with a certain brand image in mind, so your Look — your own "packaging" — says a whole lot about you, too. Just from your Look, potential employers will form opinions about your values, your attitudes, your worth, who you are, what you stand for, and what you have to offer.

Big companies put a lot of time and money into developing a brand's package design because they know how important the "outside" is to an overall brand image. They know that a brand's Character comes through loud and clear through a brand's packaging, and they know that Character has a lot to do with how well that brand actually sells.

If you think about it, doesn't packaging help you make brand choices when you're shopping? Imagine yourself standing in a grocery store aisle, and you have to choose between two brands you don't know much about. All other things being equal, if you're like most people, you're probably going to choose the brand with the packaging you like the best.

Guess what? Potential employers look at the trademarked YOU™ the same way.

Listen, I know you can't control every aspect of your Look. And I'm definitely not suggesting you head for a plastic surgeon's office! But what's key is simply to take charge of those aspects of your Look that *are* in your control. In the job search process, this means paying attention to things like the "Look" of your cover letter, the quality of your clothing, how well you're groomed, etc. Remember: You really are the Brand Manager of YOU™, and it's your job to make sure your packaging sets you up for a great impression at first glance.

> ### Watch Out!
>
> If you're like a lot of people, you may have thought that personal branding is mostly about how you look — your hairstyle, how you dress, whether or not you're wearing the "right" tie or length of skirt, etc. But smart personal branding is definitely not just about wearing the right suit. Trying to communicate a great personal brand simply by wearing the right clothing or by only thinking about how you look is just scratching the surface of who YOU™ really are ... and it definitely isn't enough to land you the job you truly want.
>
> Don't get me wrong — your Look is absolutely important to your personal brand! There's no question that Look plays a big part in helping to communicate YOU™. (I wouldn't have devoted an entire chapter to it if it didn't!) But all that said, you know by now that your personal brand is made up of so much more than *just* the way you look.

Your Look *Before* the Interview

Your Look is not just about trying to be beautiful or handsome. It's about transmitting your personal brand to the world. It's about "embodying" the brand that YOU™ want to get across. So, how should you look, and what should you wear as you're planning for an interview? It depends. If you're being interviewed for a creative job (like a graphic designer position or a writer), feel free to let loose a bit more. Use your best judgment based on what you've learned about the company. Have you found out what people usually wear at the office? Use what you know about the current employees' dress, but bear in mind that while business casual may be fine for every day at the office, it's best to dress a bit more formally in an interview. Lastly, of course, you want to take into account the job-seeking college grad personal brand you're communicating. Make your Look a great combination of who YOU™ are and what your Audience is looking for.

Here are some general guidelines that have been proven to work for your Look when it comes to college graduate job interviews:

Your Cover Letter and Resume. Before potential interviewers ever lay eyes on you, they have already had an experience of your "Look" through your cover letter and resume. These few pieces of paper or e-mailed documents are absolutely an advertisement for YOU™, so it's your opportunity to make a strong first impression before your interviewer even sees you face-to-face.

Make sure your letter and resume are not only written well, but that they *look* attractive. Are they laid out well so that the important information is easy to find? If they're printed, use white or off-white paper. If they're digital, make sure to use a white background with black print and a font that's easy to read. Unless you're applying for a job as a graphic designer or artist, avoid anything fancy to stand out from the crowd, which includes avoiding emoticons in professional e-mails. According to Liz Handlin, CEO of Ultimate-Resumes.com, "Unless you're looking for a job that values creativity above all else, you will risk coming across unprofessional if you use cute stationery, colored fonts, or smiley faces."

Your Hair. Unless you're interviewing for a rock band, keep this in mind: Spikes belong on the bottom of golf shoes, not in your hair during an interview! Not to sound too dull, but honestly, for an interview, you're better off keeping your hair simple and well-groomed. Your best bet is to communicate a solid personal brand by aiming for a hairstyle that most people would simply consider "neat and professional." Do yourself a favor, and keep it simple.

Your Skin. You may be wondering what your skin has to do with your personal brand, but keep in mind: Your skin is one of the most visible parts of your physical appearance. So, it can actually say a lot about how well you take care of yourself. "Unfair!" you might be saying. "I wasn't blessed with flawless skin." Well, join the sizable club — most of us weren't. You don't have to have perfect skin; you just need to do the best with what you have. Simply learn what your skin needs in order to look as healthy as possible ... and this goes for men, too.

For the Men. Let's face it, guys: In recent times, dozens of new male skin care products have been introduced into the market for a reason. More and more attention is being paid to how well men take care of themselves. So, guys, the (skincare) bar is rising. Step up to the plate, and check out a product or two. This means shaving daily — sorry! — and carefully (assuming your personal brand isn't Colin-Farrell-tough-boy, of course).

For the Women: Here's a startling reality: Women who wear makeup earn 20% to 30% more money than those who don't. So, women, please ignore this advice — unless, of course, you want to make more money! If you don't like to wear makeup, that's fine — just keep it light and simple. Too much is worse than too little, but too little will do nothing to help your personal brand (or your pocketbook).

Lastly, those nasty statistics about the damage that UV rays do to your skin are true! I've had family members who have suffered with serious skin cancers, so this is nothing to laugh about. Even if your personal brand is about being rugged, too much time in the sun will eventually catch up with you and can result in skin cancer. Nothing is worth that.

Your Body. Another tried-but-true piece of advice is to get regular exercise. How many times have you heard this one? But many medical studies have proven this to be right: Exercise makes you look better because it makes you healthier. Here's what else exercise has been proven to help you do:

- Makes you feel better.
- Helps your clothes fit better.
- Increases your blood circulation, which improves the color of your skin.
- Makes you sleep better, which reduces dark eye circles and puffy eyes.

Hard to refute all of that, isn't it? So, get out there and exercise. The healthier you look, the more employers will want you to be part of their team. With that in mind, doesn't your job-seeking personal brand deserve a jog around the park?

Your Clothes. The trend during the last decade and a half has been toward casual wear in offices. But a *USA Today* article I read a while back revealed that, during that same timeframe, sexual harassment lawsuits in corporate America have skyrocketed. "Why?" the article asked. The theory is that people are dressing so casually in the office — the same way they might be dressed in a bar, for example — that they've started to act in the office like they act in bars. So, how we dress sends signals to ourselves and those around us about what is and isn't proper behavior. Don't underestimate the importance of that!

The bottom line is: Unless you're applying for a job as a fashion designer, you want to be remembered for your skills, not your clothes. You want the interviewer to focus on you, not what you're wearing. So, make sure your clothes are good quality, but avoid bright colors. Whether you like it or not, more conservative blacks, grays, and navy blues work best in most interview situations. In general, if you go with one of those colors, you can't go wrong.

Actors will often tell you that they can immediately step into character when they're given the right costume. So, how you dress not only influences the way others perceive you, but it will probably impact how you perceive yourself and also how you act. And you already know how important your Actions are when it comes to communicating your college grad personal brand in an interview.

Think of it this way: If you want to "act" professionally, you need to wear the right costume for the play you're in. As a smart personal brand builder, you want to make sure everything you wear communicates your brand and says what YOU™ want to say during your all-important job search.

So, dress for success — literally — as if you're going to meet the most important V.I.P. of your life. One college recruiter told me about one graduating senior who showed up to an interview in casual clothes and said, "I had class all day. Sorry I didn't dress up more." Guess who didn't get the job? Interviewers don't care about excuses like that. He should have worn his interview suit to class or made time to change before the interview. For most jobs, an interview isn't a place where casual dress is likely to work, no matter what you may have heard about the dress code of that company. Unless the interviewer specifically tells you to dress casually, play it smart, and don't take chances. Beverly Friedman, Senior Recruiter at Google, said, "Better safe than sorry … 'business casual' does not include jeans or tennis shoes. Show respect for the process and that it mattered enough to you to dress nicely." As another recruiter put it, "How someone dresses for an interview gives a picture of how they will 'dress up' for important meetings."

Here are some other things to consider when choosing a wardrobe for YOU™:

- Invest in *quality* clothes. Spend less time worrying about the latest fashion, which is often too over-the-top for anything but the fashion industry anyway. Even if your budget isn't quite at a point where you can have a full wardrobe that's just perfect for the personal brand you want to communicate, spend the extra time and money to get some good quality items. People tend to pay more attention to quality than quantity anyway.

- Make sure your clothes are clean — not worn, torn, or missing buttons. Here is a personal story related to this: When I managed laundry brands at Procter & Gamble, all I had to do was say "I work in detergents," and everyone inevitably looked immediately at … you guessed it … my clothes. Remember our skinny chef from the opening quote of this chapter? It was the same thing. People I met expected that my clothes would be in tip-top shape because of my job. Talk about pressure! So, I started paying more attention to what I was wearing to make sure my clothing would pass a spot inspection. It actually turned out to be a good lesson in personal brand building. You owe it to your personal brand — and to your job search — to do YOU™ justice with the clothes you wear.

- Spend some time to look at your clothes objectively from an outsider's point of view. This is especially true for clothes you wear to interviews. What does your wardrobe say about YOU™? If you find it hard to be objective, ask a trusted friend or professor to give you an opinion. Then, be sure to check and recheck your interview clothes for frayed hems, rips, stains, and hanging threads.

- Wear clothes that cover up tattoos whenever possible. Tats are more accepted than they used to be, but you never know how an interviewer or a company might feel about them.

Your Accessories. When it comes to accessories, there are two key principles that great personal branders follow: First, aim for quality, not quantity. Choose your accessories carefully, and don't overdo it. Accessories (belts, ties, cufflinks, scarves, and jewelry) are just that — accessories. That means they're supposed to *add* to what you're wearing — not overpower your Look. If you wear long dangling earrings, for example, your interviewer may get distracted by them.

Second, check to see that your accessories are consistent with what YOU™ want to stand for and what your Audience will find appropriate. If your brand is "reliable with the occasional surprising edge," go ahead and clip a funny pin on your jacket lapel, or wear a bold tie to your interview. The key is to make sure your accessories are helping to communicate your personal brand during your job search without calling too much attention to themselves. After all, you want your interviewer to remember YOU™, not your brightly colored tie or your big, shiny necklace.

Your Hands. Your hands are seen in an interview a lot more than you may realize. One moment, you're using your hand to take a company brochure from your interviewer. The next moment, you're pointing at a specific bullet point on your resume. The next, you're waving at an employee that you know as you leave the interviewer's office. Unless you're a factory worker, if your fingernails are ragged or dirty or your hands are dry and scaly, your hands may just be pointing to the wrong personal brand impression. And just as we talked about watching your accessories on your ears, around your neck, etc., watch them on your fingers and your wrists, too. Interviewers pay attention to your rings, bracelets, and watches, so make sure this type of jewelry also represents your personal brand well.

One more thing: Don't underestimate the importance of having well-groomed hands — and that goes for both men and women. More and more, men are expected to have clean hands and well-groomed fingernails. So, find a place where you can treat yourself to a manicure before a big job interview. Not only will your hands look great, but it will give you that extra boost of confidence you need.

Your Shoes. I've heard it said your shoes reveal the true you, and I have to admit: When I was single, a man's shoes were often one of the first things I noticed. Were his shoes clean? Scuffed? Shined? Out of style? Cheap? I promise you I'm not one of those people who are obsessed with shoes, but I honestly felt I could judge if a guy was right for me based on his shoes. (And, by the way, I ended up with an Allen Edmonds guy through and through.)

Shoes can and do send a strong signal about your personal brand. When you're putting together your interview outfit, stop for a second and look down. Does what you see represent your personal brand? Again, unless you're entering the fashion industry, it's probably safest to wear a more conservative style of shoe. Take a look at the shoes in your closet, and make sure the "shoe represents YOU™."

The YOU™ Collage

Your Look and your job-seeking personal brand should go hand-in-hand, so go back and look again at your personal Brand Character statement. In that section of your College Graduate Personal Brand Positioning Statement, you should have five or six descriptive words or a narrative sentence that describes your Character. Keeping those words or that narrative in mind, leaf through magazines, and cut out pictures and images that you think best visualize the image you're trying to get across. You might cut out a photo of a certain type of clothing, a well-manicured hand, a certain hairstyle, a specific pair of shoes — anything you believe conveys the look YOU™ want for your college grad personal brand.

Next, find some photos of you — or better yet, take photos of yourself dressed as though you're going to an interview — and place them side-by-side next to the magazine pictures you found. Compare the two. Do you see similar "branding" coming through in your own photos as compared to what you see in the magazine pictures you cut out? If not, where are you most off-track from your desired personal brand image? Where are you spot-on? Where can you make adjustments? What one or two things could you change that would make the biggest difference in how YOU™ are perceived? Work on making changes to your Look until you more closely match what you liked in those magazine photos.

Your Look *During* the Interview

Now that you've taken time to prepare your Look for your interview, you should be just about ready to present the job-seeking YOU™ to your target companies. But there are a couple of other points to mention about your Look that are key to success when you're face-to-face with your interviewer.

Smile! According to facial expression expert Paul Ekman, a Professor Emeritus of Psychology at the University of California-San Francisco, a smile can be seen from 30 meters away and immediately indicates that the person smiling has "benign intentions." That means that the smiling person comes across as harmless — a good thing in an interview! So, don't be afraid to smile when you walk into an interview. In fact, smile the minute you walk into the building. If you make enough of an impression, the security guard at the building's entrance or the receptionist in the waiting area may just make a positive comment about you to a decision-maker. A natural, comfortable smile that says "I'm confident, I'm self-assured, and I'm friendly" can go miles (or at least 30 meters) toward communicating the personal brand image you want.

Posture. I can still hear my mother telling me: "Watch your posture! Stand up straight!" At the time, I didn't know what a strong personal brand secret she was sharing, but now I know she was right. Great personal brand builders recognize what body language experts have said for years: Powerful self-confidence is communicated by holding your shoulders straight and not slumping. Look straight ahead as you walk, not down, especially as you enter an interviewer's office, and you will convey the kind of self-assurance that — let's face it — we all want to communicate as part of our personal brand.

The same is true when you're sitting in a chair in the interviewer's office. Don't slouch! If you're wearing a suit jacket, tuck the bottom of it underneath you as you sit down so that it doesn't bunch up around your neck.

Men, make sure your suit jacket is buttoned when you first walk into the interviewer's office, but feel free to unbutton it when you sit down. Then, button it again as you're leaving. A suit jacket looks better buttoned when you're standing, but if it's buttoned while you're sitting, it will bunch up. Women can also sometimes have this problem, so take a look at yourself in the mirror while sitting in your interview outfit.

Women, if you're planning on wearing a skirt to an interview, check to make sure it doesn't ride up too high when you sit down. How about your blouse? Does it gape open when you sit? Try it on beforehand to check yourself in a mirror. This is definitely not something you want to discover for the first time in an interviewer's office!

Don't forget about the body language that we talked about in the Actions chapter. Every one of those body language tips can impact your Look during an interview. Keep your hands in your lap, or rest your elbows on the edge of a table. Body language experts say that this conveys self-confidence. They also say that it's best for men to keep their feet flat on the floor, while it's best for women to cross their ankles under the chair.

Extensions of YOU™. Just as your cover letter, resume, and e-mails represent your job-seeker personal brand, so does your briefcase, folder, notebook, or whatever else you carry in to the interview. So, if you have an old worn-out briefcase, or if you bring important documents in a ragged manila folder with writing or stickers all over it, think about how that might look to an interviewer. You don't have to spend a lot of money on a briefcase, but make sure that you carry your resume and other materials in something neat. And keep the papers orderly. The last thing you want to do is open your briefcase or folder and have a mess of disorganized papers fall out. That's not exactly the "Look" you're aiming for…

The Sweet Smell of Success. Some people don't realize that body odor is also a part of their "Look." Here are some tips to make sure YOU™ make a good "nasal" impression:

- If you have a tendency to sweat, you might want to carry a sample-size bottle of deodorant with you to an interview and apply it discreetly in the restroom after you arrive at the building where your interview will take place.

- Take breath mints with you in case you need them, and pop one in your mouth while you're sitting in the waiting room. Make sure to remove it before the interview, however, since it might get in the way of your being able to speak clearly, and chewing on a mint or gum can come across as though you're not taking the interview seriously.

- If you wear perfume or aftershave, be careful not to overdo it. You don't want your "scent" impression to be overpowering.

One Last Check. Don't forget to go into the restroom when you enter the company's office and take one last look at yourself in the mirror before the interview. Has the wind blown your hair out of place, or do you have a pen or dirt smudge on your face? Before the interview starts is the time to check just to be sure. Kate Cancro, a college recruiter for Hilton, has additional advice: "Use a lint roller before and after you get out of your car. Women need to make sure that there is no lipstick on their teeth or collar."

Your Look *After* the Interview

All of the same Look tips you've applied before and during your interview still apply after the interview. Stay consistent with your Look, and make sure that it always communicates the brand image you want — from the Look of your follow-up e-mails or letters to your own Look during any follow-up interviews or meetings.

Ashley is an example of someone who learned the hard way the importance of being consistent when it comes to your Look. Nearing the end of her time in college, Ashley was on the hunt for her first job. Within a fairly short time, she got an interview with a big bank that was at the top of her "dream company" list. That initial interview went great, and Ashley was excited about the possibilities. Even so, she held her breath for two weeks while waiting to hear about a second interview.

During the time she was waiting, Ashley and a friend of hers decided — on a whim — to change their hair colors. So, overnight, Ashley went from a brunette to a stand-out-from-the-crowd redhead. It was a big change. Her friends loved it, but when she got invited back to her dream company for her second interview, the interviewer she had met before was … well … "less than enthusiastic." In fact, when the director who interviewed Ashley the first time saw her again, he was clearly surprised and even made a comment about the change. It was then that Ashley realized how far removed her new hair color was from the personal brand she was hoping to communicate. By making a sudden and obvious change in her appearance in between interviews, she may have been communicating a brand of "unstable" or someone who changes her mind a lot (maybe even changes jobs a lot). She didn't get the job, and it was a very hard lesson to learn about the importance of communicating her personal brand consistently.

The moral of this story is that making big, noticeable changes to the way you look during the interview process — or even changing your Look frequently after you've landed a job — may not say what you want about how willing you are to be consistent in the job. Think of it from your boss's perspective. If you do something unpredictable like drastically change your hair from day to day, will you suddenly not show up for work one day? Will you quit your job with a week's notice in order to move to Tasmania? Okay, I'm exaggerating a bit here, but you get the point.

At work, your Audience — like all of us — has a lot of things to worry about and manage, like changes taking place in the organization, non-stop technology transformations, people moving around from job to job, and on and on. All of that change can cause stress. So, why add more change and stress to the work situation by constantly changing the way you look? It freaks people out! Like it or not — and call this stodgy if you want — people like to work with others they know they can depend on. So, you're better off not sending signals that could give a potential boss the impression that you could be "fly-by-night." Think about it: It's not your hairstyle you want to be remembered for anyway, right? It's your values, strengths, and passions that you want to come through the most in your interviews.

Just so you don't think I'm totally old-fashioned, if your personal brand is "raucously creative," go ahead and go for outrageous hair and occasional changes! For most of us, however, consistency in your Look is one of the best ways to communicate a steady personal brand that says "hire me." This doesn't mean you shouldn't ever change your Look or your style, of course, but try to keep the changes you make more subtle while still successfully communicating your brand.

Business Casual?

Consider this situation: You're set to have a second or third interview at a great company, and you noticed during your first interview that employees at that company dress fairly casually. Does this mean that you should also dress casually for your future interviews? Most recruiters and HR people agree that you shouldn't act as if you already have the job. It might come across as "trying too hard." So, continue to maintain a buttoned-down professional Look until you're actually hired. It's the best way to present YOU™.

Your "Look" Marketing Plan

When you sit back and think about your personal brand image from a Look standpoint, in what ways are you doing well? Where might you be falling short? What will help your Look match the personal brand you want to communicate during your job search?

To get some different perspectives on this, let's look at how Nicole and Travis plan to make sure their Looks are right in line with the personal brands they want to communicate in their job hunting process.

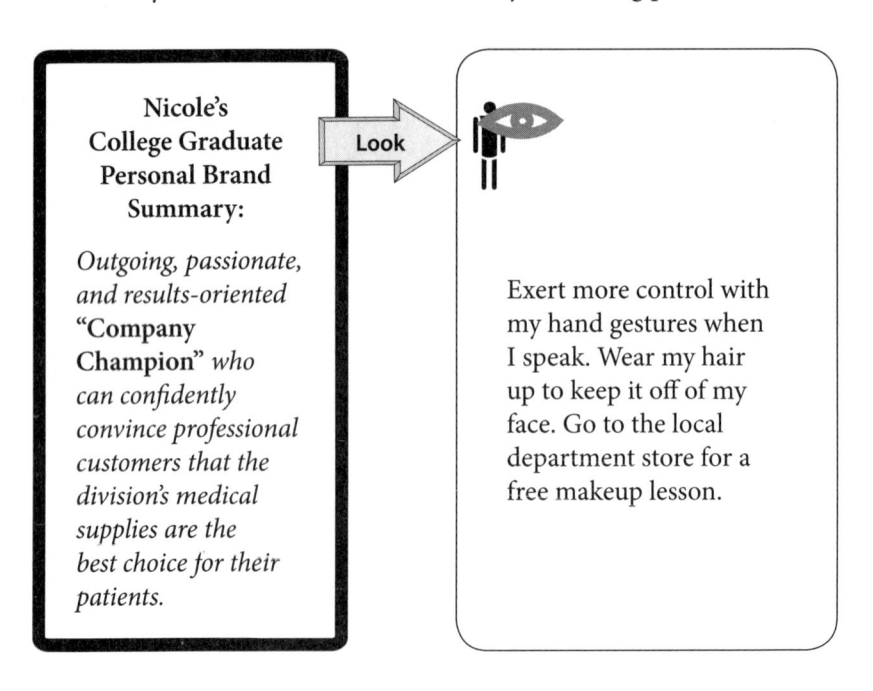

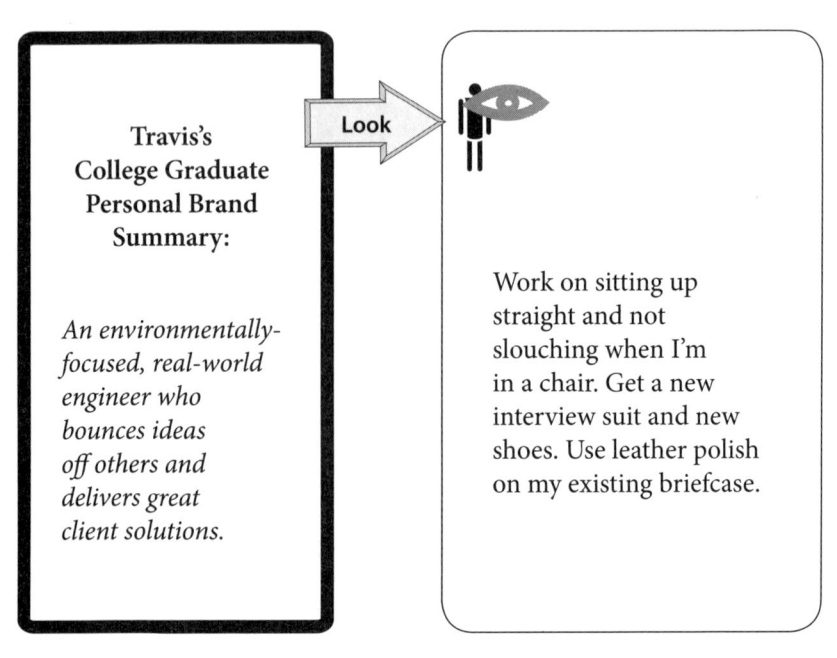

Nicole's College Graduate Personal Brand Summary:

Outgoing, passionate, and results-oriented **"Company Champion"** *who can confidently convince professional customers that the division's medical supplies are the best choice for their patients.*

Look

Exert more control with my hand gestures when I speak. Wear my hair up to keep it off of my face. Go to the local department store for a free makeup lesson.

Travis's College Graduate Personal Brand Summary:

An environmentally-focused, real-world engineer who bounces ideas off others and delivers great client solutions.

Look

Work on sitting up straight and not slouching when I'm in a chair. Get a new interview suit and new shoes. Use leather polish on my existing briefcase.

Now, think about your own job search goals. What is your Look Marketing Plan? What steps will you take to get your Look more in line with the way you want potential employers to perceive, think, and feel about YOU™?

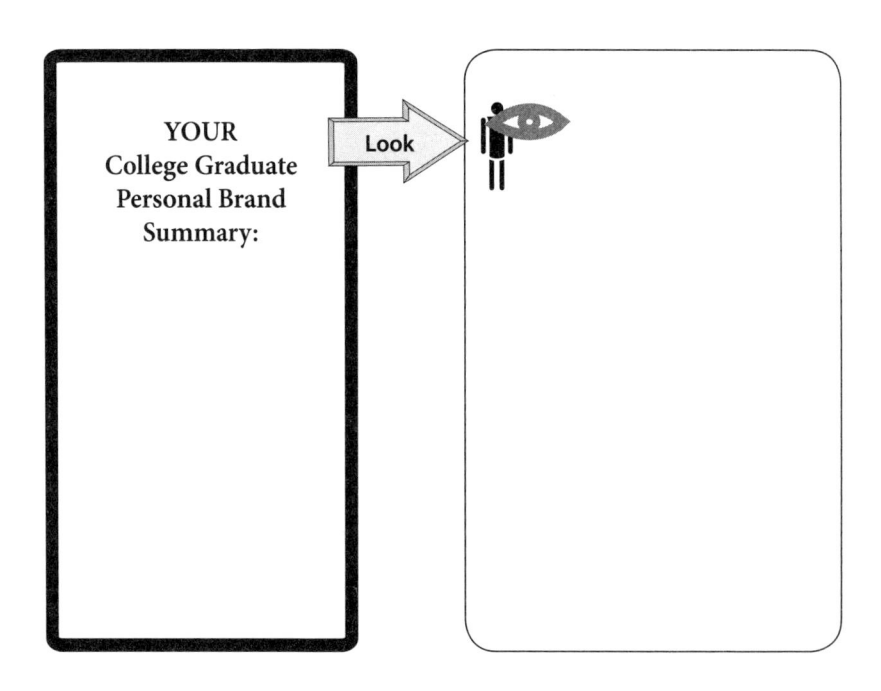

YOUR
College Graduate
Personal Brand
Summary:

Look

> " *Your Look is about 'embodying' the brand that YOU™ want to get across.* "

Communicate it

Sound

Step 2

15

Sound

College Graduate Personal Brand Marketing Plan Activity #4

Words mean more than what is set down on paper. It takes the human voice to infuse them with deeper meaning.

— Maya Angelou, Actress, poet, and author

For our purposes, your Sound is not only what you say, but how you say it. Just like your Look, your Sound is a split-second first impression that can make or break an interview. In fact, your Sound can even make or break your chances of getting the job during a phone call that takes place *before* a face-to-face interview.

Just how important is your Sound? Think about it: Sounds impact us often without even realizing it. Maybe it's the sound of fingernails scraping down a blackboard, a door slamming, a strong wind howling in the middle of the night, a chime swaying in the breeze, or waves crashing onto the beach. Many sounds—not just music—absolutely have the power to influence us.

How YOU™ sound in an interview can be just as powerful and can have just as big an impact on the person who is interviewing you. Let's talk about how to control your Sound.

Are You in Control?

There are parts of your Sound that you have control over and parts of it that are outside your control. That's because, just like your Look, your voice is a part of your physical self. So, even though you can change your Sound in some ways, you can't change it completely. Let's say that, by nature, you have a slightly nasal voice, and you've worked at it but can only change that aspect of your Sound a bit. Well, don't let your "Sound get you down!" Just do what you can to improve it, and keep those changes in mind. That alone will boost your personal brand a lot.

The good news is: There are lots of things about your Sound that you absolutely can — and should — work on improving to strengthen your job-seeking personal brand.

> **Vary Your Pitch.** While you can't change the voice you were given, you *can* alter the pitch. An overly high or low voice can really turn people off. I once had a secretary who was great, but her voice — particularly on the telephone — was always at a constant, really high pitch. It was bad enough that a few clients even complained to me about it. I began working with her to help her bring down her pitch. What finally worked involved my assistant pretending that she was a big, brawny man with a deep voice — very funny since she was just 5 feet 2 inches tall and only weighed 110 pounds! But, fortunately, the next thing we knew, her voice was no longer annoying, and no more clients called to complain. It turned out to be a lot of fun for her, too.
>
> Before you jump into interviewing, record your voice as though you were answering some potential interview questions. When you play back the recording, what do you think of your pitch? Is it just naturally high or low? If so, practice trying to move your pitch up or down. It's amazing the difference this can make. With just a little bit of practice, you'll find others listening to you more. That's how you find the pitch that best communicates the personal brand you want.
>
> If pitch turns out to be a big problem for you, and trying to change your voice on your own proves too difficult, you might want to think about working with a vocal coach if that's at all possible for you. It will do your personal brand (and your self-confidence) a lot of good!

Enunciate. Another aspect of your Sound to focus on during your job search is how you pronounce words. Stating words clearly and correctly is important, no matter what personal brand you want to communicate. If you find it difficult to say words clearly, or if you sometimes stumble to pronounce words right, three things to consider are: Practice, practice, practice!

Are you a mutterer? One way to tell is to think back on how often people ask you to repeat what you've just said. If people ask you fairly often — maybe twice a day or so — there's a good chance you're mumbling. To make sure an interviewer understands you — and to communicate your personal brand well — you need to state your words clearly. Otherwise, you run the risk of creating a personal brand image that's careless and sloppy — someone who doesn't care about being understood. Or, worse, you could come across as someone who isn't very capable, and that's a definite Personal Brand Buster®!

One way you can practice is to record yourself reading parts of your favorite blog or an online newspaper like NYTimes.com every day. Then, play it back, and listen to how well you pronounce the words. Ask others to listen to your recordings to make sure they can understand everything you say. That will tell you immediately if you're enunciating well enough.

Pace. Do you speak too quickly or too slowly? Either extreme can be a problem. If you speak too fast, the interviewer will have trouble keeping up with your words, and talking fast makes you come across as impatient, nervous, or in a rush. By linking your words together too quickly, the interviewer will probably just stop trying to understand you — a sure sign that communication has broken down. It can be easy to fall into this trap in an interview situation. Let's face it: You're trying to get across as much information about YOU™ as possible in a fairly short period of time. But if you try too hard to get everything said, you might just come across as desperate. And that doesn't serve any personal brand.

People tire quickly if they have to work to keep up with you. Take a cue from television ads for prescription drugs. After the announcer shares the information the drug company *wants* you to hear — in a patient "explaining" voice — the announcer will suddenly speed up to an unbelievably fast pace when it comes time to share the drug's side effects, speaking-as-if-there-are-no-spacebars-between-his-words. As you can imagine, the advertisers are hoping you'll tune out and/or miss that information completely even though they have to include it in the commercial because it's required by law.

If you speak too slowly, on the other hand, your interviewer will also most likely get tired, impatient, and bored. Here's a helpful clue: If you find people often finishing your sentences or jumping in to figure out what you're trying to say next, it might be a sign you're a slow talker. Work toward speeding it up just a little, and ask friends to help you figure out if your pace is improving.

Volume. In an interview situation, you want to avoid speaking too loudly or too softly. No one likes to be shouted at, so if you speak too loudly, you risk communicating a "bully" or domineering personal Brand Character. This is especially true over the phone. Do you remember a time when you were talking to someone whose vocal volume was so loud that you had to hold the receiver away from your ear? It's uncomfortable and annoying, and that's not the type of person you would want to hire.

On the other hand, speaking too softly is simply pointless. This may sound a bit harsh, but honestly, in an interview situation, you should either speak up … or shut up. Nothing is more tiring than straining to hear what someone is saying, and it doesn't take long before an interviewer will simply give up.

Unfortunately, women are often the guiltiest when it comes to low-volume speaking. I once sat on the board of a not-for-profit organization whose Chief Financial Officer was a very capable woman. But in board meetings, she spoke so softly while presenting her financial reports that the entire board would literally lean forward to try to hear her. The CEO tried coaching her to speak more loudly, but nothing seemed to work. Out of sheer frustration, she was finally asked to wear a clip microphone on her lapel which she turned on when she wanted to speak. I got the impression she thought this was a bit funny and almost cute. But it wasn't. All it communicated was a very weak personal brand. In fact, it made some board members even question her ability as a CFO because she just couldn't get past her naturally quiet voice.

If speaking too softly is your challenge, try pretending the person you're talking to is far off in a corner of the room (even if the interviewer is only four feet away). In any case, you need to work hard at increasing your volume. Being too soft of a talker can be a Personal Brand — and a career — Buster®, and it simply isn't worth it to ignore the problem.

The Power of Emotion. Think about dynamic speakers you've heard. It's the emotions they're able to get across that have everyone on the edge of their seats. Sure, the words they use may get you fired up, but if those same words were spoken without much color, they would fall flat. A great personal brand builder knows that getting their point across with just the right amount of emotion will get their Audience involved in the message, even if their Audience is just one interviewer.

Listen to your voice recording again, and ask yourself: What emotions are coming through via your voice patterns? Listen honestly. Is your voice full of energy and enthusiasm, or does it lack commitment? Is your voice convincing when you speak? If you find you have a monotone voice — the kind of voice that sounds boring after a while — practice changing the tone, and work at letting the right kinds of emotions come through with your Sound. Again, if this is a particular problem for you, and you have the opportunity to work with a voice coach or a music professor, it may have a positive impact on your job search. If you're not sure how your emotions carry through your voice, ask others for their opinions.

On the Telephone. All of the aspects of your Sound that we've talked about so far are just as important to your telephone voice as to your in-person voice. Don't think that communicating your personal brand through your Sound on the phone isn't important! It is, and this applies whether you're calling an interviewer, an HR representative, a secretary, or a receptionist. Practicing good phone etiquette with *anyone* is a great Personal Brand Booster®. Courtesy, having a clear tone, and pronouncing words well are key. Here are some great tips to communicate YOU™ by phone:

- Simple things like always thanking the person on the other end of the line and saying goodbye before hanging up go a long way toward establishing who YOU™ are.

- Practice what you're going to say beforehand, especially if you think you'll need to leave a voicemail message. It helps you to clarify what you really want to say and will prevent you from stumbling over your words.
- Speak clearly but not too quickly. If you leave your name, slow down, and spell it out. Then, repeat your telephone number to make sure it's understandable.

Your Sound *Before* the Interview

All of the above suggestions can be used before, during, *and* after an interview, but there are certain strategies for your Sound that you should specifically take care of before your interviews. Don't forget, for example, that your Sound is about more than just your voice, and it can have an impact on your job search and personal brand before you even speak to anyone at your target companies.

Your "Written Sound." It's one of the biggest mistakes that job seekers overlook: Forgetting that even though cover letters and resumes are written, they still reflect your "Sound," just like they reflect your Look. So, when you prepare your cover letters and resume — which are incredibly important introductions to YOU™ — keep them simple. Leave out large, fancy words. While you may think it makes you sound smart to use big words and share lots of information, those very same things may also make you sound like you're trying too hard.

Read through your cover letters and resume again, and keep the overall "Sound" of your college grad personal brand in mind. What is coming through? If it's not the "Sound" you want it to be, what tone would someone with your personal brand use in a letter or resume? Would it be warm? Assertive? Enthusiastic?

Have someone you trust and who knows you well read through your cover letters and resume to let you know if they really reflect YOU™. A friend of mine — who was incredibly fun-loving, outgoing, and charming in person — asked me to read through his application for a job. If I hadn't known him, I would have thought he was a completely different person based on what I read. He sounded incredibly stuffy and even snobby! His writing didn't do his personal brand justice at all. So, if you need a hand getting your job-seeker personal brand across in writing, find someone who is a good writer who can help you. (Just make sure that you choose someone who really *is* a good writer. Your roommate may not qualify!) Remember: YOU™ will get you the job, but your cover letter and resume are responsible for getting YOU™ the interview.

Your "Virtual Sound." E-mails reflect your written sound just as much as your cover letter and resume. The truth is: College grads typically pay close attention to what they write in a letter that will be printed and signed on a piece of stationery, but they can be very careless when it comes to writing e-mails. Isn't that true? I've seen people agonize over what will be printed on letterhead, but those same people will send out rapid-fire e-mails without paying much attention to content or errors.

It's critical to remember that your personal brand comes through in your e-mails just as much as it does on the phone, in person, and in your cover letter and resume. And just as with speech, communicating your Sound in e-mails is as much about *what* you write as it is about *how* you write it.

For example, do you start your e-mails with a nice greeting, or do you just write a one-line response to the previous question with no sign-off? If you phoned the person you're writing, you wouldn't just state your one-line response and hang up without a hello or goodbye, would you? It's interesting, but for some reason, we seem to communicate differently in e-mails. That can be a huge mistake! E-mails run the risk of coming across rude if you're not careful.

Remember the personal brand that you're trying to communicate, and think about how you can use your e-mails to support that. For example, take an extra ten seconds to start and end all e-mails with a simple but nice greeting, as well as a warm closing. It's an opportunity—often before the first interview—to build a professional "connection" with an interviewer. And trust me: You'll definitely stand out from others who are less careful with their e-mails. It's just one more way you can build a great job-seeker personal brand in the eyes of your interviewers. This is especially true of e-mails that you send prior to your interview. If your e-mails turn off anyone at the company, it will be hard to get past that first impression when it comes time to meet your interviewer in person.

Here are some more things to watch out for in your e-mails:

- You would never dream of sending a cover letter that contains no capital letters or punctuation, but for some reason, a fair number of people do this in e-mails. Professional job-seeker e-mails need to contain capital letters and punctuation, too.

- In your e-mails, include a signature that has your name and telephone number in it. This reminds the interviewer of who you are and makes it easy for the interviewer to contact you. Never make an interviewer search through your e-mails for the one e-mail where you included your phone number.

- Be sure to use spell check on all computer communications. With today's technology, spelling errors in interview documents are just unacceptable. All that said, don't rely on spell check entirely because it doesn't pick up every mistake. So, be sure to have a careful look yourself before hitting that "send" button.

- If writing isn't your strong suit, admit it, and ask someone who's a good writer to read through the important e-mails you've written before you send them out.

- Make sure your subject lines are clear and to the point. They should reflect exactly what your e-mail is about. Think of your subject line as a title of a document, which means, at a minimum, the first word of your subject line should be capitalized.

- Remember: E-mailing is not texting! Don't use abbreviations like "u" for "you" and "r" for "are." Spell everything out just to be on the safe side. The person receiving the e-mail may not be up to date on "text lingo."

- Don't attach any files unless you've been specifically asked to. If you do, your e-mail runs the risk of ending up in an interviewer's spam folder, and that's definitely not going to get you a job!

- Humor is great to include if you can and if it's consistent with your personal brand, but be careful with jokes. It can sometimes be hard to get the real intention across in an e-mail, so you run the risk of being misunderstood. If you're unsure if something you think is funny will work, don't take the chance — leave it out!

- Emoticons might be fun in personal e-mail communications, but don't use them in a professional e-mail, particularly if the e-mail is being sent to an interviewer or if it's at all connected to your job search. In fact, Harris Interactive surveyed employers, and 14% of them said they wouldn't hire an applicant who used emoticons in an e-mail.

Right *Before* the Interview

Back to your voice, there are two things you can do immediately before your interview to help your Sound considerably:

Wet Your Whistle. This is one of those simple things that can be easy to forget. Didn't bring a bottle of water with you to the interview? That's okay. Accept a glass of water before your interview (if you're offered). It'll keep your vocal cords flexible and strong. This is especially true if you tend to get "dry mouth" when you're nervous. Ask if it's okay to take your glass of water into the interview with you, and sip as necessary. Interviewers don't mind at all, and it's one simple way to make sure your job-seeking personal brand Sound stays strong.

Warm-Up. A chat with the receptionist or others in the waiting room can help to warm up your voice and make you more comfortable. (At the very least, it helps you come across as a friendly person!) Of course, use common sense: Don't start a conversation with someone who's reading or clearly busy with something else. But warming up your voice will avoid the possibility of sounding "croaky" when you finally make it into the interviewer's office.

Your Sound *During* the Interview

If you take the time to work on and improve your Sound before you get into interview situations, you'll be even more ready for a great job interview experience. Still, there are a few more things to watch out for with regard to your Sound when you're actually sitting across from the interviewer's desk. Consider it "game time!"

Talking Too Much. If you tend to talk too much, not letting anybody else get a word in edgewise, it's really important that you learn to stop, breathe, and listen. It's easy to forget to do this when you get excited or nervous, but if you don't, your interviewer will eventually tune you out — and you'll find yourself without a job offer. In fact, people who talk too much can come across as self-centered and unwilling to listen to others, especially if they tend to interrupt. Not a Personal Brand Booster™, that's for sure!

So, while you should tell the interviewer as much about you as needed in the interview, you definitely want your interview to be a *conversation* between two people. How do you do this? Well, for example, besides answering questions about you, don't forget to ask questions about the company, too. Remember that an interview is a two-way conversation. And don't forget that a few seconds of silence now and then can also be a great Sound.

Not Talking Enough. The opposite is a problem, too. Do you tend to be quiet most of the time? As hard as it may be at first, for the sake of your personal brand, it's really important to speak up and participate in conversations — especially in an interview. You won't get a job you really love if you're tight-lipped about yourself or your accomplishments. Learn the balance between bragging about yourself and being overly humble. Ask friends to listen to you talk about your achievements and tell you if your confidence is too much or too little. It's all about learning to communicate YOU™ in the best way possible.

Another reminder: The more prepared you are for your interviews, the less likely you are to fall into the trap of being too quiet. Do enough homework so that you're ready to make your points with just the right amount of talking — not too little and not too much.

Stay on Topic. As I mentioned earlier, it's important to think of your interview as a conversation between two people. That said, be careful not to let yourself or the interviewer go off topic while chatting. It's as much up to you as the interviewer to make sure the most important information about your experience is communicated. If you allow yourself to go off on tangents, you'll lose the valuable time you need to talk about your Unique Strengths, Reasons Why, and Brand Character. Stay focused on the key messages you want to get across, and, if you find yourself off in "la-la land," say something like: "Getting back to what we were talking about earlier…"

Be Polite. Everyday language has gotten more and more relaxed and casual over the past few decades, and that's fine. But remember: *Interview language is different.* Your language in an interview needs to be a bit more formal. For example, answer questions with "yes" rather than "yep" and with "no" rather than "nope." Say "thank you" and "please" when it fits.

In the Actions chapter, we talked about being personable and engaging in small talk on the way to the interviewer's office, but we also talked about remaining professional at all times. So, again, don't forget that it's important not to get too familiar with your interviewer. Get over your habit of saying phrases like, "How's it goin'?" If that's a problem for you, start using more appropriate phrases like "How are you?" regularly so that you don't trip up when the interview nerves hit you.

What's in a Name? Use the interviewer's name when you first shake hands, saying something like, "Hello, _____, it's great to finally meet you." Simple phrases like that get across a personable "Sound" and establish a relationship from the very start. And it lets the person know that you recognize your interviewer as his or her own personal brand. After all, as they say, everyone's favorite word is their own name, right?

Ask Questions that Will Help You Sell Yourself. You can ask questions during an interview in a way that helps emphasize your strengths. Here are some examples:

- "Given my experience as a top seller in my part-time job, what opportunities for advancement would you see here for someone like me?"

- "I took some courses in marketing and applied what I learned as a volunteer at a non-profit, helping to bring in new grant money for the organization. How open is the company to exploring new ideas like that from entry-level employees?"

Keep in mind: The questions you ask are often the last thing that happens in an interview. Just like the first impression counts, so does the "last" impression because it may be what the interviewer remembers most about you. So, a well-placed question or two at the end of an interview can leave the interviewer with a positive image of YOU™.

Those Interfering Cell Phones. It's one of those things you can easily forget about, but your cell phone is also part of your "Sound." Be sure to turn off your cell phone before you enter the company's building. Interviewer after interviewer told me that they find it incredibly annoying to be interrupted by your phone going off during an interview. On your way to the interview, turn your phone to silent, or turn the phone off altogether. If you don't — and you answer the phone — you run the risk of making the interviewer believe you think there's something more pressing or important than getting the job.

And don't even think about talking or texting on your cell phone or checking your e-mail on your Blackberry while you're in the company's waiting room! Remember: The receptionist may be listening to what you have to say to your roommate and could report it back to the interviewer. Your phone beeping and clicking is likely to annoy the receptionist and anyone else sitting in the waiting area.

"That's me. I'm texting you my resumé!"

Top Tips for Successfully Branding YOU™ On the Phone

As companies try to cut down on travel costs, doing initial interviews by phone are happening more often. So, it's important to think about how YOU™ come across over the phone. The truth is that you won't make it to the face-to-face interview unless you first ace the interview over the air waves.

Remember our college senior, Nicole? She had a telephone interview with an in-house HR recruiter prior to her in-person interview with the hiring manager. So, what are the key differences between a face-to-face interview and a telephone interview, and how do you make sure you communicate the brand you want through a phone receiver?

In an in-person interview, you can rely on all of your Actions, Reactions, Look, Sound, and Thoughts to make a good impression. In a phone interview, it can be a little more challenging because you don't have the advantages of facial expressions, body language/gestures, and just the energy of being in the same room with another person. So, it's important to use your voice as an instrument to engage, inform, and energize the conversation with your interviewer. In other words, you want to be sure your personal brand comes through "loud and clear" (every pun intended...).

- Think about whether your voice is a strength or a weakness. Be honest with yourself! If it isn't a strength, and you find it hard to communicate by phone, you know what to do—practice, practice, practice. Enlist someone to do a mock interview with you on the phone, and make a recording of it. Listen to it with someone who can give you an objective opinion. Do you come across as confident, strong, and capable? If not, practice until you get it right.

- Make sure you won't be distracted during a phone interview. If you have a room with a door that locks, close it, lock it, and put a sign on the door that says "Do not disturb." Got a roommate? Ask him or her to keep the noise down or, better yet, to give you the place to yourself during the time of the interview.

- Don't do an interview in front of your computer. You're bound to be distracted by what's on the screen or incoming e-mails, which won't help you communicate a great personal brand.
- Be sure to call the interviewer by name now and then. It personalizes the conversation and makes a connection.
- Make sure your voice conveys your interest in the job. Work with your pitch, volume, and pace. Most importantly, speak clearly and succinctly. No mumbling!
- Don't forget to watch out for "uh," "um," "yeah," "ya know," and "ya know what I'm sayin'" — all of these bad language habits will be even more noticeable on the phone. Watch out for over-use of the word "like" as well. Don't say, "Like, I took a class in economics." Say, "I took a class in economics." Remember that all interviews, even on the telephone, are more formal than an average conversation. So, say "yes" and "thank you." Speak with conviction and confidence about who YOU™ are.
- You may need to ask for more clarification than you would in person because you can't see the interviewer's facial expressions and body language. That's okay! Feel free to ask questions if you're unclear about something.
- A lack of energy may make you sound disinterested, so make sure you keep your energy up during the interview. Here are some ways you can do that:
  - Dress as though you were going to a face-to-face interview. If you dress as a professional, you'll feel and sound like a professional. This is what actors do to get into character, and it really works.

- Stand up during the interview (as long as you don't pace around the room), or at least sit up straight in your chair while you're speaking. That will give your voice enough air so that it sounds confident on the phone.
- Smile as if you were sitting across from the interviewer. Can't you tell when someone on the other end of the phone is smiling? Your interviewer will be able to tell with you, too.
- At the end of the interview, make sure to tell the interviewer you look forward to meeting him or her in person. After all, that's the goal of a phone interview!

Your Sound *After* the Interview

The same Sound tips we've talked about throughout this chapter still apply just as much after an interview and in a follow-up interview as they do before and during an interview. Don't let your "Sound" go just because you've gotten a second interview or because you've developed a more comfortable relationship with the interviewer. Stay the course, and keep up the consistency with your college grad personal brand Sound. It's key to represent your personal brand well in *all* of your communications from e-mails to telephone calls to in-person meetings.

Your Thank You Note. As we talked about in the Actions chapter, you absolutely, positively should write a thank you note to the interviewer within 24 hours after your interview. Statistics show that, on average, only about 10% of applicants write a thank you after an interview, so it's clearly a great way to stand out. And the more you can distinguish yourself in your follow-up thank you note, the more memorable your personal brand will be with the interviewer. All of that means you'll have a better chance of getting hired! In fact, if you're in the "maybe" pile when you leave the interview, a well thought-out thank you could easily move you to the "yes" pile.

Here are some tips for making your follow-up thank you a powerful statement for YOU™:

- **Personalize your thank you note.** If you send a "cookie-cutter" thank you that sounds like it's the same one you send to everyone after an interview, you could easily be moved from the "maybe" pile to the "rejected" pile. So, no cutting and pasting! Mention something specific that happened in the interview to help the interviewer remember you. One of the company recruiters I interviewed said, "It shows that you were listening and paying attention." She suggests writing something like, "I really picked up on the culture of the company, and I feel I can contribute to that kind of environment because…"

- Express your interest in the job, and be enthusiastic about it! Be willing to show your excitement and passion.

- Mention why you believe you're a great fit for the job, maybe even repeating a key Unique Strength or Reason Why that you talked about during the interview. Veda Jeffries, Assistant Director of Counseling Services at Stanford University, says a well-written thank you note "gives you an opportunity to reiterate or point out a skill you may have overlooked during the interview."

- If you interviewed with more than one person, send each of them a separate thank you note.

- Triple-check the thank you note to make sure everything is correct — especially the interviewer's name and title. A badly written thank you note with mistakes in it will do you more harm than good. Remember the statistics we mentioned on page 163 of the Actions chapter! Even one typo can ruin your chances.

- Timing is everything! If you know the company is going to make a quick hiring decision, send your thank you by e-mail.

If they're going to take a couple of weeks or longer to hire someone, stand out even more by sending your thank you note by snail mail. These days, receiving snail mail is pretty rare, so it can actually help you be remembered. Use your best handwriting, and send it in a very professional looking note card. Shannon Boehm, Manager of Undergraduate Recruitment for Sears, said this about thank you notes: "I am far more impressed when I receive follow-up handwritten thank you notes instead of e-mails. Thank you e-mails are actually very common for me to receive, and I generally just file them away. But handwritten thank you notes are posted up on my office wall. A generic one is not as impressive, but one that is well thought out can make a candidate stand out. Just make sure they are written to the right company! A few times I received thank you notes that had clearly been templates used for other companies, and the candidate forgot to paste my company name over another's. In this case, not sending a thank you note at all would have been better."

The Subsequent E-mail Trap. Don't suddenly get casual with your e-mails to the interviewer or anyone else at the company. As one of the recruiters I interviewed cautions: "Don't start forwarding jokes or funny e-mails to the interviewer or disclosing information about your personal life even if you begin to feel more comfortable with that person. It's critical to keep a professional relationship with the interviewer no matter how friendly you may have become." Acting too familiar too quickly could undermine all that you've worked hard to accomplish. Yes, you do want the interviewer to like you, but you don't want to lose the job to someone else when you're that close just because you've accidentally crossed the line.

Your "Sound" Marketing Plan

It's time to explore the Sound portion of your College Graduate Personal Brand Marketing Plan. Let's tune in to our two fellow grads to see how each of them will use Sound to communicate their personal brands during their job search process.

Nicole's College Graduate Personal Brand Summary:

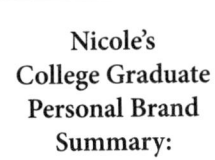

Outgoing, passionate, and results-oriented **"Company Champion"** *who can confidently convince professional customers that the division's medical supplies are the best choice for their patients.*

→ Sound →

Work on slowing down the pace of my speech and lowering my volume. Practice answering questions, staying on topic, and not talking too much.

Travis's College Graduate Personal Brand Summary:

An environmentally-focused, real-world engineer who bounces ideas off others and delivers great client solutions.

→ Sound →

Work on speaking more loudly and on trying to vary my pitch more. Practice pronouncing words clearly into a recorder and critique what I sound like.

Okay, you know the drill — it's your turn. What is your Sound Marketing Plan? What steps will you take to make sure your Sound reflects the best brand YOU™?

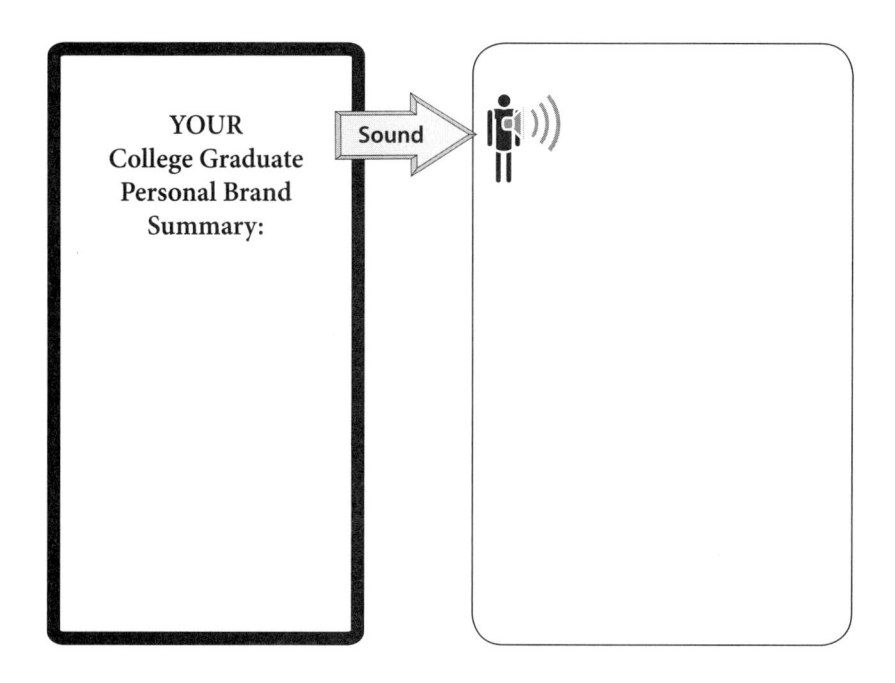

YOUR College Graduate Personal Brand Summary:

→ Sound →

> " *Many sounds — not just music — absolutely have the power to influence us.* "

Communicate it

Step 2

16

Thoughts

College Graduate Personal Brand Marketing Plan Activity #5

Whether you think you can or whether you think you can't, you're right.

— Henry Ford, Founder of the Ford Motor Company

I really believe I've saved the best for last when it comes to the five activities that communicate your personal brand: your Thoughts. Of the five activities that most successfully get across your personal brand, this is the one that can impact every other activity in your College Graduate Personal Brand Marketing Plan. Your Thoughts can influence your Actions, your Reactions, your Look, and your Sound, so they can have a major impact on the success of your job search.

Unfortunately, looking for a job after graduation and making important decisions that will impact your future professional career are both high on the list of situations that can cause stress. They're right up there not far behind the death of a parent, an illness, and moving. The uncertainty that comes with a job search can be scary and challenging. Yet, every year, millions of graduates around the world find themselves exactly where you are now. So, the trick is learning to successfully manage this stress, and one of the best ways to deal with it is to take control of your Thoughts.

Time and time again, I've witnessed job seekers struggle to find a job because they have negative Thoughts about the job search process, while those who take on a positive mindset find a great job much more quickly. So, let's explore how changing your Thoughts can take the edge off of job-hunting stress.

The Truth About Thoughts

What I'm about to write may sound a bit crazy to you, but bear with me a minute. In the 1600s, Galileo — who is today considered the "Father of Modern Science" — was interrogated for 18 days straight, tortured, imprisoned, and called a heretic. He was then placed under house arrest by the Inquisition for the rest of his life until he died, blind, at the age of 78. He was even buried without a proper monument. What horrible crime had Galileo committed that brought on this brutal treatment?

He wrote and gave lectures supporting the belief that the earth revolves around the sun.

Can you imagine that? Today, we know it's a fact that the earth revolves around the sun — we couldn't imagine it any other way — but in Galileo's time, that idea was considered outrageous.

I tell you Galileo's story in the hope that you'll open your mind as you read this chapter and consider these next words as possible, even if they challenge everything you've believed up to this point. Many scientists argue that in the future, the following three words will be as common and as accepted an idea as our sun-centered solar system is today. Here they are:

> **Thoughts are Things**

It's true: Science is beginning to prove that Thoughts exist in this world in a very real way — that Thoughts are made up of energy, just like a flower, an animal, or the human body. Even though our Thoughts may not be "seen" like a shoe or "touched" like a feather, Thoughts absolutely, positively exist. (Think about it: You can't see air either, but it's definitely there, right?) We can prove that the physical brain exists, but the "thinker" — the part of us that actually thinks our Thoughts — is still pretty much a mystery to us.

So, let's focus in this chapter on the power that your Thoughts can have on how consistently you communicate your personal brand during your job search and beyond. Just like you can make choices about which pen you use or what you do with your computer, you have choices about how you use your Thoughts to get the job you want.

Of course, the "things" in our lives that we normally see and touch are usually created by someone else — Toshiba made my computer, for example, and Mont Blanc made my pen. But to me, the most exciting thing about our Thoughts is this: *We* create them. Your thoughts are 100% yours — no one else can create them for you. And that's great news because it means you have ultimate control over your Thoughts. You and you alone are responsible for both the Thoughts you think as well as the outcome of those Thoughts — from start to finish.

In fact, if you think about it (every pun intended!), you actually have more control over your Thoughts than you do over a lot of what makes up your Look and your Sound. Even though your brain may have some involvement in your thinking, your body isn't really involved with *what* you think. So, you can change your Thoughts at will. It may not be obvious how to do this at first, but your Thoughts offer you a huge opportunity to impact each and every aspect of your College Graduate Personal Brand Marketing Plan.

In short, you can take full control of your personal brand — and your job search — through your Thoughts. It's just a matter of knowing how and making the effort.

Thoughts Are Like Chain Smoking

Psychologists believe each of us thinks about 60,000 Thoughts every day. That's 3,750 Thoughts per waking hour — a lot by anyone's estimation! But have you ever taken the time to do an "inventory" of your Thoughts? Stop and consider that for a second. What kinds of Thoughts are you creating every hour?

Psychologists also estimate that 95% to 98% of those 60,000 thoughts each day are repeated the next day, and the next day, and the next day. That means only 2% to 5% of our Thoughts are ever really different from one day to the next. Our Thoughts are like habits. We stick with the same Thought patterns and stay in the same kind of "Thought rut" day in and day out. You'd think we'd get tired of the same Thoughts, wouldn't you? But obviously, we don't even notice we're thinking the same things over and over. We don't really stop to consider what our heads are filled with day after day.

If you're like most people, your mind has probably picked up some bad habits over the years. It's no wonder that we get into patterns in our lives that we can't seem to shake. In fact, did you ever stop to chew on the idea that it might be your Thoughts that are responsible for negative patterns that play out over and over in your life?

Actually, it's nothing but a good old fashioned cause-and-effect relationship at work here. Your Thoughts are the cause, and your job, your life, your relationships — and your personal brand — are the effect. If you want to change the "effect" — the outcome — then you need to change the "cause" — your Thoughts. It's really that simple.

Okay, okay, I know it *sounds* simple, but I'm sure you're asking: "How do I actually *do* that — especially when it comes to something as stressful and potentially challenging as a job search?" Well, just like a chain smoker or someone who drinks too much can change those habits, it's up to you to change your thinking habits, too. It takes concentration, but remember that you — and only you — have the power to control what you think about at any point in time. If you don't take charge of what you think, you'll just continue the same old habits that could have a negative impact on your job search.

There are three key steps to taking charge of your Thoughts and getting better job search results:

1. Become aware of your Thoughts.
2. Turn negative Thoughts into positive Thoughts.
3. Embrace positive thinking as a new habit.

Become Aware of Your Thoughts

To change your Thoughts, the first step is to begin paying attention to what you're thinking day in and day out. Of those 3,750 Thoughts screaming in your head every hour, how many of them are you actually conscious of? What's rattling around in your brain all day?

Here's an exercise to help you become more aware of what you're thinking about:

1. Gather two highlighters of different colors, a few pieces of lined paper, and a writing pen.
2. Set a timer for five minutes. Then, put your pen to paper, and start writing everything that comes to your mind. Write down every single Thought that pops into your head for those five minutes, and

try not to let your pen stop. Don't worry about what you've written or whether it makes sense — no one has to ever read it but you.

3. Once the five minutes are up, read through the Thoughts you've written. Take the two colored highlighters, and highlight every Thought related to "job search" or "work" in one color and every Thought related to "personal" in a different color.

4. Then, go back and re-read all of your Thoughts once again. This time, with your pen, underline all of the negative Thoughts, and circle all of the positive Thoughts.

5. Now, sit back and look at the outcome. First, which color do you see the most on your pages — the color you chose for job search/work Thoughts, or the color you chose for personal Thoughts? What types of Thoughts are the most prominent in your mind? Then, look at whether there are more underlines (negative Thoughts) or more circles (positive Thoughts) on your pages. Are your negative Thoughts more related to work/your job search or to your personal life? What do you think about positively?

From that exercise, sit back and think about what you learned about your Thoughts. It's a great way to become more aware of the content of the 60,000 Thoughts you have in a day, and that kind of awareness is the first key step toward changing your Thoughts. If you've discovered that you have a lot of negative Thoughts, don't let your worry about it create yet another negative Thought! Just keep reading, and you'll learn many great tips about how to stop your thinking from getting you down.

Turn Negative Thoughts into Positive Thoughts

Once you're aware of the content of your Thoughts, the second step to managing your Thoughts is getting used to turning negative Thoughts into positive Thoughts. Maybe that sounds hard to do, but there are people all across the globe who manage to keep their Thoughts positive rather than negative.

Do you know people who are just naturally happy — people whose lives seem to always come together for them and fall into place? They have happy family lives, get good grades, and get along well with everyone. You know the kind of people I'm talking about, right? Well, I believe there's one thing that unites them all: They regularly think positive Thoughts. These people see the glass as half-full instead of half-empty. Guaranteed.

The positive results you see in their lives and in their personal brands are internally driven. People like that just naturally think about how things will turn out *well*, and their Thoughts become a reality. They don't focus on drama, details, or problems. They focus on what the positive outcome will be, and you can see the result of their Thoughts in their lives every single day. What they think actually becomes real.

So, how are your Thoughts impacting *your* life and *your* job search? Are you one of those people who wake up in the morning and say, "Ugh! Another day. I've got yet another job interview this afternoon, but I don't know why I even try. I already know I won't get the job." And, of course, because that Thought plays over and over in your mind for the next 24 hours, it's a self-fulfilling prophecy. You proved yourself right, but what did you gain from that?

Instead, what if you changed that initial Thought into something positive? What if the first thing you said to yourself when you woke up was, "Yes! Another day! The job interview I have this afternoon is going to be great. I look forward to sharing with the interviewer what I have to offer the company and also to finding out what the company has to offer me. I know how I want my personal brand to be perceived, so I'm primed and ready. It's going to be great!" Think about it: If you could start the day with that Thought, how different would your day be?

And here's the cool thing: Even if you make a positive statement before you fully believe it, you'll eventually begin to believe it. If you just allow for that small opening of possibility that you *could* have a job you'll really love, the door will soon swing wide open for you if you consistently think positively about it.

I'm not advocating that you walk around with the attitude of an over-the-top game show host, but expecting the worst will definitely deliver just that: the worst.

Homework Assignment

Every morning this week when you wake up, condition yourself to let the first thing that pops into your head be a positive thought. I guarantee you that, after doing this regularly for a while, you'll be amazed what a difference it makes in the outlook — and even outcome — of your day!

Does thinking more positively sound challenging to you? The truth is that managing your Thoughts is far from rocket science or magic. It's actually incredibly simple, and — as we said earlier — you are in charge. For example:

- Do you want company recruiters to perceive, think, and feel that your personal brand is "creative?" Then, think creative Thoughts about interviews and your personal brand.
- Do you want company recruiters to treat you nicely? Then, think nice thoughts about your interviewers.
- Do you want to feel more at peace during the job search process? Then, think more peaceful thoughts.

✓ The Six Advantages College Grads Have in a Job Search

College graduates often worry that they're automatically at a disadvantage in the job pool because they don't have as much experience as older applicants. But the truth is that you have some definite advantages just by virtue of being young and new to your job search. It's true! You may very well be chosen for a job over an older, more experienced candidate for any or all of the following six reasons:

The Millennium Generation Perspective. No one knows the needs and interests of younger customers better than … well, a younger customer! And that means you — a college grad. You can leverage this knowledge in your job interviews by helping potential employers see how you can uncover the needs of the company's young target market and find a way to respond to those needs.

IT Skills. Unlike many older job applicants, you have grown up with computers as a natural part of your life. You probably understand software, hardware, and the Internet — including social media — better than anyone who is older than you. Never underestimate the importance of this knowledge!

Multi-Tasking Abilities. If you're like most people in their late teens/early 20s, you're probably capable of listening to your MP3 player, talking on your cell phone, texting someone, checking Facebook, and answering a Skype message all at once. Studies show that people from ages 12-24 today use an average of 5.5 media at the same time, while people over 40 only use 1.7 media at the same time. This means that you're probably better at juggling a lot more things at once than an older candidate who is competing for the same job as you. And what employer wouldn't want that?

Lack of Baggage from Past Jobs. You come to the job market with very few preconceived notions, a fresh perspective, and a clean slate. Some older job candidates can get set in their ways. They learn how to do things at one job and then, find it hard to learn new ways of doing those things at a new job. So, make it clear in your job interviews that you're open to learning the company's system and that you're excited about discovering their processes.

Lower Salary Expectations. In tough economic times, older candidates often apply for lower level jobs, but companies are reluctant to hire them because they might bolt to a better job as soon as one comes along. This is why a company could actually find it more attractive to hire someone like you for a starting position. So, be open about your willingness to begin a new job at a lower salary so that you can prove yourself in that position.

Willingness and Hunger. When you're just starting out in the job market, you may have more of a "hunger" than the person who's been working for a number of years. That willingness to do "whatever it takes" is key to success, now more than ever. Companies want people with a "can-do" attitude.

> So, don't concern yourself with your title or whether you're doing work that you feel is "beneath" you. Everyone has to start somewhere, and the difference between success and failure is often the attitude and willingness you show toward helping your employer. Use every job as an opportunity to learn and grow, and you're almost sure to be rewarded in a big way.
>
> Billie Burke — the actress who played Glinda the Good Witch in the original *The Wizard of Oz* movie — once said, "Age is something that doesn't matter unless you are a cheese." Change your mindset from what you *don't* have as a college grad to what you *do* have, and remember these six advantages!

Try This Exercise

Let's do something similar to the writing exercise you did earlier, but this time, let's focus on two questions that are directly related to interviewing. Grab a pen and some paper, and find a quiet place to sit down. Take a deep breath, and ask yourself these questions:

- What are my Thoughts about interviewing?
- How do I feel about interviewing?

As you focus on these two questions, write down everything that comes to mind. Don't censor yourself, and don't stop until you've written for about three minutes.

Now, go back and look at what you wrote. How many of your Thoughts around interviewing are negative? How many of your feelings about interviews are fearful and based on worry? On the other hand, how many of your Thoughts and feelings are positive? If you're like most people, the idea of an interview produces more negative Thoughts than positive and can plant a lot of fear into your heart. How do you change that?

Remember: Thoughts are things. They exist in the world in a real way. If you find yourself thinking, "I'll never get a great job," guess what? You won't. Instead, take all of that negative energy and use it to think Thoughts like, "The best job for me is only an interview away." Replace each negative thought with a positive one. As the famous baseball player Babe Ruth once said, "Never let the fear of striking out get in your way." You must visualize and *know* that a positive outcome will be the ultimate result of your job search. That means accepting temporary setbacks as just that — temporary. They are simply there to help you learn, grow, and move closer to your goal.

Embrace Positive Thinking as a New Habit

Let's move on to our third step toward taking charge of your Thoughts — embracing positive thinking as a new habit. I can almost hear you saying, "Brenda, I've heard that stuff about controlling your Thoughts before, but it's just too hard!" A Buddhist monk in Thailand once told me that our minds can be like an untamed monkey, always jumping around, running here and there. To train it, you have to learn to reel in the monkey, as if it were on a chain, until it's fully within your control. You can choose when to reel in your "monkey mind" and when to let it run wild again. It's your mind, after all! Let's put it this way: Either you control your mind and your Thoughts, or your mind and your Thoughts control you. I know which one I like better. How about you?

Grabbing Your Monkey Mind By the Tail

There are a lot of ways you can take control of your Thoughts and reel in that monkey mind. Grab it by the tail, and make it your pet — not the other way around. Then and only then can positive thinking become your way of being — like those people you know who seem to have "charmed" lives. I'm not saying that nothing painful will ever happen to you again, but your attitude about what happens to you will become positive enough that you will get through difficult situations easier and change your circumstances sooner rather than later.

1. **Take Charge!** Tell your mind that you're the one in control here and that you won't allow any negative Thoughts to interfere with building the personal brand you want and getting a job you deserve and that you will love.

2. **Switch from Negative to Positive.** If you find that your Thoughts are running amuck with fear, wondering, questioning, and filled with "what if" scenarios when it comes to finding a new job, start training yourself to switch your thinking to something positive. Make a list of the happiest moments in your life, but write them in detail. For example, don't just write: "The day I won the award for best drama student." Instead, create a list that will really help you when you're feeling down by reminding you of exactly how you felt during that proud moment. Write something like: "The day I won the award for best drama student, the President of the College presented me with the award at a dinner. The dean and most of my professors were there, my parents, and some of my friends. Everybody applauded, and I felt like I'd accomplished a lot." Then, when you need to switch your thinking from something negative, focus your mind on one of the positive memories on your list. Relive it as best you can. Close your eyes for a minute, and remember any sights, sounds, smells, textures, or tastes to help you go back to that happier time. The more you practice this exercise, the more quickly you'll be able to transform your negative Thoughts into positive ones. In fact, eventually, all you'll have to do is think "my drama award," for example, and you'll automatically shift your focus and get rid of those negative Thoughts.

3. **Set Goals for Changing Your Thought Patterns.** Your goals should be realistic, and you should be able to measure them in some way. This way, you'll know exactly when you've reached each of them. For example: "Between now and 3:00 p.m., every time I catch myself thinking a non-personal-brand-building Thought, I'm going to switch my thinking to _____ instead." It takes focus and effort, but can you see how this will train your monkey mind over time?

4. **Reward Yourself for Reaching Your Goals and Thinking Positive Brand-Building Thoughts.** Take an inventory at the end of each day. If the majority of your Thoughts were positive ones, treat yourself to a visit to Starbucks on the way home, or take yourself to a movie. Once your mind catches on that you're going to be rewarded for thinking positive Thoughts, it will be much easier to tame. Eventually, thinking positively

will simply become a way of life for you, and remaining positive before, during, and after job interviews will just be your natural way of being.

5. **Affirm What You Want.** You've probably heard about positive affirmations, and maybe you've even used them in the past. They really are a powerful way to alter your Thoughts. Think of all of the positive affirmations you can say about yourself in the job search process. For example:

> "I do a great job of communicating my personal brand in interviews."

> "I come across as very charismatic in interviews, and interviewers see me as confident and professional."

> "I am hired by a great company for a job I love and that will help me grow both personally and professionally."

It's important that every affirmation be written or spoken in the present, as if it's already the truth. That's the point! You don't have to fully believe the affirmation for it to begin to do its good work — impacting the way you think — but the key is to strive to believe these affirmations more and more as you read and/or write them.

Make affirmations a regular part of your day. Read your affirmations first thing in the morning, at lunch time, and right before you go to sleep. If you can, read them out loud, and really "feel" what it's like to have that affirmation become real. Visualize what your life will be like when your affirmations are reality. Some people even write each affirmation in a notebook 20 or more times per day. Do whatever it takes to get your mind wrapped around the image of you living the life you want and having the job you want.

Your Thoughts *Before* the Interview

If you want to have more control of your Thoughts *during* an interview, it's important to work on your Thoughts *before* the interview. The more positive you keep your Thoughts about an interview beforehand, the more confident and relaxed you'll be when you're in an interviewer's office.

Positive Self-Talk. When you feel anxious, angry, or worried, you can bet it's a result of negative Thoughts. Psychologists say that one of the best ways to move into a better state of mind is to talk yourself out of it. Just hearing your own inner voice telling you to stay calm can take the edge off of the situation. It's a way of soothing your monkey mind and affirming the positive, and you can even do it right before you walk into the interviewer's office. But it's even better to use this skill to talk to yourself positively about the interview in the days before the appointment, the same day as the interview, and again while you sit in the waiting room. You'll be amazed by how much this can help to keep your nerves — and negative Thoughts — in check.

Face Your Fears. What are you worried about that might happen in an interview, and how can you turn those worries into a positive? For example, if your Thoughts are telling you that a potential employer might think your GPA is too low, replace that Thought with the belief that they'll hire you anyway because of your personality and determination. Maybe your worry Thought is that they'll think you have too little experience? Be prepared to share with the interviewer how you can bring a fresh perspective from the younger generation into the company and help them to understand a younger customer base. Being prepared will help to calm your fearful Thoughts significantly.

Keep Your Personal Brand Summary Near. Stash your job-seeking college grad personal brand summary in your wallet or purse, or maybe even post it on your computer or refrigerator. When you do that, it will stay top of mind at all times. This will help you to keep your Thoughts where they belong — on your job goal. Choose two or three key words from your summary, and repeat them to yourself whenever your confidence or positive Thoughts begin to fade. You can even do this in a split second before (and during) the interview to bring your Thoughts and energy back to where you want them to be.

✓ The "Picture" of Success

Top actors and athletes often say that they envision their success. They actually picture themselves getting the role, giving a great performance, winning the game, or crossing the finish line first. Many of them swear by this method for not only staying positively focused before a big event, but for turning what they picture into reality.

Let's apply this to you finding and getting the job that you want upon graduation. Try playing out "tomorrows" in your mind. What does a successful interview look like? Play it out in your head as if you're watching a movie. Really "feel" the emotions of doing a great job in an interview. How are interviewers responding to YOU™? How are YOU™ responding to them? How are you presenting yourself before, during, and after your interviews? How do you look when you walk into the interviewer's office? How does it feel when the interviewer recognizes what YOU™ have to offer? What does it feel like to be charismatic? What does it feel like to actually enjoy an interview and walk out feeling terrific?

Visualizing yourself successful in interviews will help you become excited about them. Don't overlook this as a great tool! The more energy and enthusiasm you bring to the table, the more the interviewer will feel that energy. If you walk into the room feeling defeated or depressed from the start — even if you try to hide it — I guarantee you the interviewer will feel that, too. But with sincere passion and an upbeat attitude, you have a strong chance of getting the job, even if someone else in the running may be better qualified on paper.

Picture yourself successfully putting your College Graduate Personal Brand Marketing Plan into effect and being offered the best possible job with the salary and perks you want. You can fast-forward and visualize yourself in the job you want, too. What does it feel like to be really excited about the work you do? The key is to turn your Thoughts into activities, and make your vision real. It *is* in your control, and the more you are truly able to sense this as reality in your mind, the closer you'll be to making it reality in your life and in your career.

Your Thoughts *During* the Interview

During the interview itself, you'll want to keep your mind on the conversation. So, it's important to prepare as much as possible before the interview in order to maintain a positive attitude *during* the interview. In other words, don't wait until you're sitting with the interviewer to try to have positive Thoughts. Remember: Practice makes perfect, so if you want to think positively during the interview, you need to practice beforehand.

> **Focus on Your Audience.** Even if you've been working on taming your monkey mind, old habits die hard, and you may find negative Thoughts creeping in on you while you're in an interview. If this happens, quickly bring yourself back to the moment, focusing on the interviewer and how you can fill the company's Needs. Remember: Your personal brand won't work unless it fills the Needs of your Audience! So, the more you focus on your Audience, the less time you'll have to focus on negative Thoughts.
>
> **Reactive Thoughts.** Keep in mind that Thoughts are also Reactions, just like physical Reactions. Are your Thought Reactions out of control? When something unexpected happens in an interview, you may try to control what you say and do, but do your Thoughts go wild? Do you immediately jump to conclusions or become frustrated with yourself (or the interviewer) inside your head?
>
> This kind of Thought Reaction is natural, and I'm definitely not suggesting you should never get angry or that you should try to suppress your emotions. But think seriously about how these Thought Reactions are serving you, especially if you end up "shouting" at yourself or someone else in your mind for days on end as a result. It's easy to get eaten up by emotions in your mind, but that robs you of a lot of energy and only serves to keep you focused on negative Thoughts.
>
> The next time you have a knee-jerk Thought Reaction, catch yourself. Work on letting go of the negative emotion about the situation as quickly as possible. Otherwise, you'll let the situation control you, rather than the other way around. Stop thinking in terms of who's right and who's wrong. If you're wasting your time on negative Thoughts just because you believe you'll win an

argument, you've already lost. If an interviewer doesn't think you're right for a job or doesn't choose you because of a wrong impression of you, let it go and move on to a company that can truly appreciate what you have to offer. Remember that just as you have the power to control your physical and verbal Reactions, you can also control your Thought Reactions.

Your Thoughts *After* the Interview

If you let them, your Thought Reactions can "eat at you" long after the interview. Do you obsess about what went wrong when you don't hear from a company right away? Do you get depressed when you don't get a particular job? It's natural to feel disappointment when you don't get a job you hoped for, but be careful with the direction of your Thoughts. They can run amuck and go into those negative spaces again, telling you that you're not qualified enough or that you'll never get the kind of job you want. Don't allow that!

Continue to bring yourself back to positive Thoughts. Practice Thoughts of acceptance: "The best job is out there for me, and everything is lining up just right for it to come to me at just the right time." Also, find humor in the situation, and don't take yourself too seriously. It will help you to keep your Thoughts in check and keep your eyes on the goal.

However You Slice It:
Negative Thoughts are Negative Things

Still not convinced that Thoughts are things? Whether or not you can completely buy into the science of Thought, no matter how you look at it, life is frankly just a lot more satisfying when you stay positive and in control of what you think. And it's hard to argue with the fact that people with negative attitudes are a lot less fun as friends, employees, or coworkers. There isn't any benefit in communicating a negative personal brand, and negativity will do nothing to help you get any kind of job. No matter how much work you put into the other aspects of your brand, negative Thoughts will stop you from fully making YOU™ a reality. Employers will never perceive, think, and feel good about your personal brand as long as negative Thoughts are in the way.

As the world becomes more aware of the power of our Thoughts, more books and films like *The Law of Attraction* and *The Secret* will enter the mainstream. Today, it's becoming more accepted to believe that our lives are really just reflections of our attitudes and Thoughts. We're beginning to see that simple changes within our minds can create real change in our individual lives and, collectively, in the world.

Your "Thoughts" Marketing Plan

So, how will you work on your Thoughts in your College Graduate Personal Brand Marketing Plan? Let's check in with our two grads to see what they're going to do to take charge of their Thoughts. Then, it will be your turn to complete your Thoughts Marketing Plan.

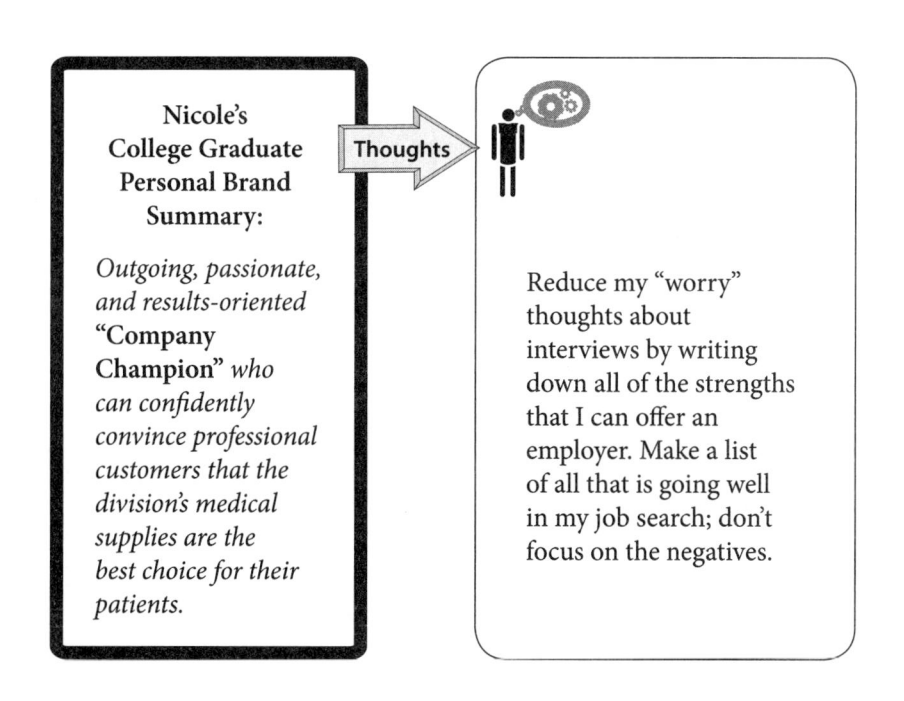

Nicole's College Graduate Personal Brand Summary:

Outgoing, passionate, and results-oriented **"Company Champion"** *who can confidently convince professional customers that the division's medical supplies are the best choice for their patients.*

→ Thoughts →

Reduce my "worry" thoughts about interviews by writing down all of the strengths that I can offer an employer. Make a list of all that is going well in my job search; don't focus on the negatives.

Travis's College Graduate Personal Brand Summary:

An environmentally-focused, real-world engineer who bounces ideas off others and delivers great client solutions.

→ Thoughts →

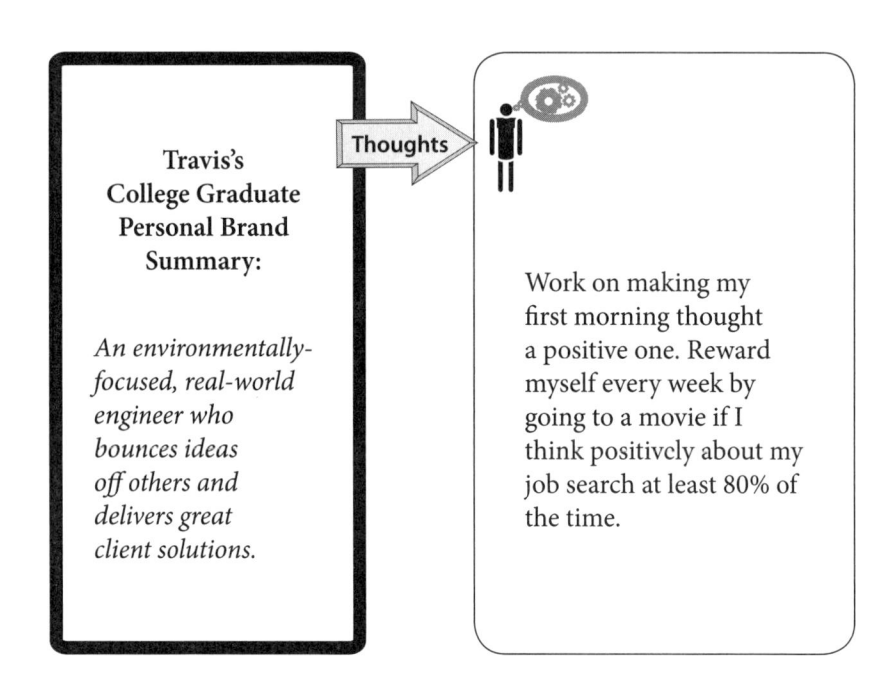

Work on making my first morning thought a positive one. Reward myself every week by going to a movie if I think positively about my job search at least 80% of the time.

Okay, now, complete the last portion of your Marketing Plan. How will you turn your Thoughts from negative to positive and energize your job search?

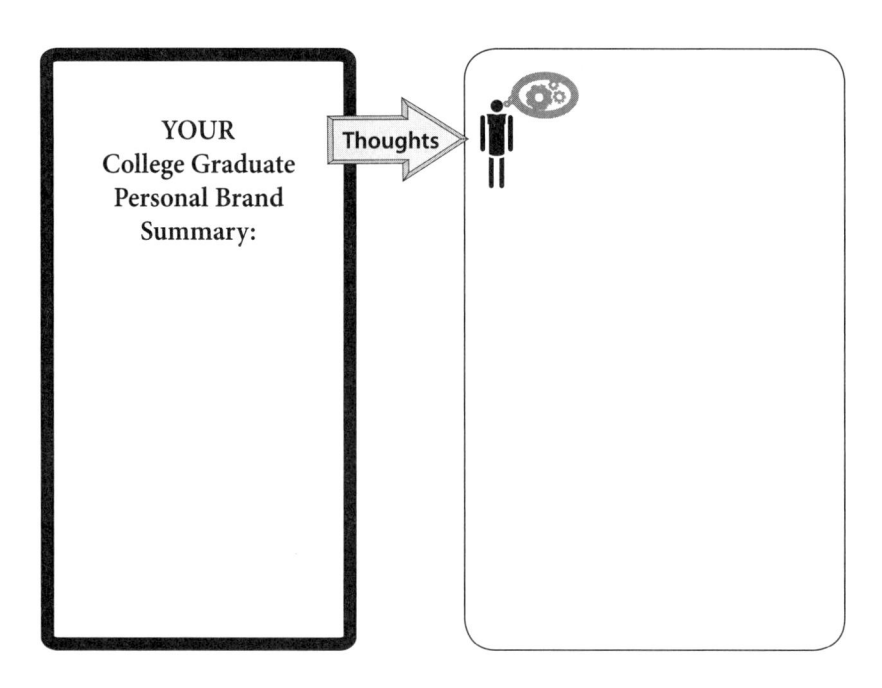

YOUR College Graduate Personal Brand Summary:

→ Thoughts →

Activity #5: Thoughts 233

You did it—you've completed all five activities of your College Graduate Personal Brand Marketing Plan! You're now ready to pull together your entire plan. This is the heart and soul of communicating your personal brand.

"They're complaining about the scarcity of decent jobs!"

Communicate it

College Graduate
Personal Brand Marketing Plan

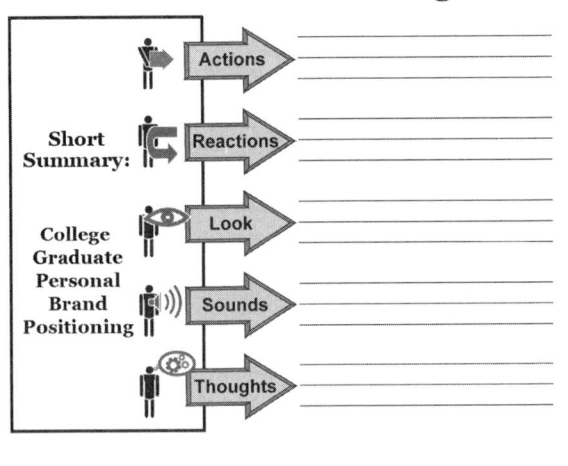

Short Summary:

College Graduate Personal Brand Positioning

- Actions
- Reactions
- Look
- Sounds
- Thoughts

Step 2

17

Your Complete College Graduate Personal Brand Marketing Plan

No one gets an iron-clad guarantee of success. Certainly, factors like opportunity, luck, and timing are important. But the backbone of success is usually found in old-fashioned, basic concepts like hard work, determination, good planning, and perseverance.

— Mia Hamm, Retired professional soccer player

You've carefully defined your personal brand using the six elements that make up YOU™. You've looked in-depth at all five activities that make up your College Graduate Personal Brand Marketing Plan. Now, it's time to combine all of the activities together to finalize your full job-search Marketing Plan. Pulling together how you will communicate your personal brand before, during, and after interviews through your Actions, Reactions, Look, Sound, and Thoughts is key to successfully mastering the job search process. This is where true success comes in the form of the job offer you want.

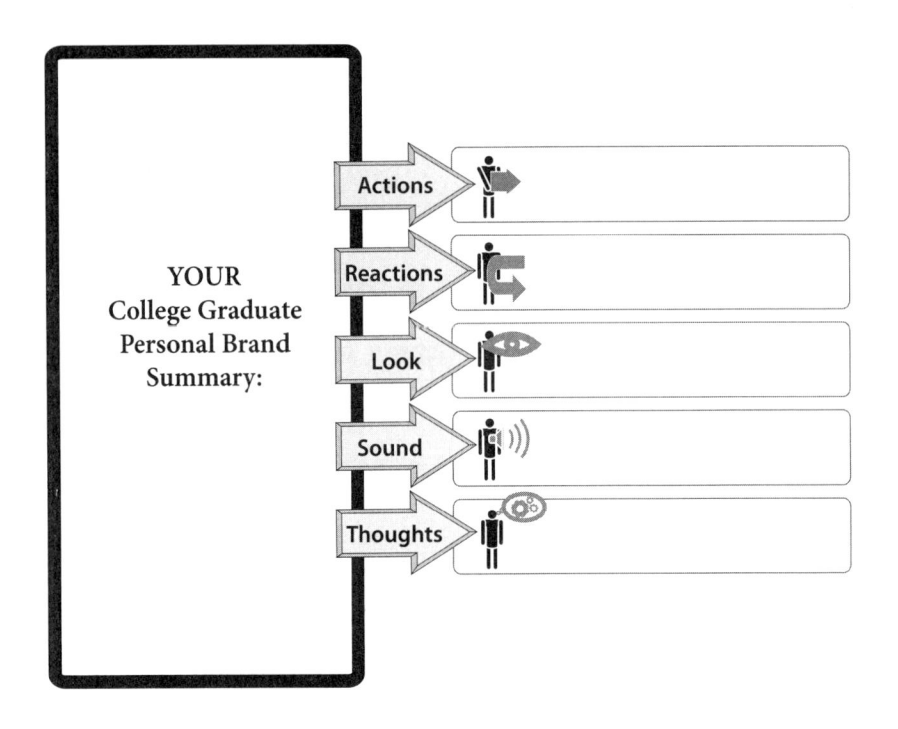

YOUR College Graduate Personal Brand Summary

YOUR College Graduate Personal Brand Summary:
- Actions
- Reactions
- Look
- Sound
- Thoughts

Take a look at the completed Marketing Plans for Nicole and Travis on the pages that follow. This is how they plan to work on their Actions, Reactions, Look, Sound, and Thoughts to drive a positive outcome from their job search.

As you look at each grad's Marketing Plan, what comes to mind? Do you see a full picture of how both of these job seekers are taking charge of their individual job searches?

What does looking at their plans tell you about your own Marketing Plan? Do you want to make any adjustments to your Plan as you review their examples? Once you see all of your five Marketing Plan activities together, does anything else come to mind that you can add to your plan that would strengthen each activity? Will each of your activities move you closer to getting a job you love?

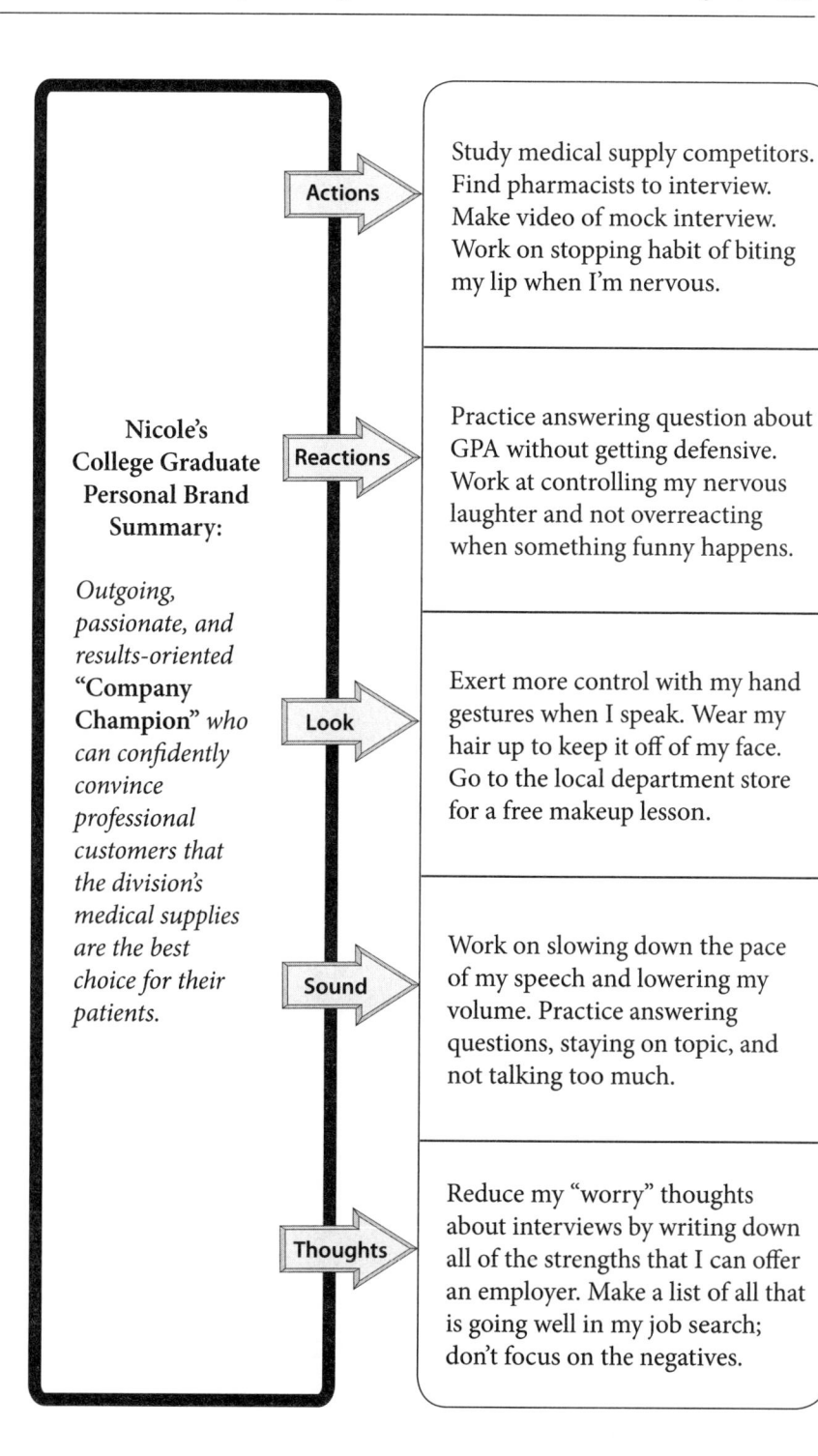

Nicole's College Graduate Personal Brand Summary:

Outgoing, passionate, and results-oriented **"Company Champion"** *who can confidently convince professional customers that the division's medical supplies are the best choice for their patients.*

Actions: Study medical supply competitors. Find pharmacists to interview. Make video of mock interview. Work on stopping habit of biting my lip when I'm nervous.

Reactions: Practice answering question about GPA without getting defensive. Work at controlling my nervous laughter and not overreacting when something funny happens.

Look: Exert more control with my hand gestures when I speak. Wear my hair up to keep it off of my face. Go to the local department store for a free makeup lesson.

Sound: Work on slowing down the pace of my speech and lowering my volume. Practice answering questions, staying on topic, and not talking too much.

Thoughts: Reduce my "worry" thoughts about interviews by writing down all of the strengths that I can offer an employer. Make a list of all that is going well in my job search; don't focus on the negatives.

Travis's College Graduate Personal Brand Summary:

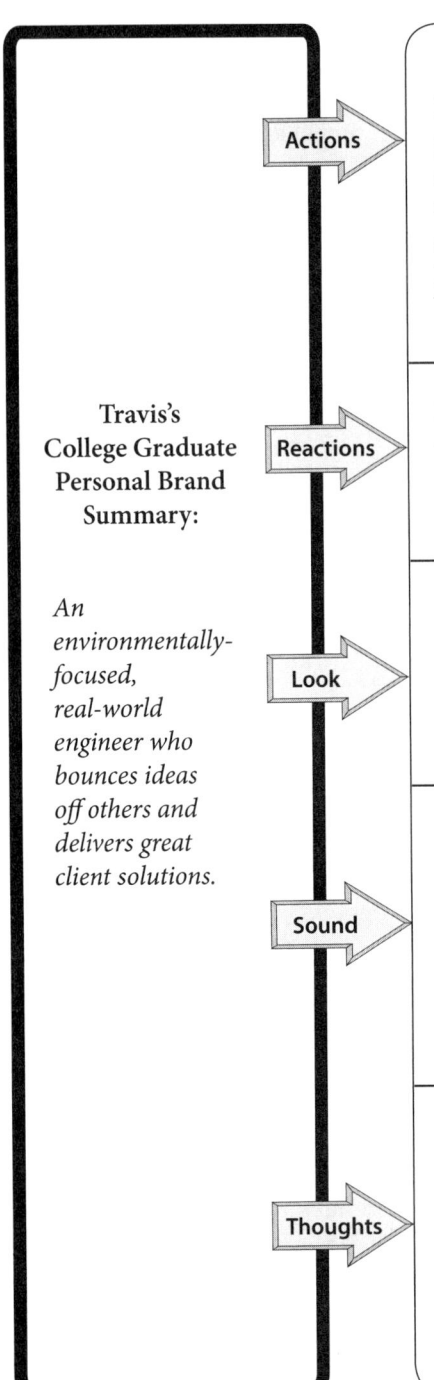

An environmentally-focused, real-world engineer who bounces ideas off others and delivers great client solutions.

Actions → Remove potentially damaging pics from my Facebook page, and delete blog entries that are too personal. Practice telling stories from my internship that highlight my Unique Strengths.

Reactions → Practice "poker face" in response to challenging questions. With a rep from Career Services, practice answering list of tough questions.

Look → Work on sitting up straight and not slouching when I'm in a chair. Get a new interview suit and new shoes. Use leather polish on my existing briefcase.

Sound → Work on speaking more loudly and on trying to vary my pitch more. Practice pronouncing words clearly into a recorder and critique what I sound like.

Thoughts → Work on making my first morning thought a positive one. Reward myself every week by going to a movie if I think positively about my job search at least 80% of the time.

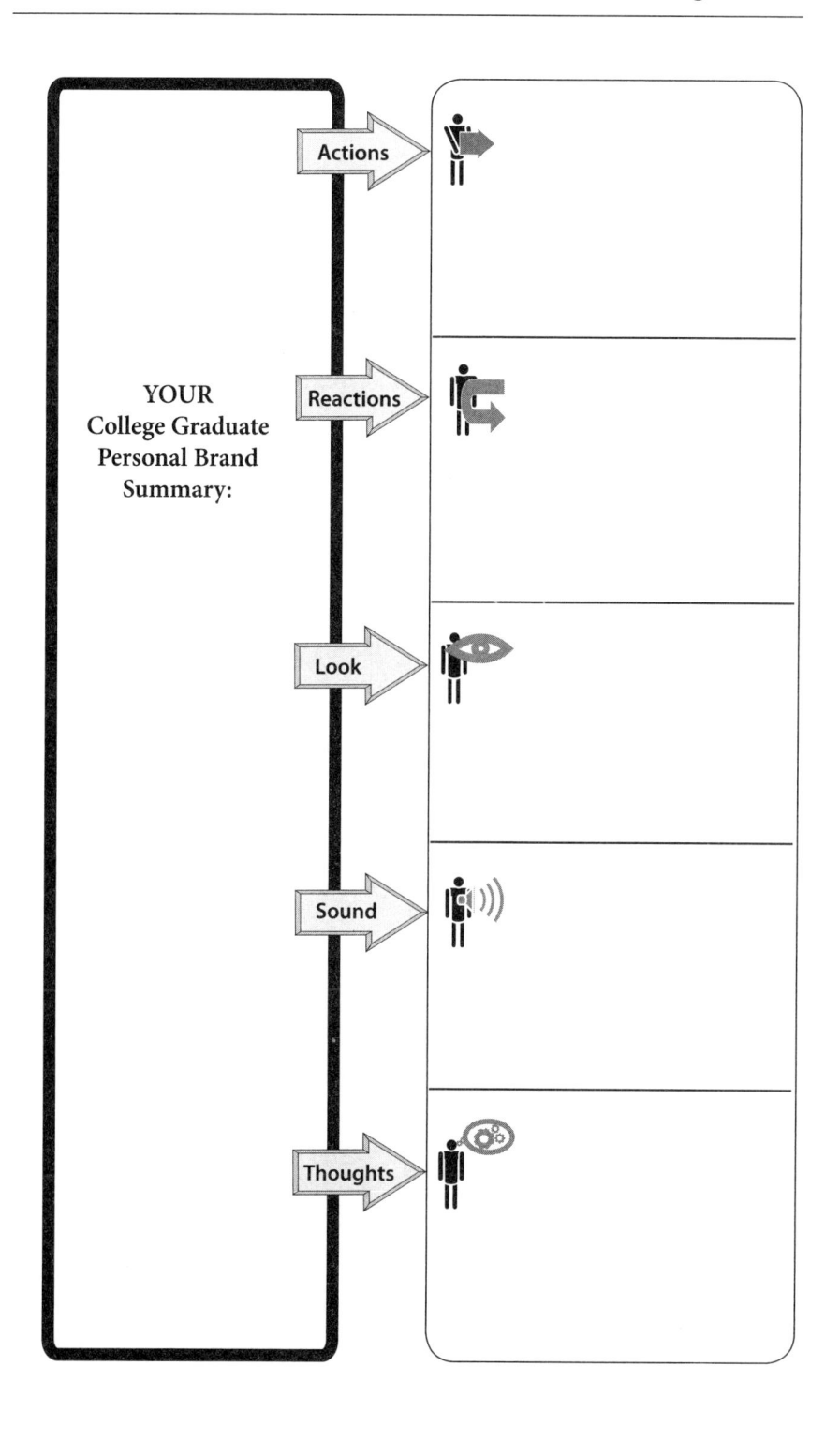

Your Complete College Graduate Personal Brand Marketing Plan 239

YOUR College Graduate Personal Brand Summary:

- Actions
- Reactions
- Look
- Sound
- Thoughts

Putting Your Marketing Plan Into Action

As we've said, putting your College Graduate Personal Brand Marketing Plan into action is about building a connection with your interviewers. But it can even go beyond that. Every single time you come in contact with anyone who works at one of your target companies, you're building a relationship with that company. Every meeting, phone call, e-mail, or letter is a chance to communicate the powerhouse personal brand you've worked so hard to define and develop. You never know what might come of a "chance" meeting here or there when you could be introduced to someone who knows an employee or executive at one of your target companies. So, make every moment count, and be consistent in communicating your job-seeking personal brand day in and day out with your Actions, Reactions, Look, Sound, and Thoughts.

That's what both Nicole and Travis did, and it paid off. They were each able to establish a connection with their target companies that got them the jobs they wanted. They did their research and learned about the companies so that they could define a personal brand that met their Audience's Needs. Then, they worked on communicating their personal brands to make a great impression in their interviews. Today, they're both doing great in their new jobs where their contributions are valued.

What about you? You've defined your personal brand and put together a plan to communicate it regularly to help you get the job you really want. You're now armed with what you need to succeed in building a powerful personal brand and creating that all-important connection with an interviewer. There's just one more step left to turn your job-seeker personal brand into the key that unlocks the door to a fantastic job and a great future. Let's do some troubleshooting and make sure you don't *damage* this personal brand called YOU™ as you continue your job hunt.

> *You're now armed with what you need to succeed in building a powerful personal brand and creating that all-important connection with an interviewer.*

Step 3
Avoid Damaging it

College Graduate Personal Brand Busters®

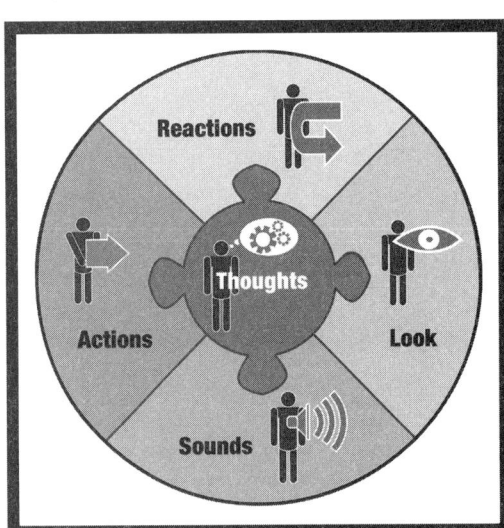

- Reactions
- Look
- Sounds
- Actions
- Thoughts

18

College Graduate Personal Brand Busters®

Learn from the mistakes of others — you can never live long enough to make them all yourself.

— John Luther Long, Author of the short story "Madame Butterfly"

You may never have heard of College Graduate Personal Brand Busters® before, but they're the critical last step to make sure your personal brand lands you the exact position you want in your desired company. Learning how to avoid these Busters® can make the difference between "we'll be in touch" and "welcome to the company!" So, what do I mean by "College Graduate Personal Brand Busters®?" They're the same five activities we talked about in Step 2 — your Actions, Reactions, Look, Sound, and Thoughts. But this time, it's the opposite of what we discussed in the chapters you just finished. These Busters® are what you *don't* want to do during your job search when it comes to your Actions, Reactions, Look, Sound, and Thoughts.

If you're not aware of them, College Graduate Personal Brand Busters® can damage all the work you've done so far to build the personal brand you desire. As Benjamin Franklin once said, "It takes many good deeds to build a good reputation and only one bad one to lose it." These Busters can lead you to bomb in your interviews, lose out on jobs you're applying for, or never even get interviews in the first place!

My College Graduate Personal Brand Busters® Collection

There are more College Graduate Personal Brand Busters® than we could possibly count.* In fact, through my years of hiring new employees at major multinational corporations all across the globe, my work as a professional career coach, and hours of discussions and interviews with dozens of human resources and recruiting experts, I have collected and developed an extensive list of College Graduate Personal Brand Busters®.

I took this full list of Personal Brand Busters® to college recruiters, HR professionals, hiring managers, and career services experts from companies and universities all across the nation to find out the "baddest of the bad." These folks have seen it all! They know the most common — and most damaging — mistakes that college graduates can make during the process of looking for a job. Many outstanding professionals took the time and energy to contribute to the list I'm about to share with you.

If you can bypass these worst Busters, you're well on your way to a job you love. We've divided them into categories based on our five College Graduate Personal Brand Marketing Plan activities — four Busters each for Actions, Reactions, Look, Sound, and Thoughts.

What these Busters are all about is helping you to learn from the mistakes of other college grad interviewees who have gone before you. The more you know what to do before, during, and after an interview — as well as what *not* to do — the better off YOU™ will be in your job search. And that will help you leapfrog from where you are now to the ultimate goal of hearing, "You're hired!"

College Graduate Personal Brand Busters® are common job search pitfalls or traps you might be falling into right now without even knowing it. Once you're aware of them, you have to keep a watchful eye out for them because they can be like stealth bombers — often under your conscious radar. And once you've learned to master them, it will feel like wearing a permanent bullet-proof vest! You'll have the confidence to know that you're not committing the worst job search sins of other college grads, and you'll feel great about your interviews.

Let's be honest: Every one of us looking for a job is guilty of a few Personal Brand Busters® from time to time. But knowledge is power.

The more you know about these Busters, the more you'll know how to avoid them, and the more you'll become aware of your own Busters as you put your Marketing Plan into action.

Keep in mind that this list is not the "complete" list of College Graduate Personal Brand Busters® by any stretch of the imagination. In fact, there really is no end to the potential list of College Graduate Personal Brand Busters® that might rear their ugly heads as you go through the job search process. No doubt you will come up with other Busters that are unique to your situation. If you do, write them down, and start your own list.

How do you know when you've come across a College Graduate Personal Brand Buster®?

1. Recognize when you've made a mistake before, during, or after an interview, and write it down. That's the best way to avoid making the same mistake again ... and it's the beginning of your own College Graduate Personal Brand Busters® list.

2. Talk with other job-seeking grads to find out what they've done or said that might have hurt their job search. You'll learn a lot about how to avoid damaging your own job-seeker personal brand.

The College Graduate Personal Brand Busters® laid out in the next chapter will work for any graduating student who faces the job search process and wants to come across as professional, confident, reliable, and in control before, during, and after any job interview. Read through each one of these Busters, think about them, and be honest with yourself. Do any of these habits sound like you?

Now, let's bust those Busters!*

---

* College Graduate Personal Brand Busters® and College Graduate Personal Brand Boosters™ are part of the Personal Brand Busters® Series. For more information on other career and on-the-job Busters, visit www.BrendaBence.com.

19

Quiz: The Top 20 College Graduate Personal Brand Busters®

I never make stupid mistakes. Only very, very clever ones.
— John Peel, British broadcaster

Mistakes aren't stupid unless we don't learn from them. In fact, I agree with Peel: Most mistakes are actually "very, very clever" because they open doors to help us get better and better at communicating our personal brands. As we said in the previous chapter, that's what College Graduate Personal Brand Busters® are all about — the mistakes other graduates have made during their job searches that you can learn from and avoid. If you keep them top of mind, they can keep you from damaging your own college grad personal brand. They're the pitfalls and traps to watch out for as you start to put your College Graduate Personal Brand Marketing Plan into action.

Through my interviews with HR managers and recruiting experts from companies all across the U.S., I have compiled the top 20 most damaging College Graduate Personal Brand Busters®. They're divided into the five College Graduate Marketing Plan Activities: Actions, Reactions, Look, Sound, and Thoughts — with four Busters each. Do you recognize yourself in any of these? After you've finished reading them, take the quiz located at the end of this chapter, and test yourself.

How well do you score? Then, you'll know exactly what to avoid as you move forward through your job search.

College Graduate Personal Brand Busters®—Actions

1. **Lying on your resume or during an interview**—even if you think they are just "little white lies." Studies show that a large number of college grads actually lie on their resumes. These lies range from overstating experience to actually making up fake "facts"—like a GPA or dates of employment—that can be easily checked by a potential employer. While it might be tempting, it's just too risky to lie! In today's electronic age, it's gotten incredibly easy to pinpoint exactly where someone didn't tell the truth. When the lie is exposed—and it will be—you'll lose your chance at a job and put your reputation at stake. If the lie is uncovered before your interview, you won't get an interview at all. If the truth comes out during your interview, you won't get the job (and you'll be embarrassed, too). And, if your lie is found out after you get the job, well, there's a good chance you'll be fired. Just try explaining *that* to your next interviewer.

   Don't get me wrong—it's normal to use your resume or an interview to frame potential negatives you might have in as positive a light as possible. But making up experiences or lying about something like your GPA or dates of employment will get you nowhere. There is 0% upside and 100% potential downside. Even if the lie feels "unimportant," people will think of you as dishonest if you're caught. And who wants to hire somebody with a dishonest personal brand? Erin Padilla of Talent Plus explains it like this: "Lying on your resume says to an employer that you have bad integrity."

   If you're remaining true to who you are, there's no reason to lie, and you'll be hired because of what YOU™ have to offer. It also just feels better knowing that you're living a life of integrity. When you're consistently honest with yourself and others, you feel better about yourself, and you save yourself the stress of worrying about getting caught. Bottom line: Lying on your resume or in an interview is a lose-lose situation. Just don't do it.

2. **Asking questions about pay and benefits during an initial interview.** Recruiters tell me they immediately read that kind of question as a sign of a college grad who's more interested in what the employer can do for them than what the grad can do for the employer. Don't forget that your *Audience's* Needs are key to success in personal

branding. Asking about pay in your first meeting may also make your interviewer think that all you care about is the money. No company wants to hire someone who's interested in nothing but how big of a paycheck comes along with the job.

Before asking about the particulars of salary, benefits, hours, overtime, etc., make sure the company and the job are a good fit for YOU™. Don't get me wrong: You definitely have every right to know eventually what a company has to offer you, but a first interview isn't the right time to ask those questions. When the company finally makes you an offer, that's when you can get more specific about salary and benefits. In the meantime, focus on showing the interviewer what a great asset you'll be to the company.

3. **Not performing a "trial run" to find out how long it takes to get to the interview site.** Don't run the risk of being late for your interview! It makes you look irresponsible and unreliable, and that's definitely not a good personal brand. As Pete Medrano of Lowe's Companies said, "This is especially unacceptable given MapQuest, Google Maps, and GPS."

Even if you're on time, you don't want to be out of breath and dripping with sweat because you had to sprint the last 50 yards. So, a trial run is key. And, be sure to do your trial run around the same time of day as the interview. If you're scheduled for an interview during rush hour traffic, a trial run during mid-morning hours won't give you a good sense of how much travel time you'll really need.

Of course, there might be times when you're late through no fault of your own. If that happens, apologize genuinely and make it clear that your being late was definitely beyond your control. But, keep your excuse brief. Protesting too much can actually come across like you're not telling the truth!

What about arriving early? Well, it's definitely better to get there early rather than late, but if you do arrive early, recruiters told me they prefer you to wait outside of the building or in the lobby of the building until ten minutes before your scheduled meeting.

4. **Trying to "fake it 'til you make it."** It's exactly what you don't want to have happen: You're in an important interview, and you think it's going well until... you're asked a question about your area of expertise that you should know, and you have *no idea* what the answer should be. What do you do? Well, no matter how tempting it may be, don't pretend that you know the answer when you really don't. There's

no upside to this! In fact, faking it might just cause you to go off on a tangent. According to one of the college recruiters I interviewed, this is one of the biggest mistakes she sees grads make in interviews. "[Faking it] just wastes good time that a candidate can use to 'sell' themselves on other skills the company may be searching for." Instead, be honest, and say that you aren't sure. Then, say you'll find out and get back to the interviewer within 24 hours. Of course, you must then absolutely follow up as promised. What's the outcome? You've built credibility, you've shown honesty and integrity, and you've shown reliability. (Plus, you'll learn something new in the process!) It turns what could be perceived as a negative — not knowing the answer to a question — into a positive.

College Graduate Personal Brand Busters®—Reactions

1. **Not listening to the question and moving into an unrelated topic.** When you're nervous in an interview, it's easy to get lost in your Thoughts. That's especially true if you're worried about something you just said, or if you find the interviewer a bit cool and unfriendly. But, it's incredibly important to focus during an interview and really listen to what the interviewer is saying and to the questions asked.

   Why? Well, if your answer isn't really related to the question, the interviewer might think you're someone who doesn't listen, and that can count against you. Kristi Oltman, Manager of Talent Acquisition at National Research Company, says, "Be 100% engaged in our conversation. Don't be a robot. Listen, think, respond." If, by chance, your mind wanders, and you lose track of the question, definitely ask the interviewer to repeat the question again. You'll have the opportunity to hear the question one more time — and this time around, of course, listen carefully!

   If you know that you have a tendency to veer off of the topic, really focus on answering questions as directly as possible. Then … STOP. That helps guard against going off on another subject or saying too much. Just answer the question to the best of your ability, and then, be quiet and wait for the next question. Wesley Thorne, Assistant Director of Business & Employer Relations at Northwestern University, says, "In my experience, poor interview reactions — from not being prepared for anticipated questions to not addressing the interviewer's specific questions — are what most often lead to candidates not landing the job."

2. **Answering a question without taking the time to think or before fully understanding the question.** Let's say you're in an interview, and you've just been asked your opinion about a topic that took you by surprise. You're not sure how to respond, but you feel the need to say something right away in order to look confident. So, you just start babbling whatever comes to mind. Does this sound familiar? If so, here's an insight: Interviewers actually prefer it if you take a moment to think before answering a question. They'd rather have a short pause and a well-thought-out answer than a rushed response to every question. And trust me: If you do rush to answer every question, you won't be at your best. In fact, you may end up saying something you don't really mean.

   What if you need some time to reflect on a challenging question? It's perfectly okay to say, "That's an interesting question. Give me a minute to think about that." Of course, don't take a *full minute* to think of your answer. (When you're sitting across from an interviewer, 60 seconds of silence can feel like an eternity!) But you should feel free to take a few seconds to think of a good answer before you speak. You're bound to have a better answer than if you just started talking without thinking. Cindy Godel, former College Recruiter for Motorola, put it this way, "Many interviewers will ask a trick or brain-teaser question just to see how the candidate will react and how they problem-solve to get the answer. The key isn't necessarily that the candidate gets the 'right' answer ... it is that the candidate at least tries and doesn't get flustered."

3. **Not asking for clarification when you don't understand a question.** One of our worst fears is to look "stupid," right? But it may look even more stupid if you fumble around answering the wrong question. In fact, I think it's stupid *not* to ask questions! There's not much upside to not asking, but there's plenty of downside. Maggie Yontz of ConAgra Foods says, "Nine times out of ten, when a candidate asks for clarification on a question I've asked, I figure that I have not communicated clearly, not that the student can't comprehend what I'm asking. I appreciate a candidate who's confident and direct enough to ask for clarification on a question that he or she doesn't understand." So, most interviewers will prefer that you ask for clarification. It lets them know you want to make sure you give a good answer. Now, who in their right mind would consider *that* stupid?

4. **Not being prepared with good, thoughtful questions to ask at the end of the interview.** In almost every interview, you should expect to be asked, "Do you have any questions?" How deep and how intelligent your questions are will show not only that you did your research on the company and the position, but that you really gave some thought as to how you could fit in to the company. It will also show that you're listening to the interviewer. Plus, paying close attention to what's being said in the interview helps you ask a related question at the end.

   Nora Bammann, Assistant Human Resources Manager of The Kroger Company, says: "*Always* have questions ready. The questions interviewees ask really tell me (a) how the interviewee processes the information they heard, and (b) if the interviewee was not only listening but if they understood what they heard." So, be ready with some questions in advance, but also feel free to ask questions in the moment based on what you're told by the interviewer. It shows you want to be a part of the organization and that you're taking the process seriously. Of course, your questions need to be relevant. Gillian Taitz, Senior Recruiter – College Relations for Staples, said, "When candidates ask me things that really just prove they are *trying* to sound intelligent and have done their online research, it really turns me off. I'd much rather we spend time talking about what is important to this candidate in terms of culture, management style, etc."

   If you need help thinking of questions to ask the interviewer, check out Appendix A on page 267 for ideas.

College Graduate Personal Brand Busters® — Look

1. **Not watching your posture.** Your posture says a lot about you. Slouching in your interview chair with your leg crossed over your knee can make you look too casual and downright unmotivated. The recruiters and HR managers I talked with said slouching during an interview is a common problem among college grads.

   On the other hand, the opposite doesn't do much for your personal brand either. If you sit up *too* straight at the edge of your chair and lean toward the interviewer, you could come across as *over*-eager. So, practice sitting in front of a mirror before heading to the interview. Is your posture professional without being "too straight?"

2. **Only looking at one interviewer when there are two or more interviewers present.** People tend to look at the person who is most expressive or seems the most receptive. But if you're interviewed by more than one person, make sure you look at everyone in the room when you speak. Make eye contact with one interviewer for a few seconds; then, shift to another. If you don't, the interviewers you ignore may not connect with you. It's simply human nature, and that lack of connection with some of your interviewers could cost you the job.

3. **Not paying attention to YOU™ on the Internet.** Chances are your interviewer or future boss will do a "Google search" on you prior to your interview. In fact, according to a survey conducted by Harris Interactive, 45% of HR professionals will go beyond Google and search for you on social networking sites like LinkedIn and Facebook. That's up from 22% just one year prior to that! More than 1/3 of the recruiters surveyed said they found information on social media that made them not hire an applicant, 53% said they wouldn't hire you if you have something "provocative" on a site, and 44% wouldn't hire you if you make reference to drugs or drinking.

So, if you aren't careful, a search like that could actually prevent you from getting an interview. The "Look" of YOU™ on the Internet could hurt your personal brand in a number of ways. Think twice before posting those wild photos from last year's spring break on your Facebook page or a picture of you passed out on your friend's living room couch on your blog. Veda Jeffries from Stanford University, says, "Students feel that Facebook, etc. is their personal thing, but it's difficult to erase negatives about who you are when it is open to anyone and everyone." Shannon Boehm of Sears had a specific experience with social media that she shared: "I received a call from my company's legal department asking me about a Facebook group our summer interns had formed. The group had used the company logo and started a group to network before the internship started. The networking part was a good idea, but using the company logo was not. So, these interns already made a name (and not a good one) with our legal department before their first day on the job. And, it then invited further scrutiny into their profiles once our attention was drawn to them (and I found *many* inappropriate pictures)."

Pay attention to what you "say" in your blog or other social media, too. In the same survey mentioned above, 35% of recruiters said they wouldn't hire you if you say something negative about someone you worked for or worked with in the past (or your former boss, if you're working now). So, avoid negative comments about other people and steer away from profanity. Don't take an overly strong stand on something controversial or share potentially embarrassing personal information about you or anyone else. Remember: Privacy is virtually non-existent on the Internet. As soon as you post it, your secret is out, and you may unconsciously damage your job-seeker personal brand faster than you can click your mouse.

4. **Dressing too casually for an interview.** Interviewers want to see how you would dress at work or in front of a client, so an interview is your best chance to prove you can be a professional. Beth Cassie of Easton Associates said, "We've been burned when we've hired someone who shows up casually dressed (like we are) but who then doesn't have the clothes or the sense to dress for a client." So, even if you know that the company normally has a "business casual" dress policy, show up in proper business clothes at the interview. It doesn't matter where you've come from before the interview. That's no excuse! If you have to feel a little silly for a day wearing a business suit to class because you have an interview immediately after school, that's just the way it is. It's worth it if it helps you ace an important interview. Beverly Friedman of Google says, "Show respect for the process and that it mattered enough to you to dress nicely. You only get *one* chance at a first impression."

College Graduate Personal Brand Busters®—Sound

1. **Speaking negatively about a past job or internship.** In a survey of interviewers and recruiters reported on Careerbuilder.com, 49% said that the worst worst offense during an interview is speaking negatively about a former boss. Saying something mean-spirited about a past job or internship will leave a bad taste in an interviewer's mouth and may just make them wonder if you'll say similar things about them behind their back if they hire you. Negativity breeds negativity. Find a way to speak positively about your past experiences. The glass is always half full!

2. **Speaking of "we" instead of "I."** Don't forget that the company is interested in hiring you, not the team you worked with! While you don't want to take full credit for something that you didn't do alone, don't forget to take credit for the role that you played in any projects at school, in community work, or in a former job or internship. An interview is a time to talk about what *you've* done and what *you* can

do, so have the confidence to sell yourself. A little humility is good, but too much will do nothing to get you a job.

3. **Letting your cell phone go off during an interview — even if it's just vibrating.** We discussed this in an earlier chapter, but I'm including it here as a Buster, too, because recruiters tell me this happens a lot! One recruiter went so far as to say, "If that were to happen in an interview, it would completely kill any chance of the candidate being hired." Letting your cell phone go off during an interview not only disrupts the meeting, but it's downright "rude." This goes for texting anywhere near the company's building, too. Tim Wilson, Partner at BDK, LLC said it makes employers wonder if you'll be able to separate your personal life from your professional life. He even added, "Receptionists are watching you." So, turn your cell phone off *before* you even get to the interview site, and put it away where it can't be seen. What you have to say to your friends and family can wait until you get back home. It's not worth losing a job over!

4. **Answering questions *too* honestly.** You definitely want to be honest in interviews, but you should be careful not to be *too* honest and share incriminating information. Use good, basic judgment and think about how the interviewer might respond to what you have to share. One college recruiter told me that a senior she interviewed admitted to having been so angry with someone once that she slashed that person's tires. Yikes! Even if the interviewer asks you for a story about a time you made a mistake, or asks you to share something you regret, be sure to choose a relatively harmless story. And this not only holds true for the first interview but for subsequent interviews, too. As one interview told me, "I've seen many students lose their job offers during our final round interview process. They feel very comfortable by the time we all go to lunch in the middle of the day, and many students reveal/say too much." So, always keep your personal brand summary top of mind, and you'll be less likely to reveal something that works against it.

College Graduate Personal Brand Busters® — Thoughts

1. **Thinking the interview only begins when you're across the desk from the interviewer.** From the moment you walk into the location where you'll be interviewed, you're "on." That means no talking on your cell phone, listening to your MP3 player, or texting in the lobby while waiting for the interviewer. It means remembering that how

you treat the receptionist may be shared with your potential boss later on. It means remembering that the time you spend following the interviewer from the reception area to the interview room is also part of your interview. Some recruiters are purposely quiet during that time just to see how you respond to the silence and if you're outgoing and personable enough to talk. So, be sure to start some conversation during that time; a little small talk will go a long way to presenting a strong personal brand.

2. **Believing a company's "greeter" at a career fair is a peer or a confidante.** A company's greeter at a college career fair is there to assess you just as much as an interviewer, even if he or she seems more casual and chats informally with you. Remember: The greeter's opinion counts! One HR professional said, "In a smaller company like ours, *everyone* checks out the candidates. How you interact with every single person at the company is important, and this includes the greeter." So, make sure that you don't say one thing to the greeter and something different to your interviewer. You'll get caught, and that could lead you to being branded as inconsistent — or worse, dishonest.

3. **Thinking that you can "wing it" when it comes to preparing for an interview.** Walking into an interview unprepared is a good way to blow it. As Brigid McMahon of IBM put it, "In 12 years of recruiting, the #1 faux pas I see in interviews is a candidate's failure to do his/her homework. They should be able to articulate what excites/interests them about the work and what attributes and skills they possess that will align and add value. It boggles my mind how many candidates don't do their homework. It's a sure fire way to eliminate yourself from the competition."

You should walk in knowing as much about that company as possible, and you need to be prepared with answers and questions based on your Audience's Needs, your Unique Strengths, your Reasons Why, and your Brand Character traits. This means having stories ready that will show what you've done in your past experiences in jobs, internships, courses, volunteer work, and community/school involvement. Kristi Oltman says, "Using examples is huge for me. It creates validity." Another recruiter said that stories are necessary to bring your resume to life: "Not doing this sells you short and makes the interviewer question the depth of experiences listed on your resume."

So, practice, practice, practice! Rehearsing is guaranteed to help you when it comes time for the "real deal." You'll feel more confident, and you won't be as easily thrown by tough questions that come your way. Of course, don't overdo it. One interviewer I spoke with said, "A student can also be *too* rehearsed in an interview. Interviewers are looking for genuine, sincere responses to questions." So, practice what you want to communicate, but don't memorize it word for word.

4. **Beating yourself up if you don't do well in an interview or if you don't get the job.** It makes no sense to jump to conclusions. You may have done better in the interview than you think and/or maybe the company simply decided to hire fewer college grads this year than they had planned. So, not getting chosen for a job may not have anything at all to do with you. Wesley Thorne from Northwestern University puts it this way: "There could be any number of reasons why a candidate does not get a job offer. While it's important to reflect on what could be improved upon, it is also important not to take the process personally, as it could lead to self-doubt. It is important to always move forward; when one door closes, another one will open."

So, whatever you do, don't allow your Thoughts to become negative. It will only get you down and make the rest of your interview process more difficult. Review the Thoughts chapter for productive ways to handle a disappointment. Then, learn from it, move on, and stay positive.

The Quiz

So, what College Graduate Personal Brand Busters® do *you* need to avoid? On the next page is a quiz to help you better understand how YOU™ do in interviews with our top 20 most damaging College Graduate Personal Brand Busters®. If you think you commit a particular College Graduate Personal Brand Buster® at least 50% of the time or more, mark it "yes." If you think you commit that particular Buster less than 50% of the time, mark it "no."

At the end of the quiz is a key to score your answers. When you're finished, you'll have a very clear idea of how much work you need to do to keep from damaging your college grad personal brand before, during, and after job interviews. But even if your score is a bit disappointing, take heart. As author F. Wikzek said, "If you don't make mistakes, you're not working on hard enough problems. And *that's* a big mistake."

If you haven't started interviewing yet, you may want to save this quiz for later, but you can take it over and over throughout your job search process to keep tabs on how well you're doing.

No matter your score, with this book and the *How YOU™ are like Shampoo for College Graduates* personal branding system, you have a guide for getting your personal brand in shape for a great job search. After each Buster, jot down action steps that you'll take to truly bust that particular Buster. What will you do to make sure you don't commit that Buster again?

Quiz

Do You Occasionally Commit These College Graduate Personal Brand Busters®

Actions

Yes   No   Action Steps

☐   ☐   1. Lying on your resume or during an interview — even if you think they are just "little white lies."

☐   ☐   2. Asking questions about pay and benefits during an initial interview.

☐   ☐   3. Not performing a "trial run" to find out how long it takes to get to the interview site.

☐   ☐   4. Trying to "fake it 'til you make it."

Reactions

Yes	No		Action Steps
☐	☐	5. Not listening to the question and moving into an unrelated topic.	
☐	☐	6. Answering questions without taking the time to think or before fully understanding the question.	
☐	☐	7. Not asking for clarification when you don't understand a question.	
☐	☐	8. Not being prepared with good, thoughtful questions to ask at the end of the interview.	

Look

Yes	No		Action Steps
☐	☐	9. Not watching your posture.	
☐	☐	10. Only looking at one interviewer when there are two or more interviewers present.	
☐	☐	11. Not paying attention to YOU™ on the Internet.	
☐	☐	12. Dressing too casually for an interview.	

Sound

Yes No   Action Steps

☐ ☐ 13. Speaking negatively about a past job or internship.

☐ ☐ 14. Speaking of "we" instead of "I."

☐ ☐ 15. Letting your cell phone go off during an interview — even if it's just vibrating.

☐ ☐ 16. Answering questions *too* honestly.

Thoughts

Yes No   Action Steps

☐ ☐ 17. Thinking the interview only begins when you're across the desk from the interviewer.

☐ ☐ 18. Believing a company's "greeter" at a career fair is a peer or confidante.

☐ ☐ 19. Thinking that you can "wing it" when it comes to preparing for an interview.

☐ ☐ 20. Beating yourself up if you don't do well in an interview or if you don't get the job.

Scoring Your College Graduate Personal Brand Busters® Quiz

Now, it's time to check out your score. Count the number of times you responded "yes," and compare your final number against this College Graduate Personal Brand Busters® scorecard.

If the number of "yes" responses you gave is…

0 to 5   **Great job!** You're obviously a strong job-seeking personal brand builder. Keep up the good work, and don't stop until you have zero "yes" responses.

6 to 10   Choose one or two areas which you think could make the biggest difference in your college grad personal brand image, and set up a plan to focus on changing those behaviors in your upcoming job interviews.

11 to 20   The good news is: You've uncovered a number of ways to improve how well you communicate your college graduate personal brand throughout your job search. Identify three to four areas where you want to focus in the near future. Then, find a mentor or coach to give you feedback and encouragement along the way as you work on changing your personal brand image before, during, and after interviews. You have the power to change your personal brand. Well done for taking this first step!

So, how did you do? Whatever your score on the quiz, I tip my hat to you because you've done a lot of work toward making your job-seeking college grad personal brand a reality and toward getting a great position that you will truly love each and every day.

Now, let's make sure you take the steps you need to in order to guarantee you'll be successful at building your personal brand *long-term*. You don't want to leave anything to chance…

The Proven Pathway to Getting YOU™ a Great Job

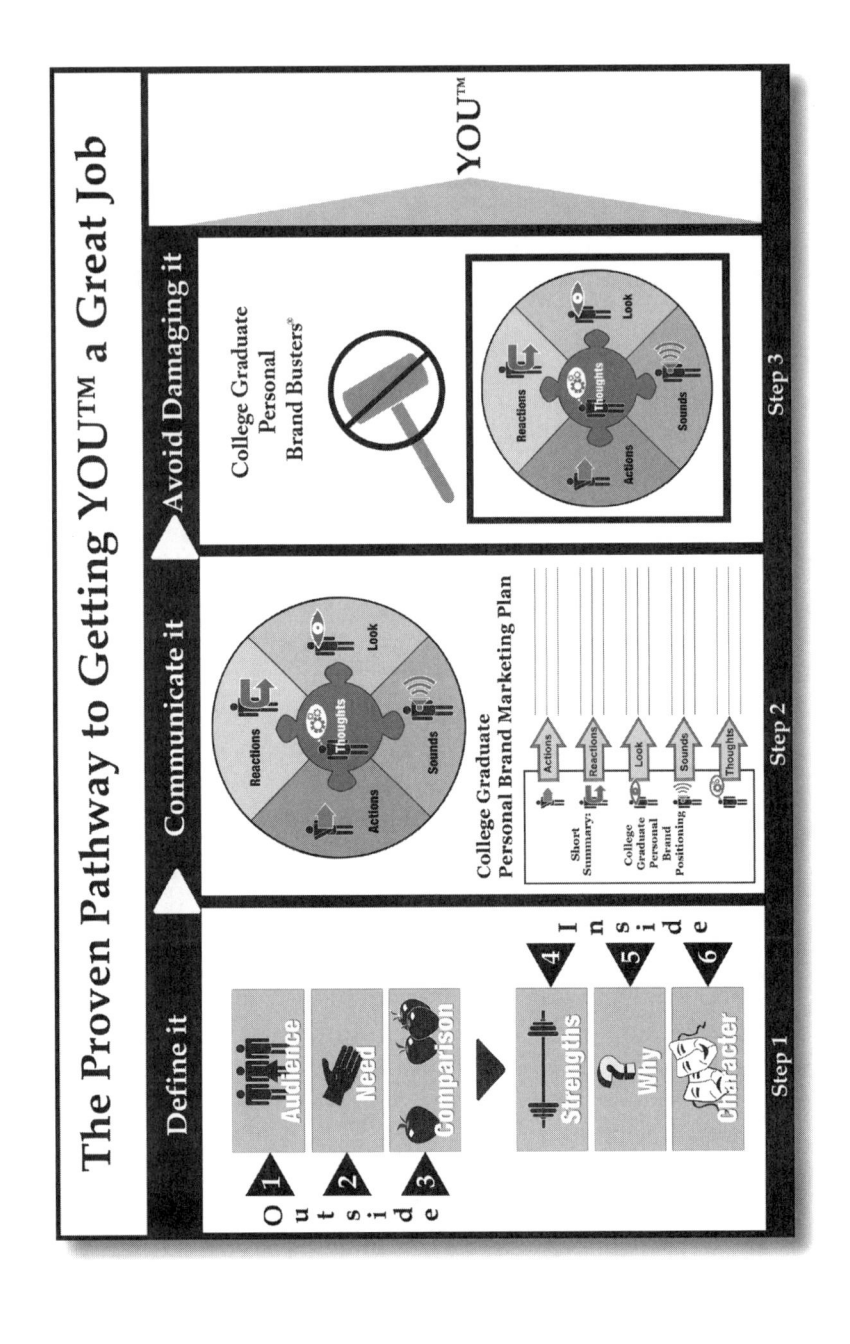

Step 1: Define it

Outside
1. Audience
2. Need
3. Comparison

Inside
4. Strengths
5. Why
6. Character

Step 2: Communicate it

College Graduate Personal Brand Marketing Plan

- Short Summary
- College Graduate Personal Brand Positioning
  - Actions
  - Reactions
  - Look
  - Sounds
  - Thoughts

Step 3: Avoid Damaging it

College Graduate Personal Brand Busters®

- Look
- Sounds
- Actions
- Reactions
- Thoughts

YOU™

20

Assuring Long-Term Success

Obstacles don't have to stop you. If you run into a wall, don't turn around and give up. Figure out how to climb it, go through it, or work around it.

— Michael Jordan, Retired professional basketball player

As we near the end of this journey, it's a good idea to sit back and reflect on just how far you've come in developing your own unique college graduate personal brand called YOU™. Together, we've applied this unique personal branding system to help you develop an individual personal brand that you can apply to a successful job search as you get ready to graduate. We have:

- Looked at what personal branding is and what impact it can have on your ability to find and keep the best job for you.

- Defined the six core elements that make up your college graduate personal brand — Audience, Need, Comparison, Unique Strengths, Reasons Why, and Brand Character — and we've pulled these elements together to create your unique College Graduate Personal Brand Positioning Statement.

- Explored how to best communicate your well-defined personal brand through the five activities that most impact how potential employers perceive, think, and feel about YOU™ — your Actions, your Reactions, your Look, your Sound, and your Thoughts.

- Developed a College Graduate Personal Brand Marketing Plan specific to YOU™ that outlines the Actions, Reactions, Look, Sound, and Thoughts you will use to make sure YOU™ come across consistently before, during, and after your interviews.

- Reviewed how to avoid harming your personal brand by watching out for key College Graduate Personal Brand Busters® — including the top 20 most damaging Busters from our quiz, as well as Busters from your own personal list.

Along the way, you've asked yourself and others some tough questions. You've had the chance to look at your personal brand from an objective viewpoint. You've been able to craft a vision of your future in a job you love. The bottom line is that you've become a great job-seeking personal brand builder, working toward building your brand with an Audience focus. Good work! All of this effort will not only help you land the job you want, but can also help you develop a powerful personal brand in your new job that brings you greater opportunities for advancement and salary increases.

Of course, like any good marketer with a strong strategy, it isn't enough to simply have a plan. You have to follow through and stick to that plan consistently — day in and day out.

Make Success a Done Deal

Be *confident* you can get the job you want within the company you like. A study done by the University of Washington found that participants who simply had more confidence in themselves were more likely to keep their New Year's resolutions. In other words, the study participants who believed they could achieve their goals did achieve them!

You're trying to create new habits and new ways of behaving in interviews, so be patient with yourself — but don't give up. If you make a mistake or two, don't beat yourself up. In that same University of Washington study, only 40% of the people who successfully achieved their top New Year's resolution managed it on their first try. The rest tried many times, and 17% finally succeeded after more than six tries. Persistence pays off, especially when it comes to looking for a job. Just learn from your mistakes to avoid spinning your wheels, and refocus as fast as you can.

The work you've done to define and communicate your college graduate personal brand will help you to stay committed to the vision of finding a great job. One idea to keep you focused is to come up with something visual that stands for your brand image. Keep it somewhere near you as a reminder, and look at it before you walk into an interview. You could put it in your pocket or in your wallet on the same paper as your personal brand summary so that you see or feel it every time you reach in for some money. Every time that symbol is brought to mind, you'll remember your personal brand objectives.

Find a trusted friend to become your job-seeking personal brand buddy as you both look for jobs. You can help each other stay on track with your individual College Graduate Personal Brand Marketing Plans and support each other along the way. If you can't find a buddy to help you, consider finding a mentor or a college professor, if possible, to guide and coach you during your job search. That kind of outside, unbiased viewpoint can be priceless.

Evolve Your Personal Brand

As human beings, we're not static, and we're not supposed to be. After you've successfully used your personal brand to get the job you desire, you'll want to make adjustments to your brand. It will become your "on-the-job" brand which caters to your new company's Needs. This is where the first book in The YOU™ Series—*How YOU™ are like Shampoo*—can help you in developing your personal brand for your new job. (See page 279.) So, your personal brand will continue to grow and evolve over time, just as your favorite name brands evolve.

Apple used to stand for just the Macintosh computer. Now, Apple stands for much, much more. It has evolved its brand considerably in the past few years. Kodak, on the other hand, hung its hat on film and took too long to respond to the growing digital camera trend years ago. That's a brand that didn't evolve as quickly as it should have.

Just like these name brands, you have to evolve your own personal brand to fit with the changes that are happening around you. Once you get a new job (and any time you change jobs after that), you'll want to create a new Personal Brand Positioning Statement based on new information. Even if you stay in the same job for a long time, your brand will change as circumstances around you and within the company change. Stay alert for how those changes — such as a new boss or a new focus within the company — might mean that parts of your personal brand need to be adjusted.

My Personal Note to YOU™

It's been great to ride along with you on this road toward your personal brand — YOU™! I hope to hear from you about your job search successes, challenges, and questions as you build your College Graduate Personal Brand Positioning Statement and put your College Graduate Personal Brand Marketing Plan into action. Please write me at Brenda@BrendaBence.com. I would love to hear how your job search is going and how the *How YOU™ are like Shampoo For College Graduates* personal branding system helped you land a great first position as you start your career.

Also, please check out our online coaching modules for any help you might want along the way. Visit us at www.BrendaBence.com for more information.

Congratulations on taking control of your job search success by learning to craft and communicate your college graduate personal brand! I wish for YOU™ nothing less than a job you love, a lifetime of fulfillment, and great achievements along the way.

Appendix A

Great Interview Questions for YOU™

Many thanks go out to the recruiters and HR experts all across the nation who shared their favorite questions to ask during an interview.

Twenty Questions Coming Your Way

To ace an interview, nothing beats preparation. Here are 20 questions you'll want to be ready to answer:

1. I looked at your resume, but I'd like to get a 2-3 minute summary of who you are. Please highlight what you most want me to know about you.

2. What made you want to major in _____? What sparked your interest in this field?

3. Why did you decide to apply to our company for this job?

4. What are you looking for in a job and a company?

5. From what you know at this point about the job and our company, what appeals to you most? What appeals to you least?

6. How have your experiences at work, at school, or in your community prepared you to take on the responsibilities and challenges of this job?

7. What are the three most important things you've learned from your work or volunteer experiences to date?

8. How do you stay organized?

9. Tell me about a time when you successfully juggled a lot of responsibilities and deadlines. How did you do it?

10. What do you regard as the top three major achievements in your life — what you are most proud of?

11. If we asked people who know you well to describe you, what five adjectives would most frequently come up? What three reasons would they give as to why we should hire you?

12. For what have you been most frequently praised … and most frequently criticized?

13. Of all the students on campus, what's the one thing that sets you apart from the others?

14. What decisions or actions that you've taken during your college years have disappointed you? If you could change them, what would you have done differently?

15. How do you deal with personal stress and/or the stressful situations that you have experienced on the job or at school?

16. Give us an example of a major challenge or chaotic situation you've faced in your life and what you did to manage it.

17. What do you like to do outside of work?

18. What do you want to be doing five years from now? What is your ultimate career goal?

19. If you could wave a magic wand so that this position turned out to be your dream job, what specific things would you want the wand to ensure?

20. What do you want me to remember most about this interview?

A Dozen Queries to Pose

Here are 12 great questions you can ask any interviewer during an interview. Remember that you probably won't be able to ask all of these in every interview, so make a priority list, and ask the most important questions first.

1. *(If not already clear…)* What kinds of tasks and responsibilities would I have in this position?

2. What are the major challenges, opportunities, and risks of this job?

3. Why is the position open now, and what is the history of the position and of the people who have held it?

4. How do management and others in the department perceive this position?

5. *(If not already clear…)* Who would I be reporting to in this position? What can you tell me about this person?

6. Please explain to me how training works here. Is it more on-the-job training or formal training courses?

7. I've visited your website, and here's something I'd like to know more about: _____.

8. How would you describe the culture of the company? What are the typical working relationships like between and among individuals, departments, and divisions (if applicable).

9. What interests you most about me? What do you think I might be able to accomplish and contribute? What about me might cause you concern?

10. What would success look like after one year in this job? What would you expect to have been accomplished by then? And what would that expectation be after three years?

11. What opportunities for advancement are there within the company?

12. When will you be making a decision about the position?

Appendix B

Personality Profiles and Tests

Assessment.com
www.assessment.com

MAPP is a personal assessment that takes about 20 minutes to complete. MAPP identifies your true motivations toward work and allows you to match yourself to job categories to see where you best fit. It's been used by job seekers, companies, schools, workforce centers, and coaches. Job seekers who want to learn more about their strengths and motivations toward work can take the MAPP assessment and receive a free sample report of their top motivators and job areas. If you like what you see, you can choose to purchase a full report. There are four options with retail prices starting at $19.95. You can view report options and choose the best one for you.

Keirsey
www.keirsey.com

Retail Price: $19.95 for the Career Temperament Report which assists career professionals, job seekers, and students in the career exploration process. This report is designed to help people align their career preparation and choices with their innate strengths and preferences. It includes expert advice on career options, tips on communication/interpersonal skills, and insight on navigating the job market based on personality type. The Temperament Report provides suggested career matches based on research surveys conducted across a wide spectrum of industries.

Personality 100
www.personality100.com

PHD-certified personality test based on over 60 years of research and three years of analysis. The questionnaire measures 32 dimensions. According to the website, millions have taken the test — which is free — but getting the results costs $29.95. Once you pay, you receive 100 pages of "objective and scientific" feedback.

Strengths Finder
www.strengthsfinder.com

After you purchase the book *Now, Discover Your Strengths*, there is a code inside which allows you to access the StrengthsFinder assessment tool online. Gallup introduced the first version of StrengthsFinder in 2001. In StrengthsFinder 2.0, Gallup unveiled the new and improved version of this popular assessment, Language of 34 Themes, and much more. You can read the book in one sitting, but they say "you'll use it as a reference for decades." These highly customized Strengths Insights will help you understand how each of your top five themes plays out in your life on a much more personal and professional level. The Strengths Insights describe what makes you stand out when compared to the millions of people that Gallup has studied.

Strong Interest Inventory (SII)

Used by many college career service centers, this psychological test is one of the most popular. SII shows you how your interests compare with the interests of people successful in specific jobs. Answering the questions usually takes about 25 minutes after which your results are scored by computer. Fees to take this test depend upon the website you visit. You may want to try www.PersonalityDesk.com which offers a student price of $89 to take both the SII along with the Myers-Briggs personality test. [Note: The original form of the SII is the test which pointed me in the direction of Marketing as a business focus!]

This information, while verified and correct at the time of printing, is subject to change at any time. Please contact each provider directly to inquire about current tests and pricing. Thank you!

Suggested Books

What Color Is Your Parachute? A Practical Manual for Job-Hunters and Career-Changers by Richard N. Bolles

Body Language for Dummies by Elizabeth Kuhnke

Leaving Campus and Going to Work by T. Jason Smith

200 Best Jobs for College Graduates by Michael Farr and Laurence Shatkin

How to Survive the Real World: Life After College Graduation—Advice from 774 Graduates Who Did by Hundreds of Heads and Andrea Syrtash, Editor

The Complete Resume Job Search Book for College Students: The A-To-Z Career Guide for College Students and Recent Grads Who Want to Stand Out From the Crowd, Get Off on the Right Foot, Land the Best Job Possible by Bob Adams and Laura Morin

Resumes for First-Time Job Hunters by the Editors of McGraw-Hill Publishers

Acing the Interview: How to Ask and Answer the Questions That Will Get You the Job by Tony Beshara

Best Answers to the 201 Most Frequently Asked Interview Questions by Matthew Deluca

About the Author

Brenda S. Bence is in demand as an internationally-recognized branding expert, popular trainer, professional speaker, certified executive coach, and author of the award-winning *How YOU™ are like Shampoo* series of personal branding books.

With an MBA from Harvard Business School, Brenda spent the bulk of her career building mega brands for companies like Procter & Gamble and Bristol-Myers Squibb, where she was a senior executive responsible for billion-dollar businesses across four continents and 50 countries.

In 2002, Brenda left the corporate world and founded **Brand Development Associates (BDA) International, Ltd.** Now doing business in 20 countries with offices in both the U.S. and Asia, Brenda speaks, trains, and coaches clients located all across North America, Asia, Europe, Australia, and New Zealand.

As a magazine and a newspaper columnist, Brenda writes articles on a variety of topics related to corporate and personal branding and executive coaching. She has been featured in more than 100 media outlets around the globe including NBC, *Reader's Digest, Financial Times, Investor's Business Daily, Entrepreneur Magazine, Kiplinger's Personal Finance, SmartMoney,* and *Los Angeles Times*. Brenda is also a frequent guest on radio and television shows.

Brenda has an Honorary Doctor of Laws degree as well as a Bachelor of Arts degree in English and French from Nebraska Wesleyan University.

Splitting her time between homes in Thailand and the U.S., Brenda sits on a number of boards of public and private companies and not-for-profit organizations. Having traveled to 70 countries, Brenda enjoys studying foreign languages and is an avid Mahjong player.

Brenda has been happily married to her husband, Daniel, for the past 12 years. And, she really would choose him over her favorite toothpaste brand.

DRESS FOR SUCCESS®
Suits to Self-Sufficiency

Dress for Success® is an international non-profit organization dedicated to improving the lives of disadvantaged women. The professional clothing, employment retention programs, and ongoing support that Dress for Success provides its clients symbolize their faith in every woman's ability to be self-sufficient and successful in her career.

Founded in New York City in 1997 as an answer to the needs of low-income women who are seeking employment and self-sufficiency, Dress for Success is a 501(c)(3) not-for-profit organization. In the same year that Dress for Success was founded, the welfare overhaul set time restrictions for public assistance recipients, which in turn quickly forced heads of households into low wage jobs. Because of the rapid increase in the number of poor working women, they became an underserved segment of society, and many lacked the skills and support to retain their employment. Dress for Success has responded to the needs of the women that they serve by providing professional attire, career development tools, and a network of support to help women succeed in work and in life.

Over the past 13 years, Dress for Success has grown into a thriving international not-for-profit organization that has supported more than 500,000 disadvantaged women at over 100 affiliates worldwide. Dress for Success serves, on average, 45,000 clients each year throughout the United States, Canada, Mexico, Poland, New Zealand, the Netherlands, the United Kingdom, and the West Indies. To make a donation, you may contact Dress for Success, 32 East 31st Street, 7th Floor, New York, NY 10016, or gift online at www.DressForSucess.org.

Acknowledgments

Thank you to so many who have offered their incredible talents to help this book become a reality:

- Melanie Votaw — for her outstanding editing and supportive partnership in the book-birthing process
- Maggie Stanton and Kelsey Steinmeyer — for their help with research, development, and editing, and for their keen insights into today's college life
- Eric Myhr — for excellent typesetting and great attention to detail
- Graham Dixhorn — for spot-on book cover copy
- George Foster — for fresh book cover design
- Kurt Heck — for book cover photography
- Brenda Brown — for entertaining cartoon development
- Swas Siripong "Kwan" — for interior graphic assistance

I also owe a debt of thanks to so many corporate experts, recruiters, advisors, HR specialists, and university career services professionals who patiently answered my questions. Their inputs are an invaluable resource for the readers of this book, and I am enormously grateful to them for their generosity: Janelle Schutte Andreini, Nora Bammann, Mary Banks, Matt Beran, Susan Berg, Shannon Boehm, Ann Breetzke, Kay Byers, Kate Cancro, Beth Cassie, Laura Dominguez Chan, Angela Cherry, Joanna Clark, Maria Curry, Meredith Daw, Kaylea Dunn, Carolyn Ersland, Nicole Uhrmacher Figard, Travis Figard, Beverly Friedman, Sigmund Ginsburg, Cindy Godel, Desiree Hack, Liz Handlin, Mary Hawk, Noelle Heinrich, Barbara Hewitt, Heather Hoops, Charles Hunt, Veda Jeffries, Sheryl Kalash, Amy Kloefkorn, Sandra Kovar, Jim Lafferty, Lian Li, Fontez Mark, Brigid McMahon, Pete Medrano, Liz Michaels, Nanci Mickelsen, Robin Mount, Kristi Oltman, Erin Padilla, Maura Quinn, Norm Saale, Karen Smith, Gillian Taitz, Chris Talley, Wesley Thorne, Matthew Travis, Tim Wilson, Gary Woollacott, Maggie Yontz.

The people listed in the previous paragraph come from an impressive array of companies and universities: ABB, Aperio Group, AT & T, BKD LLP, ConAgra Foods, Deloitte LLP, Disney, Doane College, Easton Associates, GE Healthcare, Goldman Sachs, Google,

Harvard University, Hewlett-Packard Company, Hilton Worldwide, IBM, Intel, Liberty Mutual, Lincoln Public Schools, Lowe's, MasterCard, McDermott & Miller P.C., Motorola, MSD, National Research Company, Nebraska State Department of Roads, Nebraska Wesleyan University, Nestle Purina PetCare Company, Northwest Mutual, Northwestern University, Olsson Associates, Opus Recruitment, Procter & Gamble, RadioShack, Sears, Seim Johnson, Sony, Stanford University, Staples, Talent Plus, The Kroger Corporation, T-Mobile, Tyco, Ultimate-Resumes.com, University of Chicago, University of Colorado, University of Pennsylvania.

In addition to experts from industry, I have another group of experts to thank — a terrific team of college students who served as my advisory board over the past few months. Their participation gave me wonderful insights into the world of the college student today and helped me stay on track. Thanks so much to each of them for their help: Sam Acker, Sarah Adams, Adrianna Choquette, Jennifer Crunk, Kristen Erthum, Tracy Fessler, Andrew Gatzemeyer, Kesha Grenemeier, Tyler Jackman, Troy Lewellen, Sadie Martin, Caitlynn McGreer, Natalie Nickel, Kristin Osmera, Cady Russell, Pakiza Shirinova, Stefanie Skrdla, Maggie Stanton, Kelsey Steinmeyer, Paul Drake Stockard, Michael Vargas, Megan Van Winkle.

Besides those who actually worked "on" the book, there were many others who have helped by supporting me behind the scenes. My sincere gratitude goes to:

Daniel — my husband, business partner ... and the brand I am most loyal to.

Danielle — best friend of 35 years who is also one of the most gifted photographic artists I know.

My wonderful family and the staff at BDA International — for all their help and support during these months of book development.

My Team — you're the best.

Brenda S. Bence
Professional Speaker, Trainer, and Coach

Invite Brenda to speak at your college!

Help guide upcoming college graduates to greater job search success by inviting Brenda Bence to speak at your campus. Brenda is in demand as a speaker not only for her unique approach to personal branding, but also for her warm, funny, and entertaining personality.

Her popular talks about personal branding draw on Brenda's decades of experience as a marketer and coach. Her ability to communicate complex ideas simply and practically helps college graduates to discover and leverage the core elements of her groundbreaking personal branding system that has been designed especially for them. Through her easy-to-understand, no-nonsense approach to personal branding, Brenda has guided and motivated audiences around the world to better interview success, higher job satisfaction, and greater career fulfillment.

Contact Brenda@BrendaBence.com today to inquire about Brenda's availability to speak at your campus.

The How YOU™ are like Shampoo Personal Branding System for College Graduates is also available as a college course!

To help college students prepare for a successful job search, Brenda Bence's personal branding system can be offered as a course in two ways:

1. A Professor and/or a Career Services professional can facilitate the course on your campus. Instruction manuals and student workbooks are available to assist in the process. Write to CollegeCourse@BrendaBence.com to find out more.

2. Students can sign up individually and take the course remotely via online access. Write to OnlineCourse@BrendaBence.com for more information.

Bring the powerful college graduate personal branding system outlined in How YOU™ are like Shampoo to your university today!

To book Brenda Bence as a speaker or trainer on your campus, please contact:

Telephone in North America (Chicago, U.S.A.):	1-312-242-1830
Facsimile in North America (Chicago, U.S.A.):	1-312-277-9211
Telephone in Asia (Bangkok, Thailand):	+662-711-9215
Facsimile in Asia (Bangkok, Thailand):	+662-711-9210

E-mail Brenda at:

>Brenda@BrendaBence.com

To find out more about Brenda's programs, products, and clients, visit her website at:

>www.BrendaBence.com

Brenda would love to hear how this book has impacted your job search, your career, and your life. To share your personal brand stories, insights, and experiences with Brenda, e-mail:

>Comments@BrendaBence.com

Other Books and Products
by Brenda Bence

How YOU™ are like Shampoo

The breakthrough Personal Branding System based on proven big-brand marketing methods to help you earn more, do more, and be more at work

Available in Paperback, e-Book, 5-CD Audio Set, MP3, and Accompanying Manual of Exercises

How YOU™ are like Shampoo for Job Seekers

The proven Personal Branding System to help you succeed in any interview and secure the job of your dreams

Available in Paperback, e-Book, and Accompanying Manual of Exercises

The Power of the Platform: Speakers on Purpose

Brenda Bence, along with many of the world's other finest keynote speakers, have come together in one book to help you achieve your goals, find your purpose, and live the life of your dreams!

Available in Paperback and e-Book